WORKPLACE LEARNING & PERFORMANCE ROLES

The
INTERVENTION
SELECTOR
DESIGNER & DEVELOPER
IMPLEMENTOR

WILLIAM J. ROTHWELL

A Self-Guided Job Aid With Assessments Based on
ASTD Models for Workplace Learning and Performance

© 2000 by the American Society for Training & Development.

All rights reserved. Printed in the United States of America.

No part of this publication may be reproduced, distributed, or transmitted in any form or by any means, including photocopying, recording, or other electronic or mechanical methods, without the prior written permission of the publisher, except in the case of brief quotations embodied in critical reviews and certain other noncommercial uses permitted by copyright law. For permission requests, write to ASTD, Publications Department, Box 1443, Alexandria, VA 22313-2043.

Ordering information: Books published by the American Society for Training & Development can be ordered by calling 800.628.2783 or 703.683.8100, or via the Website at www.astd.org.

Library of Congress Catalog Card Number: 00-107112

ISBN: 1-56286-142-5

TABLE OF CONTENTS

                                                                                     Page

List of Tables and Figures vi

Section 1   **Getting Started** 1
- What Is the Background of This Project 3
- What Does This Job Aid Contain, and How Do You Use It? 3

Section 2   **Defining the Roles** 5
- The Role of the Intervention Selector 7
  — Definition of the Role of Intervention Selector 7
  — Importance of the Intervention Selector's Role 7
  — The Relationship Between This and Other Roles 8
  — The Place of Intervention Selection in the Human Performance Improvement Process 8
  — What Are Competencies, and Why Are They Important? 8
  — Competencies Associated With the Role of Intervention Selector . 8
  — Outputs Associated With the Role of Intervention Selector 11
  — Who Performs the Role of Intervention Selector? 12
  — When Do They Perform This Role? 12
  — What Projects Do Intervention Selectors Carry Out? 18
- The Role of the Intervention Designer and Developer 18
  — Definition of the Role of Intervention Designer and Developer . 18
  — Importance of the Intervention Designer and Developer's Role .. 19
  — The Relationship Between This and Other Roles 19
  — The Place of Intervention Designer and Developer in the Human Performance Improvement Process 19
  — Competencies Associated With the Role of Intervention Designer and Developer 20
  — Outputs Associated With the Role of Intervention Designer and Developer 22
  — Who Performs the Role of Intervention Designer and Developer? . 22
  — When Do They Perform This Role? 27
  — What Projects Does the Intervention Designer and Developer Carry Out? 28
- The Role of the Intervention Implementor 28
  — Definition of the Role of Intervention Implementor 28
  — Importance of the Role of Intervention Implementor 29
  — The Relationship Between This and Other Roles 29
  — The Place of the Intervention Implementor in the Human Performance Improvement Process 29
  — Competencies Associated with the Role of Intervention Implementor 29
  — Outputs Associated with the Role of Intervention Implementor .. 31
  — Who Performs the Role of Intervention Implementor? 31
  — When Do They Perform This Role? 35
  — What Projects Does the Intervention Implementor Carry Out? 35

Section 3	**Enacting the Role of Intervention Selector** 37	
	♦ A Model of the Intervention Selection Process 39	
	♦ Steps in the Intervention Selection Process 44	
	— *Step 1*: Verify That the Root Causes of the Performance Problem Have Been Distinguished From the Symptoms or Consequences 44	
	— *Step 2*: Consider the Range of Possible Interventions to Close the Performance Gap By Addressing the Root Causes 50	
	— *Step 3*: Identify Constraints or Limitations on the Choice of the Interventions 56	
	— *Step 4*: Identify Possible Changes in the Performance Problem That May Influence the Interventions 58	
	— *Step 5*: Consider Possible Side Effects of Interventions if Implemented and Plan for Addressing Them 58	
	— *Step 6*: Determine Necessary Stakeholder Support, Involvement, and Ownership 61	
	— *Step 7*: Select Appropriate Interventions to Close the Performance Gap and Thereby Address the Performance Problem 64	
	— *Step 8*: Clarify the Initial and Eventual Scope of the Performance Interventions ..67	
	♦ Section Summary 68	
Section 4	**Enacting the Role of Intervention Designer and Developer** 69	
	♦ A Model of the Intervention Design and Development Process 71	
	♦ Steps in the Intervention Design and Development Process 74	
	— *Step 1*: Examine the Characteristics of the Participants in the Intervention 74	
	— *Step 2*: Examine the Competencies Necessary for Successful Achievement 76	
	— *Step 3*: Examine the Characteristics of the Work Environment 78	
	— *Step 4*: Formulate Performance Objectives to Guide the Intervention 78	
	— *Step 5*: Formulate Specific Methods by Which to Measure Performance Objectives 83	
	— *Step 6*: Create a Detailed Project Plan 84	
	— *Step 7*: Create a Detailed Communication and Marketing Plan to Clarify What Is Happening, Has Happened, and Will Happen 86	
	— *Step 8*: Make, Buy, or Buy and Modify Materials and Media to Support the Implementation of the Intervention 86	
	♦ Section Summary 89	
Section 5	**Enacting the Role of Intervention Implementor** 91	
	♦ A Model of the Intervention Implementation Process 93	
	♦ Steps in the Intervention Implementation Process 97	
	— *Step 1*: Work With Participants and Stakeholders on a Daily Basis to Implement the Action Plan 97	
	— *Step 2*: Use Materials and Media Supplied by the Intervention Designers and Developers and Provide Feedback to Them About Ways to Improve Their Use 99	
	— *Step 3*: Deliver, or Facilitate Delivery of, the Intervention to Targeted Participants 101	

- *Step 4*: Ensure That Communication about the Intervention Is Carried out Effectively 103
- *Step 5*: Track Short-Term Results Against the Intervention Performance Objectives 104
- *Step 6*: Surmount Barriers to Implementation and Ensure That the Intervention Is Implemented as Planned 106
- *Step 7*: Provide Clear, Specific, and Continuing Feedback to Stakeholders about the Results of the Intervention 108
- ♦ Section Summary 108

Section 6 **Tools for Conducting Intervention Selection, Design and Development, and Implementation** 111
- ♦ Introduction to the Tools Section 113

Section 7 **Afterword** 133
- ♦ Why Is It Important to Master These Roles and Competencies? 135
- ♦ How Does It Feel to Perform These Roles? 135
- ♦ What Should You Do Next? 135

Section 8 **Bibliography** 137

About the Author 145

LIST OF TABLES AND FIGURES

Section 2	Table 2.1: Competencies Associated with the Intervention Selector's Role	9
	Table 2.2: Sample Outputs Associated with the Intervention Selector's Role	11
	Table 2.3: Competencies Associated with the Intervention Designer and Developer's Role	20
	Table 2.4: Sample Outputs Associated with the Intervention Designer and Developer's Role	22
	Table 2.5: Competencies Associated with the Intervention Implementor's Role	30
	Table 2.6: Sample Outputs Associated with the Intervention Implementor's Role	31
	Figure 2.1: The Human Performance Improvement Process Model for the Role of Intervention Selector	9
	Figure 2.2: Worksheet to Organize Your Thinking on the Work Expectations of Your Organization for the Intervention Selector's Role	13
	Figure 2.3: The Human Performance Improvement Process Model for the Role of Intervention Designer and Developer	19
	Figure 2.4: Worksheet to Organize Your Thinking on the Work Expectations of Your Organization for the Intervention Designer and Developer's Role	23
	Figure 2.5: Steps in the Action Learning Model	28
	Figure 2.6: The Human Performance Improvement Process Model for the Role of Intervention Implementor	29
	Figure 2.7: Worksheet to Organize Your Thinking on the Work Expectations of Your Organization for the Intervention Implementor's Role	32
Section 3	Table 3.1: Relationship Between Intervention Selection and the Competencies of the Intervention Selector	41
	Figure 3.1: Model of Intervention Selection	40
	Figure 3.2: Step 1: Verify That the Root Causes of the Performance Problem Have Been Distinguished From the Symptoms or Consequences	45
	Figure 3.3: Assessment for Pinpointing the Causes of a Performance Problem	47
	Figure 3.4: Instrument for Assessing Stakeholder Agreement About the Causes of a Performance Problem	48
	Figure 3.5: Step 2: Consider the Range of Possible Interventions to Close the Performance Gap by Addressing the Root Causes	51
	Figure 3.6: Summary of Force Field Analysis	52
	Figure 3.7: Instrument for Assessing Possible Interventions to Solve a Performance Problem By Addressing Its Causes	53
	Figure 3.8: Step 3: Identify Constraints or Limitations on the Choice of the Interventions	57
	Figure 3.9: Step 4: Identify Possible Changes in the Performance Problem That May Influence the Interventions	59
	Figure 3.10: Step 5: Consider Possible Side Effects of Interventions if Implemented and Plan for Addressing Them	60

Figure 3.11: Step 6: Determine Necessary Stakeholder Support, Involvement, and Ownership 62

Figure 3.12: Step 7: Select Appropriate Interventions to Close the Performance Gap and Thereby Address the Performance Problem 64

Figure 3.13: Another Way to Think About the Intervention Selection Process 66

Figure 3.14: Step 8: Clarify the Initial and Eventual Scope of the Performance Interventions 67

Section 4

Table 4.1: Relationship Between Intervention Design and Development and the Competencies of the Intervention Designer and Developer 73

Figure 4.1: Model of Intervention Design and Development 72

Figure 4.2: Step 1: Examine the Characteristics of the Participants in the Intervention 75

Figure 4.3: Step 2: Examine the Competencies Necessary for Successful Achievement 77

Figure 4.4: Step 3: Examine the Characteristics of the Work Environment 79

Figure 4.5: Step 4: Formulate Performance Objectives to Guide the Intervention 80

Figure 4.6: Relationship Between Instructional Objectives and Performance Objectives 81

Figure 4.7: Worksheet for Preparing Performance Objectives for an Intervention 82

Figure 4.8: Step 5: Formulate Specific Methods by Which to Measure Performance Objectives 84

Figure 4.9: Step 6: Create a Detailed Project Plan 85

Figure 4.10: Step 7: Create a Detailed Communication and Marketing Plan to Clarify What Is Happening, Has Happened, and Will Happen 87

Figure 4.11: Step 8: Make, Buy, or Buy and Modify Materials and Media to Support the Implementation of the Intervention 88

Figure 4.12: Model for Selecting Materials and Media for a Performance Intervention 90

Section 5

Table 5.1: The Relationship Between Intervention Implementation and the Competencies of the Intervention Implementor 95

Figure 5.1: Model of Intervention Implementation 94

Figure 5.2: Step 1: Work with Participants and Stakeholders on a Daily Basis to Implement the Action Plan 98

Figure 5.3: Step 2: Use Materials and Media Supplied by the Intervention Designers and Developers and Provide Feedback to Them About Ways to Improve Their Use 100

Figure 5.4: Step 3: Deliver, or Facilitate Delivery of, the Intervention to Targeted Participants 102

Figure 5.5: Step 4: Ensure That Communication About the Intervention Is Carried Out Effectively 104

	Figure 5.6: Step 5: Track Short-Term Results Against the Intervention Performance Objectives 105
	Figure 5.7: Step 6: Surmount Barriers to Implementation and Ensure That the Intervention Is Implemented as Planned 107
	Figure 5.8: Step 7: Provide Clear, Specific, and Continuing Feedback to Stakeholders About the Results of the Intervention 109
Section 6	**Figure 6.1:** Worksheet to Guide Intervention Selection 114
	Figure 6.2: Worksheet to Guide Intervention Design and Development 121
	Figure 6.3: Worksheet to Guide Intervention Implementation 128

| **SECTION 1** | GETTING STARTED |

- What Is the Background of This Project?
- What Does This Job Aid Contain, and How Do You Use It?

| **SECTION 2** | DEFINING THE ROLES |

| **SECTION 3** | ENACTING THE ROLE OF INTERVENTION SELECTOR |

| **SECTION 4** | ENACTING THE ROLE OF INTERVENTION DESIGNER AND DEVELOPER |

| **SECTION 5** | ENACTING THE ROLE OF INTERVENTION IMPLEMENTOR |

| **SECTION 6** | TOOLS FOR CONDUCTING INTERVENTION SELECTION, DESIGN AND DEVELOPMENT, AND IMPLEMENTATION |

| **SECTION 7** | AFTERWORD |

| **SECTION 8** | BIBLIOGRAPHY |

SECTION 1   GETTING STARTED

What Is the Background of This Project?

The Intervention Selector, Designer and Developer, and Implementor is an outgrowth of *ASTD Models for Workplace Learning and Performance* (Rothwell, Sanders, and Soper, 1999). It is a self-study job aid for the workplace learning and performance (WLP) practitioner that describes the competencies essential to success in the WLP field and contains information about the practitioner's roles as intervention selector, designer and developer, and implementor. (Additional volumes in this ASTD series focus on the practitioner's other roles.)

As in other self-study job aids in this series, the term *role* should not be confused with *job title*. Instead, the word *role* refers to the part that an actor plays, just as it does in the theater. In WLP a role is a part that the practitioner plays in the human performance improvement (HPI) process. Following is a complete list of WLP roles (see also Rothwell, Sanders, and Soper, 1999, pages xv-xvii):

- The *manager* plans, organizes, schedules, and leads the work of individuals and groups to attain desired results; facilitates the strategic plan; ensures that workplace learning and performance is aligned with organizational needs and plans; and ensures the accomplishment of the administrative requirements of the function.

- The *analyst* isolates and troubleshoots the causes of "human performance gaps" or identifies areas in need of improvement.

- The *intervention selector* chooses appropriate learning and performance interventions (that is, corrective actions), both in and out of the workplace, to address the causes of these performance gaps.

- The *intervention designer and developer* formulates learning and performance interventions that address these causes and complement similarly targeted interventions.

- The *intervention implementor* ensures that the interventions that have been selected are carried out in an effective and appropriate way and complements similarly targeted interventions. In this capacity, the intervention implementor may serve as, for example, administrator, instructor, organization development practitioner, career development specialist, process redesign consultant, workspace designer, compensation specialist, or facilitator.

- The *change leader* inspires the workforce to embrace the interventions implemented, creates a direction for the effort, and ensures that the interventions are continuously monitored and directed in ways that are consistent with stakeholders' desired results.

- The *evaluator* assesses the changes made, the actions taken, the results achieved, and the impact experienced, and apprises participants and stakeholders accordingly.

What Does This Job Aid Contain, and How Do You Use It?

The Intervention Selector, Designer and Developer, and Implementor is designed to enhance your knowledge. Read the written material, practice using the worksheets and activities, and (above all) apply it on the job so that your training will transfer from this job aid to on-the-job performance improvement. For additional input, be sure to ask mentors or knowledgeable co-workers for one-on-one coaching.

SECTION 1   GETTING STARTED

SECTION 2   DEFINING THE ROLES

- ♦ The Role of the Intervention Selector
  - — Definition of the Role of Intervention Selector
  - — Importance of the Intervention Selector's Role
  - — The Relationship Between This and Other Roles
  - — The Place of Intervention Selection in the Human Performance Improvement Process
  - — What Are Competencies, and Why Are They Important?
  - — Competencies Associated With the Role of Intervention Selector
  - — Outputs Associated With the Role of Intervention Selector
  - — Who Performs the Role of Intervention Selector?
  - — When Do They Perform This Role?
  - — What Projects Do Intervention Selectors Carry Out?

- ♦ The Role of the Intervention Designer and Developer
  - — Definition of the Role of Intervention Designer and Developer
  - — Importance of the Intervention Designer and Developer's Role
  - — The Relationship Between This and Other Roles
  - — The Place of Intervention Designer and Developer in the Human Performance Improvement Process
  - — Competencies Associated With the Role of Intervention Designer and Developer
  - — Outputs Associated With the Role of Intervention Designer and Developer
  - — Who Performs the Role of Intervention Designer and Developer?
  - — When Do They Perform This Role?
  - — What Projects Does the Intervention Designer and Developer Carry Out?

- ◆ The Role of the Intervention Implementor
  - — Definition of the Role of Intervention Implementor
  - — Importance of the Role of Intervention Implementor
  - — The Relationship Between This and Other Roles
  - — The Place of the Intervention Implementor in the Human Performance Improvement Process
  - — Competencies Associated with the Role of Intervention Implementor
  - — Outputs Associated with the Role of Intervention Implementor
  - — Who Performs the Role of Intervention Implementor?
  - — When Do They Perform This Role?
  - — What Projects Does the Intervention Implementor Carry Out?

SECTION 3   ENACTING THE ROLE OF INTERVENTION SELECTOR

SECTION 4   ENACTING THE ROLE OF INTERVENTION DESIGNER AND DEVELOPER

SECTION 5   ENACTING THE ROLE OF INTERVENTION IMPLEMENTOR

SECTION 6   TOOLS FOR CONDUCTING INTERVENTION SELECTION, DESIGN AND DEVELOPMENT, AND IMPLEMENTATION

SECTION 7   AFTERWORD

SECTION 8   BIBLIOGRAPHY

SECTION 2   DEFINING THE ROLES

This section defines the roles of *intervention selector, intervention designer and developer,* and *intervention implementor.* This section also explains the importance of each role, describes how each role is related to other roles, shows the placement of each role in the human performance improvement (HPI) process, lists the competencies and outputs of each role, and reviews who performs each role, when those roles are carried out, and what projects are carried out by each role.

The Role of the Intervention Selector

Definition of the Role of Intervention Selector

The WLP practitioner's role as intervention selector is to facilitate the choice of the most appropriate interventions to address the root causes of performance problems and thereby narrow or close performance gaps between what is and what should be. Relying on the results of the analyst's role, the intervention selector apprises stakeholders about the most appropriate interventions for solving a performance problem by addressing its root cause or causes. It is the intervention selector's task to determine—or help others to determine—what should be done to solve a performance problem.

If the analyst's role is akin to that of the medical doctor serving as diagnostician, then the intervention selector's role is akin to that of the medical doctor serving as prescriptor—the one who offers the medicine intended to treat the illness. Some intervention selectors are empowered to choose a performance intervention without consulting other people. In many cases, however, intervention selectors recommend appropriate action by means of a written proposal and then await decisions by organizational superiors for approval to take action.

Intervention selection is the process of examining the ways by which to solve a performance problem over the long term or short term. (The term *intervention* is typically used instead of *solution* to imply more than a quick fix.)

The intervention selector faces a great temptation to assume that every performance problem has just one solution and can be solved by only one intervention. Some years ago, Adams (1986, p. ix) explained this issue:

Few people like problems. Hence, the natural tendency in problem-solving is to pick the first solution that comes to mind and run with it. The disadvantage of this approach is that you may run either off a cliff or into a worse problem than you started with. A better strategy in solving problems is to select the most attractive path from many ideas, or concepts.

The temptation to pick one solution stems from a bias toward action ("Let's do something now and then clean up the mess later") or an inability to apply creativity to solution finding. There can be dangers to thinking so narrowly. Consider the situation of a medical doctor who diagnoses an illness but then sees only one treatment or medicine as capable of curing it. That is, of course, a problematic assumption. The reason? Every medical treatment creates the risk of dangerous side effects that could end up making the patient more ill than he or she was to begin with. (That is one reason why the Hippocratic oath requires doctors to do no harm.)

In the intervention selection process, selectors are most effective when they are most creative. Then, they are able to facilitate a process of solution finding that is not imperiled by such fallacies as *stereotyping* (seeing only what you want to see), *misdiagnosis* (failing to isolate the causes of a problem or delimiting the problem too much), *misperception* (failing to see the problem from the viewpoints of different but relevant stakeholder groups), or *sensory overload* (seeing too much information to arrive at a conclusion or seeing too much information to make it possible to focus on the most important issues).

In a sense, the intervention selector's role focuses on finding many creative, cost-effective ways to solve a performance problem and deciding upon the most efficient, effective, and workable approach that is likely to yield performance improvement. The results of this process, made by the intervention selector alone or by key decision makers, should be useful in identifying what to do to solve a performance problem by addressing its causes, whether one or many, not its symptoms. Of special importance to success in the intervention selector's role is persistence, an unwillingness to give up in the face of resistance (Blair and Price, 1998).

Importance of the Intervention Selector's Role

No intervention can be selected until a proper analysis has been conducted. Always remember that it is essential to know as much as possible about the problem and its causes before selecting an appropriate intervention to solve the problem by addressing its root causes. It falls to the intervention selector to make use of the results of analysis by discovering—or helping stakeholders to discover—the most efficient and effective ways of solving the problem by addressing its root causes.

The intervention selector's role is important because most decision makers want results. They are not interested in the mere appearance of action taken to address problems (which is called *window dressing*) or a quickly chosen solution that eventually causes more problems than it solves (*shooting-from-the-hip decision making*). The intervention selector's role is thus key because it ensures that many possible solutions to a problem are considered and that their relative costs, benefits, advantages, and disadvantages are reviewed before a decision is made about what to do and how to do it to solve the problem. While many WLP practitioners may associate intervention selection with a simple choice between using a learning or a nonlearning intervention, the choice is rarely that simple. In fact, to address some problems, both types of interventions may be necessary and may need to be integrated. Without intervention selection, WLP professionals and others would not choose the most appropriate way to solve a performance problem. In that event, the work of the analyst would be rendered useless and the work of the evaluator would be rendered joyless.

The Relationship Between This and Other Roles

The intervention selector's role depends on the work results of the analyst and is measured by evaluators. If the analyst does not do a good job in isolating the root causes of a performance problem, it is unlikely that even the most skilled intervention selector could find the most appropriate interventions to address that problem. The results of the intervention selector's role influence the subsequent work of intervention designers and developers, who scope the intervention, and intervention implementors, who take steps to implement the intervention action plans and use materials and media created by intervention designers and developers.

The Place of Intervention Selection in the Human Performance Improvement Process

Intervention selection appears near the beginning of the HPI process model, the guiding model for WLP, as shown in figure 2.1. Note that intervention selection should only be undertaken after performance analysis and cause analysis.

What Are Competencies, and Why Are They Important?

Competencies are characteristics underlying successful performance. Competencies have commanded growing attention because they distinguish *exemplary performers* (best in class) from *the fully successful* (standard, but nothing more) performers. In other words, competencies are any knowledge, skill, attitude, motivation, or personal characteristic that leads to successful performance.

A *competency model* is a narrative description of the requirements for success in a job, occupation, department, or organization. It is an expression of what should be. It provides a basis against which to assess individuals or groups for development, serving as a foundation for (among other things) multirater, full-circle assessment; individual development planning; and career counseling. By building competencies, individuals, including WLP practitioners, can position themselves for career success (Dubois and Rothwell, 2000; Rothwell and Lindholm, 1999).

Competencies Associated With the Role of Intervention Selector

Descriptions of the research-based competencies associated with the intervention selector's role can be found in Rothwell, Sanders, and Soper (1999) and are shown in table 2.1.

The competencies in the table represent a formidable skill set. To summarize what they mean in practice, intervention selectors should be able to apply analytical and creative thinking to each of the causes of a performance problem. First, intervention selectors should interpret performance data and determine the effect of interventions on customers, suppliers, and employees (*analyzing performance data*).

Second, intervention selectors should have an excellent grasp of the range available of learning and nonlearning interventions, including (among others) career development (*career development theory and application*), organization development (*organization*

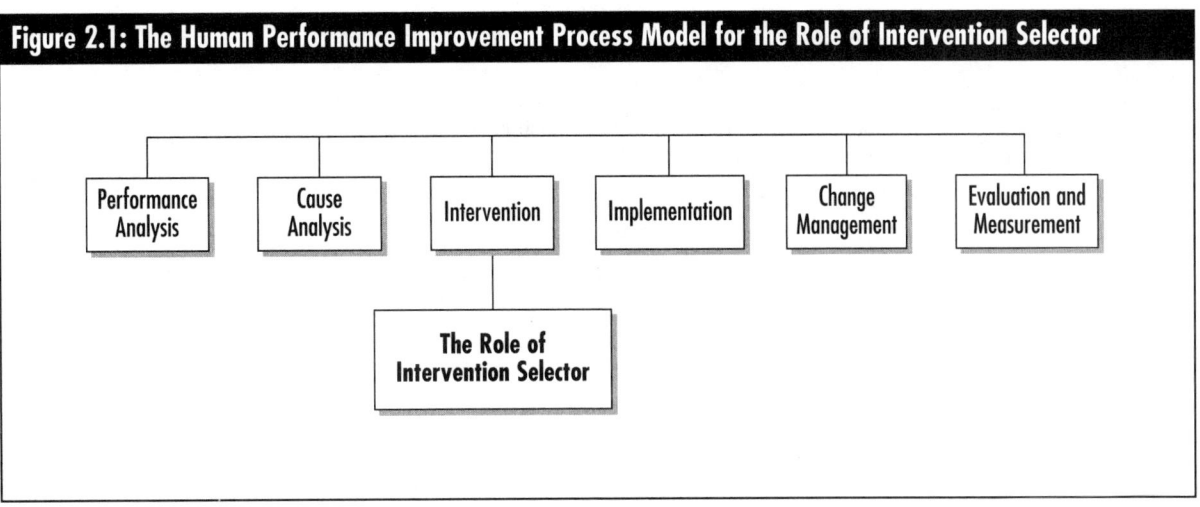

Figure 2.1: The Human Performance Improvement Process Model for the Role of Intervention Selector

Table 2.1: Competencies Associated with the Intervention Selector's Role

- *Adult learning:* Understanding how adults learn and how they use knowledge, skills, and attitudes.
- *Analyzing performance data:* Interpreting performance data and determining the effect of interventions on customers, suppliers, and employees.
- *Buy-in advocacy:* Building ownership and support for workplace initiatives.
- *Career development theory and application:* Understanding the theories, techniques, and appropriate applications of career development interventions used for performance improvement.
- *Communication:* Applying effective verbal, nonverbal, and written communication methods to achieve desired results.
- *Communication networks:* Understanding the various methods through which communication is achieved.
- *Computer-mediated communication:* Understanding the implication of current and evolving computer-based electronic communication.
- *Consulting:* Understanding the results that stakeholders desire from a process and providing insight into how they can best use their resources to achieve goals.
- *Cost-benefit analysis:* Accurately assessing the relative value of performance improvement interventions.
- *Distance education:* Understanding the evolving trends in technology-supported delivery methods and the implications of separating instructors and learners in time and location.
- *Diversity awareness:* Assessing the impact and appropriateness of interventions on individuals, groups, and organizations.
- *Electronic performance support systems:* Understanding current and evolving performance support systems and their appropriate applications.
- *Ethics modeling:* Modeling exemplary ethical behavior and understanding the implications of this responsibility.

(continued on next page)

Table 2.1: Competencies Associated with the Intervention Selector's Role *(continued)*

- *Identification of critical business issues:* Determining key business issues and forces for change and applying that knowledge to performance improvement strategies.
- *Industry awareness:* Understanding the current and future climate of the organization's industry and formulating strategies that respond to that climate.
- *Interpersonal relationship building:* Effectively interacting with others in order to produce meaningful outcomes.
- *Intervention selection:* Selecting performance improvement strategies that address the root cause or causes of performance gaps rather than treat symptoms or side effects.
- *Knowledge management:* Developing and implementing systems for creating, managing, and distributing knowledge.
- *Organization development theory and application:* Understanding the theories, techniques, and appropriate applications of organization development interventions as they are used for performance improvement.
- *Outsourcing management:* Ability to identify and select specialized resources outside of the organization; identifying, selecting, and managing technical specifications for these specialized resources.
- *Performance gap analysis:* Performing a front-end analysis by comparing actual and ideal performance levels in the workplace; identifying opportunities and strategies for performance improvement.
- *Performance theory:* Recognizing the implications, outcomes, and consequences of performance interventions to distinguish between activities and results.
- *Quality implications:* Identifying the relationships and implications among quality programs and performance.
- *Reward system theory and application:* Understanding the theories, techniques, and appropriate applications of reward system interventions used for performance improvement.
- *Staff selection theory and application:* Understanding the theories, techniques, and appropriate applications of staff selection interventions used for performance improvement.
- *Systems thinking:* Recognizing the interrelationship among events by determining the driving forces that connect seemingly isolated incidents within the organization; taking a holistic view of performance problems in order to find root causes.
- *Technological literacy:* Understanding and appropriately applying existing, new, or emerging technology.
- *Training theory and application:* Understanding the theories, techniques, and appropriate applications of training interventions for performance improvement.

Source: Rothwell, W., Sanders, E., and Soper, J. (1999). *ASTD Models for Workplace Learning and Performance: Roles, Competencies, and Outputs.* Alexandria, VA: ASTD, pp. 53–56. Used by permission.

development theory and application), reward systems (*reward system theory and application*), staff selection (*staff selection theory and application*), and training (*training theory and application*).

Third, intervention selectors should select performance improvement strategies that address the root cause or causes of performance gaps, rather than treat symptoms or side effects (*intervention selection*).

Fourth, intervention selectors should develop and implement systems for creating, managing, and distributing knowledge (*knowledge management*).

Fifth, intervention selectors should be able to perform front-end analysis by comparing actual and ideal performance levels in the workplace; identifying opportunities and strategies for performance improvement (*performance gap analysis*).

Sixth, intervention selectors should recognize the implications, outcomes, and consequences of performance interventions to distinguish between activities and results (*performance theory*).

Seventh, intervention selectors should recognize the interrelationship among events by determining the driving forces that connect seemingly isolated incidents within the organization, taking a holistic view of performance problems in order to find root causes (*systems thinking*).

Eighth, intervention selectors should accurately assess the relative value of interventions (*cost-benefit analysis*).

Ninth, intervention selectors should be able to determine business issues and forces for change and apply that knowledge to performance improvement strategies (*identification of critical business issues*).

Tenth, intervention selectors should understand the current and future climate of the organization's industry and formulate strategies that respond to that climate (*industry awareness*).

Eleventh, intervention selectors should possess the ability to identify and select specialized resources outside of the organization as well as identify, select, and manage technical specifications for those specialized resources (*outsourcing management*).

Twelfth, intervention selectors should be able to identify the relationships and implications among quality programs and performance (*quality implications*).

Thirteenth, intervention selectors should be able to apply effective verbal, nonverbal, and written communication methods to achieve desired results (*communication*) and understand the various methods through which communication is achieved (*communication networks*).

Fourteenth, intervention selectors should understand the results that stakeholders desire from a process and provide insight into how they can best use their resources to achieve goals (*consulting*) and effectively interact with others in order to produce meaningful outcomes (*interpersonal relationship building*).

Fifteenth, intervention selectors should build ownership and support for workplace initiatives (*buy-in advocacy*), assess the impact and appropriateness of interventions on individuals, groups, and organizations (*diversity awareness*), model exemplary ethical behavior and understand the implications of this responsibility (*ethics modeling*), and understand how adults learn and how they use knowledge, skills, and attitudes (*adult learning*).

Sixteenth and finally, intervention selectors should be able to understand the implication of current and evolving computer-based electronic communication (*computer-mediated communication*), evolving trends in technology-supported delivery methods and the implications of separating instructors and learners in time and location (*distance education*), current and evolving performance support systems and their appropriate applications (*electronic performance support systems*), and appropriately apply existing, new, or emerging technology (*technological literacy*).

Outputs Associated With the Role of Intervention Selector

Output is the term used to refer to the results of intervention selection processes. (For outputs of evaluation, see table 2.2.) However, the particular work outputs necessary in the intervention selector's role depend upon the unique requirements of

---

Table 2.2: Sample Outputs Associated with the Intervention Selector's Role

- Recommendations to others about selecting interventions to address or avert problems or seize opportunities
- Recommendations to others about ways to combine interventions
- Assessments of the expected impact of interventions
- Objectives for interventions that are aligned with desired business results

Source: Rothwell, W., Sanders, E., and Soper, J. (1999). *ASTD Models for Workplace Learning and Performance: Roles, Competencies, and Outputs*. Alexandria, VA: ASTD, p. 61. Used by permission.

key stakeholders, an organization's corporate culture, and work expectations. Take a moment to consider the corporate culture and work expectations of your own organization by completing the worksheet in figure 2.2.

Who Performs the Role of Intervention Selector?

The role of intervention selector may be played by one or more of the following: WLP practitioners serving as external or internal consultants, line managers, or employees. The choice of who performs the intervention selector's role has distinctive advantages and disadvantages.

External consultants often possess expertise and command credibility in the subject in question and experience in selecting appropriate interventions. These are distinct advantages. Evidence of expertise like an academic degree, a successful track record, or publications on the subject may make it easier for external consultants to gain access to key stakeholders. They may also have license to ask questions or recommend approaches that an internal consultant in the corporate culture might not have.

But external consultants may also possess disadvantages. They are not as familiar with an organization's corporate culture, power structure, or work processes as internal consultants, line managers, or employees are. Nor do they know the personalities or value systems of the organization's key decision makers. External consultants must find ways to familiarize themselves with such matters quickly and effectively.

The use of internal consultants for intervention selection also has advantages. Internal consultants are usually more familiar with the particular industry or business, the organization's corporate culture, and its work processes than external consultants are. Additionally, internal consultants can afford the time and effort to follow through on intervention selection in a way that may not be possible for external consultants, who have other clients and other demands on their time.

But internal consultants are just as imperfect, in their own way, as external consultants. They may not be able to gain access to key decision makers, and they may not be considered as credible as external consultants. Further, internal consultants sometimes lack real or perceived objectivity in selecting interventions, especially if they are trying to "sell" their own services. They may even be accused of manipulating the analysis results to sell their consulting services—a "crime" that external consultants are likewise accused of doing.

Of course, line managers and employees are most familiar with the performance problems and their causes that give rise to the need for interventions. But that familiarity has its downside. While they may know what causes a problem, they may not possess the competencies essential to solve it. Nor may they think of a full range of possible solutions. Of course, line managers and employees alike can be trained in the competencies of the intervention selector's role, just as they can be trained in the competencies of other WLP roles.

Often the most powerful approach for intervention selection, as with other steps in the HPI process model, is to field a team of people to select an intervention. That team may include external consultants working along with internal ones, external consultants working with line managers and employees, or internal consultants working with line managers and employees.

When Do They Perform This Role?

As with other roles, the intervention selector's role may be requested by others or initiated by intervention selectors themselves.

When Requested by Others. WLP practitioners are familiar with being asked to decide what to do to solve a performance problem. Unfortunately, managers and others sometimes approach them when they have already decided the intervention that they want. Their decision is not always correct. Consider the following vignettes and decide for yourself how well the intervention selection process was handled in each situation.

Vignette 1: An hourly worker walks into the office of a WLP practitioner. She says, "Our process improvement team has just met. We decided that our team needs training to solve the problem of tardiness that seems to be so prevalent on our team. (We just can't seem to get people to work on time in the team.) Could you prepare a one-hour course on time management for our team members so that they can get to work on time?"

Figure 2.2: Worksheet to Organize Your Thinking on the Work Expectations of Your Organization for the Intervention Selector's Role

Directions: Use this worksheet to organize your thinking about the work expectations your organization has for you in your role as intervention selector. Remember that the role of the intervention selector "chooses appropriate interventions to address root causes of human performance gaps" (Rothwell, Sanders, and Soper, 1999, p. 43). However, the outputs and quality requirements of the intervention selector role may vary from one corporate culture to another. For each competency listed in column 1, describe in column 2 what results—outputs—you believe your organization expects. (You may need to discuss this issue with your organization's key decision makers and stakeholders.) Then, in column 3, describe what behaviors and quality requirements would demonstrate success with that competency. In short, what results would you have to obtain to be considered successful by your customers and stakeholders? While there are no "right" or "wrong" answers to these questions in any absolute sense, they are important for building the appropriate expectations among your customers and stakeholders. Take the time to discuss these issues.

	Column 1 Competency	Column 2 What do you believe are the organization's expectations for results—the outputs—for your functioning in the intervention selector role?	Column 3 What behavior and quality requirements would demonstrate success with this competency in this organization? In short, what results would you have to obtain to be considered successful by your customers and stakeholders?
1	*Adult learning:* Understanding how adults learn and how they use knowledge, skills, and attitudes.		
2	*Analyzing performance data:* Interpreting performance data and determining the effect of interventions on customers, suppliers, and employees.		
3	*Buy-in advocacy:* Building ownership and support for workplace initiatives.		
4	*Career development theory and application:* Understanding the theories, techniques, and appropriate applications of career development interventions used for performance improvement.		

(continued on next page)

Figure 2.2: Worksheet to Organize Your Thinking on the Work Expectations of Your Organization for the Intervention Selector's Role *(continued)*

	Column 1 Competency	Column 2 What do you believe are the organization's expectations for results—the outputs—for your functioning in the intervention selector role?	Column 3 What behavior and quality requirements would demonstrate success with this competency in this organization? In short, what results would you have to obtain to be considered successful by your customers and stakeholders?
5	*Communication:* Applying effective verbal, nonverbal, and written communication methods to achieve desired results.		
6	*Communication networks:* Understanding the various methods through which communication is achieved.		
7	*Computer-mediated communication:* Understanding the implication of current and evolving computer-based electronic communication.		
8	*Consulting:* Understanding the results that stakeholders desire from a process and providing insight into how they can best use their resources to achieve goals.		
9	*Cost-benefit analysis:* Accurately assessing the relative value of performance improvement interventions.		
10	*Distance education:* Understanding the evolving trends in technology-supported delivery methods and the implications of separating instructors and learners in time and location.		

11	*Diversity awareness:* Assessing the impact and appropriateness of interventions on individuals, groups, and organizations.		
12	*Electronic performance support systems:* Understanding current and evolving performance support systems and their appropriate applications.		
13	*Ethics modeling:* Modeling exemplary ethical behavior and understanding the implications of this responsibility.		
14	*Identification of critical business issues:* Determining key business issues and forces for change and applying that knowledge to performance improvement strategies.		
15	*Industry awareness:* Understanding the current and future climate of the organization's industry and formulating strategies that respond to that climate.		
16	*Interpersonal relationship building:* Effectively interacting with others in order to produce meaningful outcomes.		
17	*Intervention selection:* Selecting performance improvement strategies that address the root causes of performance gaps, rather than treat symptoms or side effects.		
18	*Knowledge management:* Developing and implementing systems for creating, managing, and distributing knowledge.		

(continued on next page)

Figure 2.2: Worksheet to Organize Your Thinking on the Work Expectations of Your Organization for the Intervention Selector's Role *(continued)*

	Column 1 Competency	Column 2 What do you believe are the organization's expectations for results—the outputs—for your functioning in the intervention selector role?	Column 3 What behavior and quality requirements would demonstrate success with this competency in this organization? In short, what results would you have to obtain to be considered successful by your customers and stakeholders?
19	*Organization development theory and application:* Understanding the theories, techniques, and appropriate applications of organization development interventions as they are used for performance improvement.		
20	*Outsourcing management:* Ability to identify and select specialized resources outside of the organization; identifying, selecting, and managing technical specifications for these specialized resources.		
21	*Performance gap analysis:* Performing front-end analysis by comparing actual and ideal performance levels in the workplace; identifying opportunities and strategies for performance improvement.		
22	*Performance theory:* Recognizing the implications, outcomes, and consequences of performance interventions to distinguish between activities and results.		
23	*Quality implications:* Identifying the relationships and implications among quality programs and performance.		

24	*Reward system theory and application:* Understanding the theories, techniques, and appropriate applications of reward system interventions used for performance improvement.		
25	*Staff selection theory and application:* Understanding the theories, techniques, and appropriate applications of staff selection interventions used for performance improvement.		
26	*Systems thinking:* Recognizing the interrelationship among events by determining the driving forces that connect seemingly isolated incidents within the organization; taking a holistic view of performance problems in order to find root causes.		
27	*Technlogical literacy:* Understanding and appropriately applying existing, new, or emerging technology.		
28	*Training theory and application:* Understanding the theories, techniques, and appropriate applications of training interventions for performance improvement.		

Vignette 2: A line manager is talking to his colleagues in a management meeting. He remarks, "The turnover in this company is getting way out of hand. Do you know that I just lost three people this month? It is intolerable. Now I have to find and train many replacements, and that's not easy right now. Every one of these people is leaving for a job at a higher rate of pay. That proves what I have known all along: Our pay rates are far too low. We need to do something about that problem. When will the human resources department get our pay rates up to speed? We are not competitive."

Vignette 3: "Our company has a morale problem," began the CEO in a management meeting. "It is clear from the exit interview report I just reviewed. Departing employees are complaining that their supervisors never make clear enough what performance is expected—and then the workers get zapped at appraisal time for not meeting expectations that were never made clear until rating time. It's clear to me that we need to do something about our supervisors. Should we improve their training? I wonder. We could also make our selection process more rigorous, promoting fewer people to supervision from within and increasing the number of people hired as supervisors with experience from outside. Yes, I think those actions will solve the problems."

As you continue reading about the intervention selector's role, think about these vignettes. What questions would an intervention selector ask in these situations, and how should an intervention selector handle them?

When Initiated by the Intervention Selector. Although other people often ask WLP practitioners to enact the role of intervention selector, WLP practitioners also have an obligation to be proactive—that is, to recommend interventions even when others do not request them. In these situations they are said to initiate the role of intervention selector.

WLP practitioners who initiate intervention selection on their own, just like those who initiate analysis or evaluation on their own, face a greater challenge than do those who simply react to the requests of others. Nobody has asked for their opinion or recommendations. And sometimes stakeholders view such efforts as mere grandstanding by self-interested WLP practitioners who want to justify their existence. Like analysts or evaluators who act proactively, intervention selectors who do so must first find a sponsor or change champion to build awareness of the value of the intervention.

What Projects Do Intervention Selectors Carry Out?

Intervention selectors may independently make recommendations about what interventions to select, why they are appropriate, how they compare with other possible interventions, and what results to expect. Alternatively, they may serve as facilitators for task forces, project teams, or other groups from an organization that is formed to find solutions to identified problems. Intervention selection projects, like analysis or evaluation projects, can range in scope from the small scale to the large scale. Projects can also be carried out as isolated and stand-alone efforts, or they can be integrated with other efforts. The central question governing scope is this: What is the size of the group that will participate, is participating, or has participated in the intervention?

Many WLP practitioners are familiar with small-scale projects. Typical small-scale projects are those in which managers request help in solving a problem with one worker. Such projects are often carried out as one step in a process having many steps. For example, a manager may request help with a worker who has been arriving at work late every day, always with a good excuse. The manager may suggest training—or perhaps even disciplinary action—as a solution. However, the cause of the problem is unknown and, therefore, the appropriate solution is also unknown. Consequently, finding out the cause of the problem is one step in a small-scale project that affects only one person.

The intervention selector role, much like other roles, can also be carried out as large-scale projects. Examples might include situations in which WLP practitioners are asked to participate on a team to improve feedback in the organization, improve incentives and rewards, improve selection methods, and so forth. In each case, intervention selectors may be leading a long-term improvement effort.

The Role of Intervention Designer and Developer

Definition of the Role of Intervention Designer and Developer

The WLP practitioner's role as intervention designer and developer is to prepare the plan for the intervention and the materials and media to support it. In learning interventions, the intervention designer and developer's role is associated with that of instructional designer or materials developer, one who makes decisions about what training materials to use and how to deliver them. In nonlearning interventions, the intervention designer and developer's role is sometimes associated with that of human resource specialist, one who makes decisions about how to implement improvements in compensation and benefit programs, selection methods, feedback systems, and many other possible interventions. As noted in *ASTD Models for Workplace Learning and Performance*, "some examples of the work of the intervention designer and developer include serving as instructional designer, media specialist, materials developer, process engineer, ergonomics engineer, instructional writer, and compensation analyst" (Rothwell, Sanders, and Soper, 1999, p. 43). In short, it is the instructional designer and developer's task to determine how to implement the intervention chosen by the intervention selector based on the results provided by the analyst. The intervention designer and developer's role focuses around intervention planning.

Importance of the Intervention Designer and Developer's Role

No intervention can be designed and developed until the intervention is selected to address the root causes of performance problems. It is the intervention designer and developer's role to scope the intervention and prepare—or help others prepare—an action plan to make it a reality.

The intervention designer and developer's role is important because grand ideas sometimes founder on crude procedures. Resources misapplied are worse than no resources at all.

The intervention designer and developer's role is key because it ensures that an intervention will be implemented as it was supposed to be and will achieve intended results. Without the work of intervention designers and developers, there would be no action plan to govern implementation. Nor would there be materials—such as leader guides, participant guides, Websites, surveys, assessment instruments, procedure manuals, job aids, or other materials—available to support implementation.

The Relationship Between This and Other Roles

The role of intervention design and developer is closely related to that of intervention selector and intervention implementor. Without the work of intervention selectors, intervention designers and developers would not know what intervention to implement. Without the work of intervention implementors, the action plans and materials of intervention designers and developers would not be used. While intervention selectors decide what interventions to choose to address performance problems, intervention designers and developers decide how to implement those interventions. And while intervention designers and developers decide how to implement, intervention implementors actually follow through to ensure that the actions taken on a daily basis match up to plans.

The Place of Intervention Designer and Developer in the Human Performance Improvement Process

Intervention design and development occurs near the beginning of the HPI process model, the guiding model for WLP, as shown in figure 2.3.

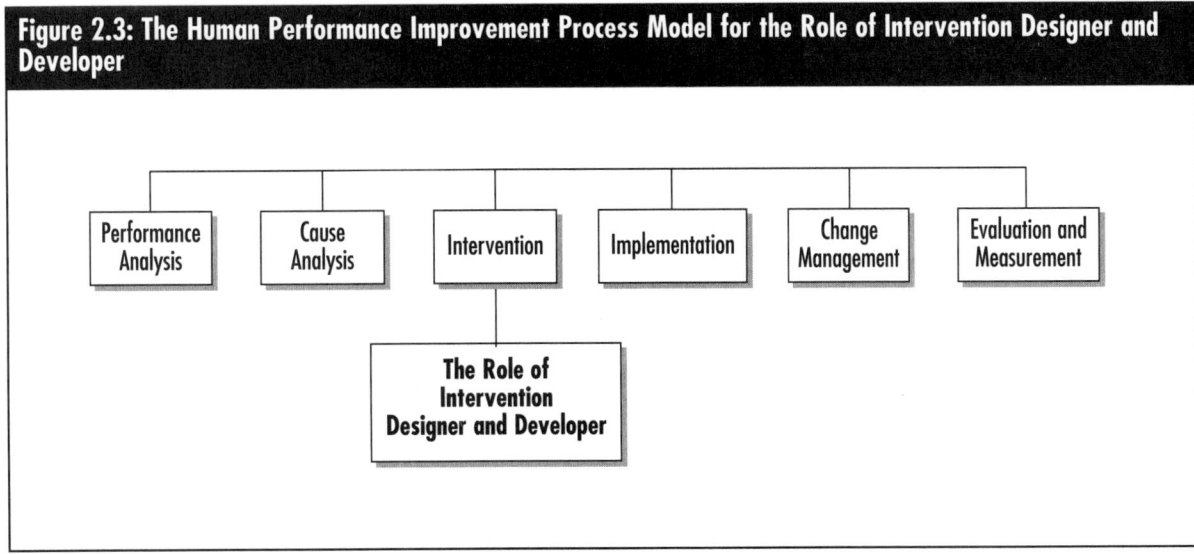

Figure 2.3: The Human Performance Improvement Process Model for the Role of Intervention Designer and Developer

Competencies Associated With the Role of Intervention Designer and Developer

Descriptions of the competencies associated with the intervention designer and developer's role can be found in Rothwell, Sanders, and Soper (1999) and are shown in table 2.3.

The competencies listed in table 2.3 represent a formidable skill set. To summarize what they mean in practice, intervention designers and developers should be able to prepare (or help others prepare) an action plan to guide a performance intervention.

Table 2.3: Competencies Associated with the Intervention Designer and Developer's Role

- *Adult learning:* Understanding how adults learn and how they use knowledge, skills, and attitudes.
- *Analyzing performance data:* Interpreting performance data and determining the effect of interventions on customers, suppliers, and employees.
- *Career development theory and application:* Understanding the theories, techniques, and appropriate applications of career development interventions used for performance improvement.
- *Communication:* Applying effective verbal, nonverbal, and written communication methods to achieve desired results.
- *Communication networks:* Understanding the various methods through which communication is achieved.
- *Computer-mediated communication:* Understanding the implication of current and evolving computer-based electronic communication.
- *Distance education:* Understanding the evolving trends in technology-supported delivery methods and the implications of separating instructors and learners in time and location.
- *Diversity awareness:* Assessing the impact and appropriateness of interventions on individuals, groups, and organizations.
- *Electronic performance support systems:* Understanding current and evolving performance support systems and their appropriate applications.
- *Ethics modeling:* Modeling exemplary ethical behavior and understanding the implications of this responsibility.
- *Industry awareness:* Understanding the current and future climate of the organization's industry and formulating strategies that respond to that climate.
- *Interpersonal relationship building:* Effectively interacting with others in order to produce meaningful outcomes.
- *Intervention selection:* Selecting performance improvement strategies that address the root causes of performance gaps, rather than treat symptoms or side effects.
- *Knowledge management:* Developing and implementing systems for creating, managing, and distributing knowledge.
- *Model building:* Conceptualizing and developing theoretical and practical frameworks that describe complex ideas.
- *Organization development theory and application:* Understanding the theories, techniques, and appropriate applications of organization development interventions as they are used for performance improvement.
- *Performance theory:* Recognizing the implications, outcomes, and consequences of performance interventions to distinguish between activities and results.
- *Project management:* Planning, organizing, and monitoring work.

- *Reward system theory and application:* Understanding the theories, techniques, and appropriate applications of reward system interventions used for performance improvement.
- *Standards identification:* Determining what constitutes success for individuals, organizations, and processes.
- *Survey design and development:* Creating survey approaches that use open-ended (essay) and closed-style questions (multiple choice and Likert items) for collecting data; preparing instruments in written, verbal, or electronic formats.
- *Systems thinking:* Recognizing the interrelationship among events by determining the driving forces that connect seemingly isolated incidents within the organization; taking a holistic view of performance problems in order to find root causes.
- *Technological literacy:* Understanding and appropriately applying existing, new, or emerging technology.
- *Training theory and application:* Understanding the theories, techniques, and appropriate applications of training interventions for performance improvement.
- *Workplace performance, learning strategies, and intervention evaluation:* Continually evaluating and improving interventions before and during implementation.

Source: Rothwell, W., Sanders, E., and Soper, J. (1999). *ASTD Models for Workplace Learning and Performance: Roles, Competencies, and Outputs.* Alexandria, VA: ASTD, pp. 53–56. Used by permission.

First, the intervention designer and developer role should interpret performance data and determine the effect of interventions on customers, suppliers, and employees *(analyzing performance data)*.

Second, the intervention designer and developer should understand the theories, techniques, and appropriate applications of career development interventions used for performance improvement *(career development theory and application)*, select performance improvement strategies that address the root causes of performance gaps, rather than treat symptoms or side effects *(intervention selection)*, develop and implement systems for creating, managing, and distributing knowledge *(knowledge management)*, and conceptualize and develop theoretical and practical frameworks that describe complex ideas *(model building)*.

Third, intervention designers and developers should understand the theories, techniques, and appropriate applications of organization development interventions used for performance improvement *(organization development theory and application)*, recognize the implications, outcomes, and consequences of performance interventions to distinguish between activities and results *(performance theory)*, and understand the theories, techniques, and appropriate applications of reward system interventions used for performance improvement *(reward system theory and application)*.

Fourth, intervention designers and developers should determine what constitutes success for individuals, organizations, and processes *(standards identification)*, recognize the interrelationship among events by determining the driving forces that connect seemingly isolated incidents within the organization and by taking a holistic view of performance problems in order to find root causes *(systems thinking)*.

Fifth, intervention designers and developers should understand the theories, techniques, and appropriate applications of training interventions used for performance improvement *(training theory and application)*, continually evaluate and improve interventions before and during implementation *(workplace performance, learning strategies, and intervention evaluation)*, and understand the current and future climate of the organization's industry and formulate strategies that respond to that climate *(industry awareness)*.

Sixth, intervention designers and developers should plan, organize, and monitor work *(project management)*, apply effective verbal, nonverbal, and written communication methods to achieve desired results (*communication*), and understand the various methods through which communication is achieved (*communication networks*).

Seventh, intervention designers and developers should effectively interact with others in order to produce meaningful outcomes (*interpersonal relationship building*), assess the impact and appropriateness of interventions on individuals, groups, and organizations (*diversity awareness*), and model exemplary ethical behavior and understanding the implications of this responsibility (*ethics modeling*).

Eighth, intervention designers and developers should understand how adults learn and how they use knowledge, skills, and attitudes (*adult learning*) and create survey approaches that use open-ended (essay) and closed-style questions (multiple choice and Likert items) for collecting data and should prepare instruments in written, verbal, or electronic formats (*survey design and development*).

Ninth and finally, intervention designers and developers should understand the implication of current and evolving computer-based electronic communication (*computer-mediated communication*), understand the evolving trends in technology-supported delivery methods and the implications of separating instructors and learners in time and location (*distance education*), understand current and evolving performance support systems and their appropriate applications (*electronic performance support systems*), and understand and appropriately apply existing, new, or emerging technology (*technological literacy*).

Outputs Associated With the Role of Intervention Designer and Developer

Output is the term used to refer to the results of intervention design and development processes. (For outputs of this role, see table 2.4.) However, the particular work outputs necessary in the role depend upon the unique requirements of key stakeholders, an organization's corporate culture, and work expectations. Take a moment to consider the corporate culture and work expectations of your own organization by completing the worksheet in figure 2.4.

Who Performs the Role of Intervention Designer and Developer?

The intervention designer and developer role, like that of other WLP roles, may be played by one or more of the following: WLP practitioners serving as external or internal consultants, line managers, or employees.

It is possible, for instance, to design and develop training interventions using an action learning model in which an instructional designer serves as a facilitator with a group consisting of a programmer and technologist (for Web-based or other high-tech applications), a graphic artist, and subject matter specialists representing different stakeholder groups (Rothwell, 1999a). The same basic approach may be used with other performance interventions as well. Unlike the traditional instructional systems design

---

Table 2.4: Sample Outputs Associated with the Intervention Designer and Developer's Role

- Intervention designs
- Action plans for interventions
- Lists of stakeholders and participants for interventions
- Links intervention design to business objectives

Source: Rothwell, W., Sanders, E., and Soper, J. (1999). *ASTD Models for Workplace Learning and Performance: Roles, Competencies, and Outputs.* Alexandria, VA: ASTD, p. 61. Used by permission.

Figure 2.4: Worksheet to Organize Your Thinking on the Work Expectations of Your Organization for the Intervention Designer and Developer's Role

Directions: Use this worksheet to organize your thinking about the work expectations your organization has for you in your role as intervention designer and developer. Remember that the role of the intervention designer and developer "creates learning and other interventions that help to address the specific root causes of human performance gaps" (Rothwell, Sanders, and Soper, 1999, p. 43). However, the outputs and quality requirements of the intervention designer and developer role may vary from one corporate culture to another. For each competency listed in column 1, describe in column 2 what results—outputs—you believe your organization expects. (You may need to discuss this issue with your organization's key decision makers and stakeholders.) Then, in column 3, describe what behaviors and quality requirements would demonstrate success with that competency. In short, what results would you have to obtain to be considered successful by your customers and stakeholders? While there are no "right" or "wrong" answers to these questions in any absolute sense, they are important for building the appropriate expectations among your customers and stakeholders. Take the time to discuss these issues.

	Column 1 Competency	Column 2 What do you believe are the organization's expectations for results—the outputs—for your functioning in the intervention designer and developer role?	Column 3 What behavior and quality requirements would demonstrate success with this competency in this organization? In short, what results would you have to obtain to be considered successful by your customers and stakeholders?
1	*Adult learning:* Understanding how adults learn and how they use knowledge, skills, and attitudes.		
2	*Analyzing performance data:* Interpreting performance data and determining the effect of interventions on customers, suppliers, and employees.		
3	*Career development theory and application:* Understanding the theories, techniques, and appropriate applications of career development interventions used for performance improvement.		
4	*Communication:* Applying effective verbal, nonverbal, and written communication methods to achieve desired results.		

(continued on next page)

Figure 2.4: Worksheet to Organize Your Thinking on the Work Expectations of Your Organization for the Intervention Designer and Developer's Role *(continued)*

	Column 1 Competency	Column 2 What do you believe are the organization's expectations for results—the outputs—for your functioning in the intervention designer and developer role?	Column 3 What behavior and quality requirements would demonstrate success with this competency in this organization? In short, what results would you have to obtain to be considered successful by your customers and stakeholders?
5	*Communication networks:* Understanding the various methods through which communication is achieved.		
6	*Computer-mediated communication:* Understanding the implication of current and evolving computer-based electronic communication.		
7	*Distance education:* Understanding the evolving trends in technology-supported delivery methods and the implications of separating instructors and learners in time and location.		
8	*Diversity awareness:* Assessing the impact and appropriateness of interventions on individuals, groups, and organizations.		
9	*Electronic performance support systems:* Understanding current and evolving performance support systems and their appropriate applications.		
10	*Ethics modeling:* Modeling exemplary ethical behavior and understanding the implications of this responsibility.		

11	*Industry awareness:* Understanding the current and future climate of the organization's industry and formulating strategies that respond to that climate.		
12	*Interpersonal relationship building:* Effectively interacting with others in order to produce meaningful outcomes.		
13	*Intervention selection:* Selecting performance improvement strategies that address the root causes of performance gaps, rather than treat symptoms or side effects.		
14	*Knowledge management:* Developing and implementing systems for creating, managing, and distributing knowledge.		
15	*Model building:* Conceptualizing and developing theoretical and practical frameworks that describe complex ideas.		
16	*Organization development theory and application:* Understanding the theories, techniques, and appropriate applications of organization development interventions as they are used for performance improvement.		
17	*Performance theory:* Recognizing the implications, outcomes, and consequences of performance interventions to distinguish between activities and results.		

(continued on next page)

Figure 2.4: Worksheet to Organize Your Thinking on the Work Expectations of Your Organization for the Intervention Designer and Developer's Role *(continued)*

	Column 1 Competency	Column 2 What do you believe are the organization's expectations for results—the outputs—for your functioning in the intervention designer and developer role?	Column 3 What behavior and quality requirements would demonstrate success with this competency in this organization? In short, what results would you have to obtain to be considered successful by your customers and stakeholders?
18	*Project management:* Planning, organizing, and monitoring work.		
19	*Reward system theory and application:* Understanding the theories, techniques, and appropriate applications of reward system interventions used for performance improvement.		
20	*Standards identification:* Determining what constitutes success for individuals, organizations, and processes.		
21	*Survey design and development:* Creating survey approaches that use open-ended (essay) and closed-style questions (multiple choice and Likert items) for collecting data; preparing instruments in written, verbal, or electronic formats.		
22	*Systems thinking:* Recognizing the interrelationship among events by determining the driving forces that connect seemingly isolated incidents within the organization; taking a holistic view of performance problems in order to find root causes.		

23	*Technlogical literacy:* Understanding and appropriately applying existing, new, or emerging technology.		
24	*Training theory and application:* Understanding the theories, techniques, and appropriate applications of training interventions for performance improvement.		
25	*Workplace performance, learning strategies, and intervention evaluation:* Continually evaluating and improving interventions before and during implementation.		

(ISD) model approach in which instructional designers bear most responsibility for analyzing the problem, designing and developing instruction, implementing instruction and evaluating results (Rothwell and Kazanas, 1998), this approach places primary responsibility on the stakeholders who own the problem.

The action learning model has been widely described elsewhere (for example, Boshyk, 2000; Dotlich and James, 1998; Marquardt and Revans, 1999; Weinstein, 1998). The following review of that model illustrates how the role of the intervention designer and developer may be handled by professionally trained experts (such as individuals with graduate degrees in instructional design), subject matter experts, or a team representing many talents and abilities. Its basic premise begins with a problem, issue, vision, or goal to be achieved, as shown in figure 2.5. A team is formed to address that problem, issue, vision, or goal. Team members must collectively have the competencies necessary to address the matter at hand, and they must each need broader development by exposure to other disciplines, approaches, or methods. They are then briefed on the matter by those who first recognized it. The designer leads them through a facilitated process in which they may do benchmarking with other organizations to see how those organizations have addressed the problem. The team members are then free to experiment with solutions or interventions within previously imposed constraints on time, money, and people. If they resolve the matter, the action learning is concluded; if they do not, their efforts are viewed as experiments from which the organization has derived important lessons. The point of this discussion is that the role of the intervention designer and developer may be handled by professionally trained experts (such as individuals with graduate degrees in instructional design), subject matter experts, or a team representing many talents and abilities.

When Do They Perform This Role?

Just like other roles, the intervention designer and developer's role is either requested by others or initiated by designers themselves. However, given the unique nature of intervention design and development as a process that stems from the work of previous roles, most designers do their work only after other people have analyzed the performance

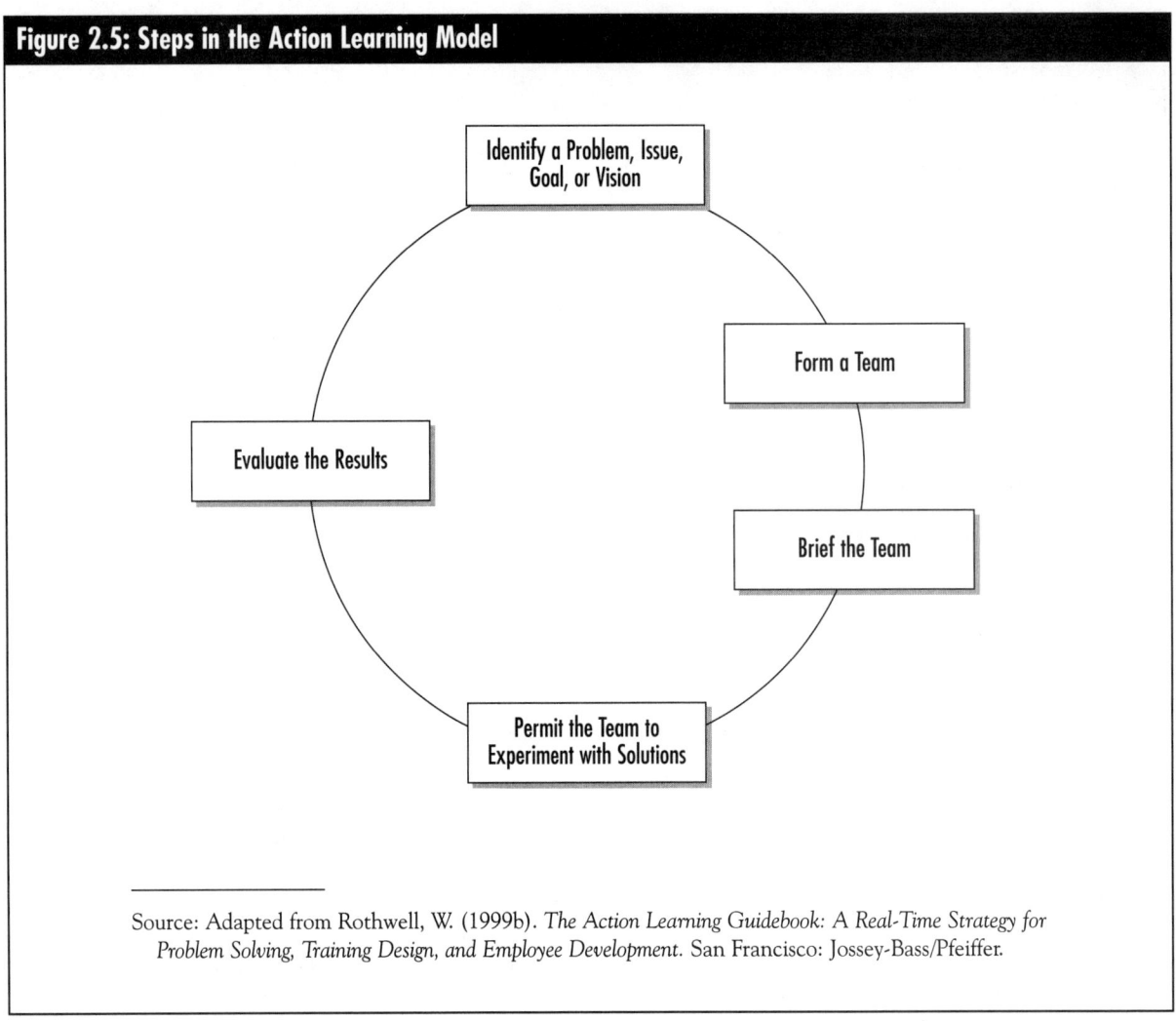

Figure 2.5: Steps in the Action Learning Model

Source: Adapted from Rothwell, W. (1999b). *The Action Learning Guidebook: A Real-Time Strategy for Problem Solving, Training Design, and Employee Development.* San Francisco: Jossey-Bass/Pfeiffer.

problem and reached agreement on the interventions necessary to solve it. Of course, designers may be either employed by the organization for which they work (internal consultants) or hired from outside as contractors (external consultants) based on their specialized expertise with the intervention they are to plan.

What Projects Does the Intervention Designer and Developer Carry Out?

Intervention designers and developers are responsible for planning all aspects of an intervention. In learning interventions such as training, their work is comparable to that of the instructional designer (Rothwell and Kazanas, 1998). In nonlearning interventions such as making improvements in selection, incentive, reward, or other systems, their work is comparable to that of organization development practitioners involved in action planning (Warrick, 1995). They can prepare materials to guide all aspects of an instructional or a noninstructional intervention and devise, or facilitate the preparation of, an action plan for the intervention.

The Role of the Intervention Implementor

Definition of the Role of Intervention Implementor

The intervention implementor "ensures the appropriate and effective implementation of desired interventions that address the specific root causes of human performance gaps. Some examples of the work of the intervention implementor include serving as administrator, instructor, organization development practitioner, career development specialist, process re-designed consultant, workspace designer, compensation specialist, and facilitator" (Rothwell, Sanders, and Soper, 1999, p. 43). It is worth emphasizing that no one WLP practitioner is expected to function at an expert level in all these roles. However, it is also worth emphasizing that WLP practitioners should have enough fundamental knowledge so they could serve as intervention implementors on a daily basis. Their knowledge should be sufficient for them to supervise other staff or contractors. It is the intervention implementor's task to guide the daily activities necessary to ensure that the action plan formulated by the intervention designer and developer is installed as planned.

Importance of the Role of Intervention Implementor

No intervention can be successful if it is not implemented successfully. Orchestrating the activities essential for making an action plan a reality is a difficult and stressful role, but it is essential. It is the intervention implementor's role to do just that.

The intervention implementor's role is important because someone must spearhead and facilitate the daily efforts to make the intervention successful. (In short, someone has to work the magic.) Without continuing action, stakeholders forget long-term goals. As a consequence, the performance problem is not solved, and the organization's performance problems persist. Without implementation, the efforts of all other roles would be pointless—since there would be no action taken on analysis, there would be no results to evaluate, and the actions taken to select and design and develop interventions would be rendered pointless.

The Relationship Between This and Other Roles

The intervention implementor's role is closely linked to those that preceded it in the HPI process. The intervention implementor acts on the results of analysis, intervention selection, and intervention design and development and helps others to act. The intervention implementor also provides the basis for subsequent evaluation of intervention results.

The Place of Intervention Implementor in the Human Performance Improvement Process

Intervention implementation appears about in the middle of the HPI process model, the guiding model for WPL, as shown in figure 2.6. It follows performance and cause analysis and intervention selection.

Competencies Associated With the Role of Intervention Implementor

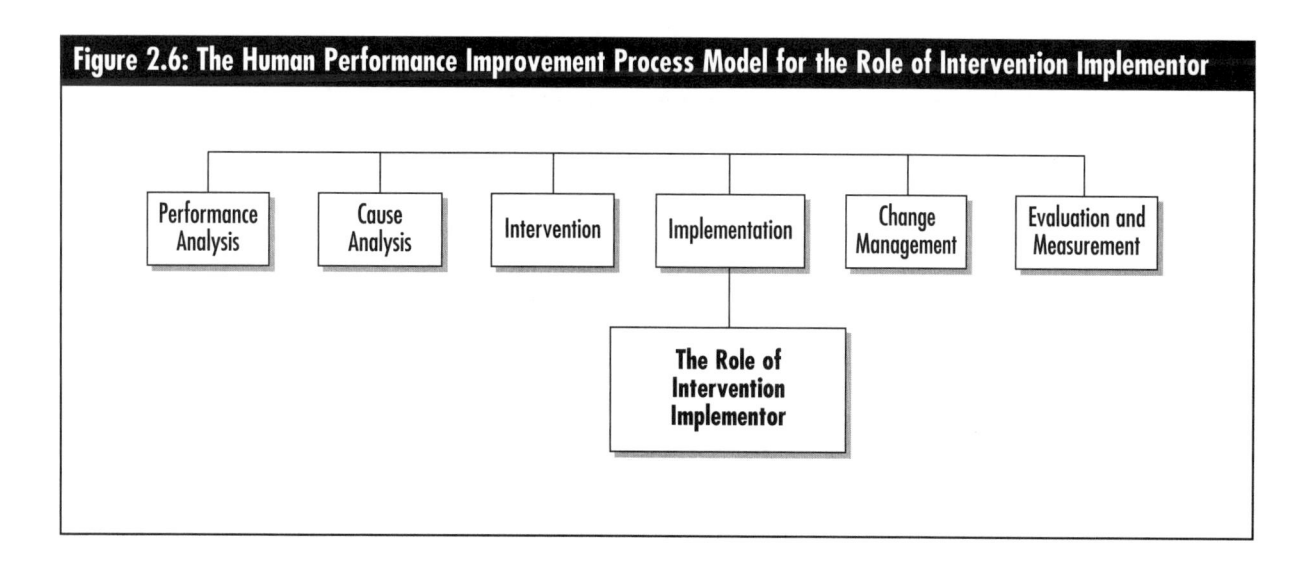

Descriptions of the competencies associated with the intervention implementor's role can be found in Rothwell, Sanders, and Soper (1999) and are shown in table 2.5.

Figure 2.6: The Human Performance Improvement Process Model for the Role of Intervention Implementor

Performance Analysis — Cause Analysis — Intervention — Implementation — Change Management — Evaluation and Measurement

Implementation → The Role of Intervention Implementor

Table 2.5: Competencies Associated with the Intervention Implementor's Role

- *Adult learning:* Understanding how adults learn and how they use knowledge, skills, and attitudes.
- *Buy-in and advocacy:* Building ownership and support for workplace initiatives.
- *Communication:* Applying effective verbal, nonverbal, and written communication methods to achieve desired results.
- *Communication networks:* Understanding the various methods through which communication is achieved.
- *Computer-mediated communication:* Understanding the implication of current and evolving computer-based electronic communication.
- *Consulting:* Understanding the results that stakeholders desire from a process and providing insight into how they can best use their resources to achieve goals.
- *Coping skills:* Dealing with ambiguity and stress resulting from conflicting information and goals; helping others deal with ambiguity and stress.
- *Diversity awareness:* Assessing the impact and appropriateness of interventions on individuals, groups, and organizations.
- *Electronic performance support systems:* Understanding current and evolving performance support systems and their appropriate applications.
- *Facilitation:* Helping others discover new insights.
- *Group dynamics:* Assessing how groups of people function and evolve as they seek to meet the needs of their members and of the organization.
- *Interpersonal relationship building:* Effectively interacting with others in order to produce meaningful outcomes.
- *Intervention monitoring:* Tracking and coordinating interventions to ensure consistency in implementation and alignment with organizational strategies.
- *Process consultation:* Using a monitoring and feedback method to continually improve the productivity of work groups.
- *Technological literacy:* Understanding and appropriately applying existing, new, or emerging technology.
- *Training theory and application:* Understanding the theories, techniques, and appropriate applications of training interventions for performance improvement.
- *Workplace performance, learning strategies, and intervention evaluation:* Continually evaluating and improving interventions before and during implementation.

Source: Rothwell, W., Sanders, E., and Soper, J. (1999). *ASTD Models for Workplace Learning and Performance: Roles, Competencies, and Outputs*. Alexandria, VA: ASTD, pp. 53–56. Used by permission.

The competencies listed in table 2.5, like those of other roles, represent a formidable skill set. To summarize what they mean in practice, intervention implementors should be able to assess the value of interventions.

First, intervention implementors should use a monitoring and feedback method to continually improve the productivity of work groups (*process consultation*).

Second, intervention implementors should understand the theories, techniques, and appropriate applications of training interventions used for performance improvement (*training theory and application*).

Third, intervention implementors should continually evaluate and improve interventions before and during implementation (*workplace performance, learning strategies, and intervention evaluation*).

Fourth, intervention implementors should apply effective verbal, nonverbal, and written communication methods to achieve desired results (*communication*).

Fifth, intervention implementors should understand the various methods through which communication is achieved (*communication networks*).

Sixth, intervention implementors should understand the results that stakeholders desire from a process and provide insight into how they can best use their resources to achieve goals (*consulting*).

Seventh, intervention implementors should deal with ambiguity and stress resulting from conflicting information and goals, helping others deal with ambiguity and stress (*coping skills*).

Eighth, intervention implementors should effectively interact with others in order to produce meaningful outcomes (*interpersonal relationship building*) and build ownership and support for workplace initiatives (*buy-in and advocacy*).

Ninth, intervention implementors should assess the impact and appropriateness of interventions on individuals, groups, and organizations (*diversity awareness*), assess how groups of people function and evolve as they seek to meet the needs of their members and of the organization (*group dynamics*), and understand how adults learn and how they use knowledge, skills, and attitudes (*adult learning*).

Tenth, intervention implementors should help others discover new insights (*facilitation*) and track and coordinate interventions to ensure consistency in implementation and alignment with organizational strategies (*intervention monitoring*).

Eleventh, intervention implementors should understand the implication of current and evolving computer-based electronic communication (*computer-mediated communication*), understand current and evolving performance support systems and their appropriate applications (*electronic performance support systems*), and understand and appropriately apply existing, new, or emerging technology (*technological literacy*).

Outputs Associated With the Role of Intervention Implementor

Output is the term used to refer to the results of intervention implementation processes. (For outputs of intervention implementation, see table 2.6.) However, as in enacting other roles, the particular work outputs necessary in the intervention implementor's role depend upon the unique requirements of key stakeholders, an organization's corporate culture, and work expectations. Take a moment to consider the corporate culture and work expectations of your own organization by completing the worksheet in figure 2.7.

Who Performs the Role of Intervention Implementor?

The intervention implementor role, like other roles, may be played by one or more of the following: WLP practitioners serving as external or internal consultants, line managers, or employees. Each choice of who will conduct intervention implementation, just like the choice of who will enact other roles, has distinctive advantages and disadvantages, as described elsewhere in this section.

Table 2.6: Sample Outputs Associated with the Intervention Implementor's Role

- Plans and schedules for implementing interventions
- Facilitation methods that will deliver the intervention appropriately
- Consulting services
- Contributions to business goals and objectives
- Measurable return-on-investment

Source: Rothwell, W., Sanders, E., and Soper, J. (1999). *ASTD Models for Workplace Learning and Performance: Roles, Competencies, and Outputs.* Alexandria, VA: ASTD, p. 61. Used by permission.

Figure 2.7: Worksheet to Organize Your Thinking on the Work Expectations of Your Organization for the Intervention Implementor's Role

Directions: Use this worksheet to organize your thinking about the work expectations your organization has for you in your role as intervention implementor. Remember that the role of the intervention implementor "ensures the appropriate and effective implementation of desired interventions that address the specific root causes of human performance gaps" (Rothwell, Sanders, and Soper, 1999, p. 43). However, the outputs and quality requirements of the intervention implementor role may vary from one corporate culture to another. For each competency listed in column 1, describe in column 2 what results—outputs—you believe your organization expects. (You may need to discuss this issue with your organization's key decision makers and stakeholders.) Then, in column 3, describe what behaviors and quality requirements would demonstrate success with that competency. In short, what results would you have to obtain to be considered successful by your customers and stakeholders? While there are no "right" or "wrong" answers to these questions in any absolute sense, they are important for building the appropriate expectations among your customers and stakeholders. Take the time to discuss these issues.

	Column 1 Competency	Column 2 What do you believe are the organization's expectations for results—the outputs—for your functioning in the intervention implementor role?	Column 3 What behavior and quality requirements would demonstrate success with this competency in this organization? In short, what results would you have to obtain to be considered successful by your customers and stakeholders?
1	*Adult learning:* Understanding how adults learn and how they use knowledge, skills, and attitudes.		
2	*Buy-in and advocacy:* Building ownership and support for workplace initiatives.		
3	*Communication:* Applying effective verbal, nonverbal, and written communication methods to achieve desired results.		
4	*Communication networks:* Understanding the various methods through which communication is achieved.		
5	*Computer-mediated communication:* Understanding the implication of current and evolving computer-based electronic communication.		

6	*Consulting:* Understanding the results that stakeholders desire from a process and providing insight into how they can best use their resources to achieve goals.		
7	*Coping skills:* Dealing with ambiguity and stress resulting from conflicting information and goals; helping others deal with ambiguity and stress.		
8	*Diversity awareness:* Assessing the impact and appropriateness of interventions on individuals, groups, and organizations.		
9	*Electronic performance support systems:* Understanding current and evolving performance support systems and their appropriate applications.		
10	*Facilitation:* Helping others discover new insights.		
11	*Group dynamics:* Assessing how groups of people function and evolve as they seek to meet the needs of their members and of the organization.		
12	*Interpersonal relationship building:* Effectively interacting with others in order to produce meaningful outcomes.		
13	*Intervention monitoring:* Tracking and coordinating interventions to ensure consistency in implementation and alignment with organizational strategies.		

(continued on next page)

Figure 2.7: Worksheet to Organize Your Thinking on the Work Expectations of Your Organization for the Intervention Implementor's Role *(continued)*

	Column 1 Competency	Column 2 What do you believe are the organization's expectations for results—the outputs—for your functioning in the intervention implementor role?	Column 3 What behavior and quality requirements would demonstrate success with this competency in this organization? In short, what results would you have to obtain to be considered successful by your customers and stakeholders?
14	*Process consultation:* Using a monitoring and feedback method to continually improve the productivity of work groups.		
15	*Technological literacy:* Understanding and appropriately applying existing, new, or emerging technology.		
16	*Training theory and application:* Understanding the theories, techniques, and appropriate applications of training interventions for performance improvement.		
17	*Workplace performance, learning strategies, and intervention evaluation:* Continually evaluating and improving interventions before and during implementation.		

When Do They Perform This Role?

The intervention implementor's role is enacted only after analysts have isolated the performance problem and its underlying causes, intervention selectors have pinpointed the appropriate interventions to solve the problem by addressing the causes, and intervention designers and developers have formulated intervention action plans and prepared appropriate materials and chosen appropriate media by which to deliver them.

What Projects Does the Intervention Implementor Carry Out?

The intervention implementor carries out any intervention designed to improve human performance by closing performance gaps and addressing their causes. That may involve delivering learning interventions—such as delivering instruction or overseeing such other learning interventions as employee educational reimbursement efforts, job rotation programs, or leadership development initiatives.

That may also involve delivering nonlearning interventions, such as improved employee recruitment and selection efforts, incentive and reward programs, feedback efforts, or ergonomic design.

SECTION 1 — GETTING STARTED

SECTION 2 — DEFINING THE ROLES

SECTION 3 — ENACTING THE ROLE OF INTERVENTION SELECTOR

- ◆ A Model of the Intervention Selection Process
- ◆ Steps in the Intervention Selection Process
  - — *Step 1:* Verify That the Root Causes of the Performance Problem Have Been Distinguished From the Symptoms or Consequences
  - — *Step 2:* Consider the Range of Possible Interventions to Close the Performance Gap By Addressing the Root Causes
  - — *Step 3:* Identify Constraints or Limitations on the Choice of the Interventions
  - — *Step 4:* Identify Possible Changes in the Performance Problem That May Influence the Interventions
  - — *Step 5:* Consider Possible Side Effects of Interventions if Implemented and Plan for Addressing Them
  - — *Step 6:* Determine Necessary Stakeholder Support, Involvement, and Ownership
  - — *Step 7:* Select Appropriate Interventions to Close the Performance Gap and Thereby Address the Performance Problem
  - — *Step 8:* Clarify the Initial and Eventual Scope of the Performance Interventions
- ◆ Section Summary

SECTION 4 — ENACTING THE ROLE OF INTERVENTION DESIGNER AND DEVELOPER

SECTION 5 — ENACTING THE ROLE OF INTERVENTION IMPLEMENTOR

SECTION 6 — TOOLS FOR CONDUCTING INTERVENTION SELECTION, DESIGN AND DEVELOPMENT, AND IMPLEMENTATION

SECTION 7 — AFTERWORD

SECTION 8 — BIBLIOGRAPHY

SECTION 3 ENACTING THE ROLE OF INTERVENTION SELECTOR

The intervention selector role "chooses appropriate interventions to address root causes of human performance gaps" (Rothwell, Sanders, and Soper, 1999, p. 43). When WLP practitioners or others enact this role, they make the switch from focusing on performance problems and their causes to solutions and their implementation.

A *model* helps describe or clarify an otherwise complex object or process. Model building is as important in intervention selection as it is in other roles of the WLP practitioner. An intervention selection process model helps WLP practitioners and other people carry out effective intervention selection. Each step in the model requires that action be taken. Various models for intervention selection have been proposed or described, and much has been written about what interventions should be chosen to narrow or close performance gaps resulting from performance problems. (The bibliography in Section 8 lists numerous publications on the topic. See, for example, Langdon, Whiteside, and McKenna, 1999; Rosenheck, 1997; and Rothwell, 1996a; Rothwell, 1996b.)

A Model of the Intervention Selection Process

One way to think of the intervention selection process is as a series of general steps, as follows:

1. Verify that the root causes of the performance problem have been distinguished from the symptoms or consequences.
2. Consider the range of possible interventions to close the performance gap by addressing the root causes.
3. Identify constraints or limitations on the choice of the interventions.
4. Identify possible changes in the performance problem that may influence the interventions.
5. Consider possible side effects of interventions if implemented and plan for addressing them.
6. Determine necessary stakeholder support, involvement, and ownership.
7. Select appropriate interventions to close the performance gap and thereby address the performance problem.
8. Clarify the initial and eventual scope of the performance interventions.

These steps are depicted in figure 3.1, and their relationship to the intervention selector's competencies are depicted in table 3.1. This section addresses these steps and provides guidance for applying them. As you think about selecting an intervention, use figure 6.1, "Worksheet to Guide Intervention Selection," on page 114 to help pose questions related to each step of the model.

Figure 3.1: Model of Intervention Selection

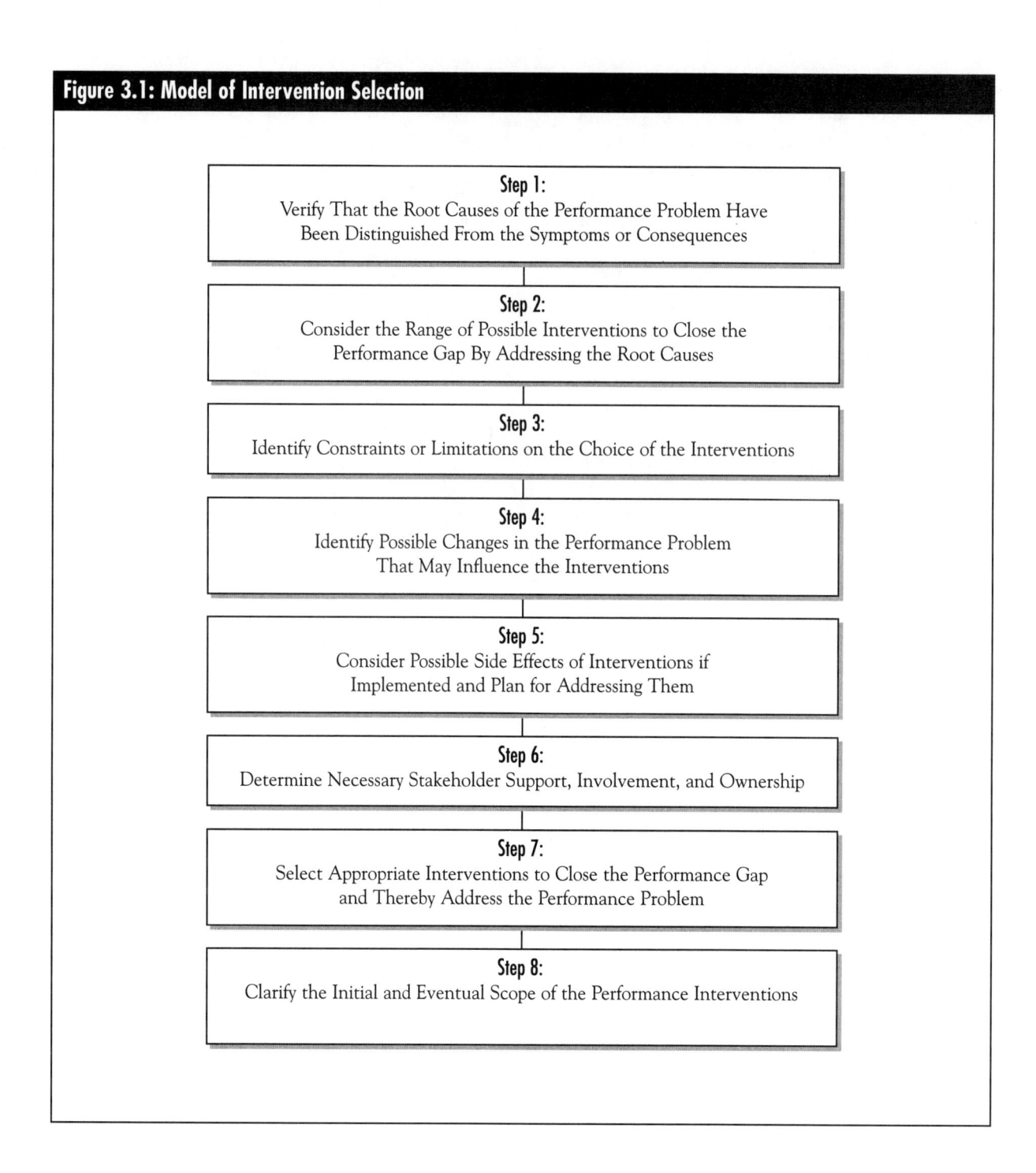

Step 1:
Verify That the Root Causes of the Performance Problem Have Been Distinguished From the Symptoms or Consequences

Step 2:
Consider the Range of Possible Interventions to Close the Performance Gap By Addressing the Root Causes

Step 3:
Identify Constraints or Limitations on the Choice of the Interventions

Step 4:
Identify Possible Changes in the Performance Problem That May Influence the Interventions

Step 5:
Consider Possible Side Effects of Interventions if Implemented and Plan for Addressing Them

Step 6:
Determine Necessary Stakeholder Support, Involvement, and Ownership

Step 7:
Select Appropriate Interventions to Close the Performance Gap and Thereby Address the Performance Problem

Step 8:
Clarify the Initial and Eventual Scope of the Performance Interventions

Table 3.1: Relationship Between Intervention Selection and the Competencies of the Intervention Selector*

Model of Intervention Selection	Competencies of the Intervention Selector Role
Verify that the root causes of the performance problem have been distinguished from the symptoms or consequences	◆ *Consulting:* Understanding the results that stakeholders desire from a process and providing insight into how they can best use their resources to achieve goals ◆ *Knowledge management:* Developing and implementing systems for creating, managing, and distributing knowledge ◆ *Performance gap analysis:* Performing front-end analysis by comparing actual and ideal performance levels in the workplace; identifying opportunities and strategies for performance improvement ◆ *Systems thinking:* Recognizing the interrelationship among events by determining the driving forces that connect seemingly isolated incidents within the organization; taking a holistic view of performance problems in order to find root causes
Consider the range of possible interventions to close the performance gap by addressing the root causes	◆ *Adult learning:* Understanding how adults learn and how they use knowledge, skills, and attitudes ◆ *Career development theory and application:* Understanding the theories, techniques, and appropriate applications of career development interventions used for performance improvement ◆ *Consulting:* Understanding the results that stakeholders desire from a process and providing insight into how they can best use their resources to achieve goals ◆ *Cost-benefit analysis:* Accurately assessing the relative value of performance improvement interventions ◆ *Identification of critical business issues:* Determining key business issues and forces for change and applying that knowledge to performance improvement strategies ◆ *Industry awareness:* Understanding the current and future climate of the organization's industry and formulating strategies that respond to that climate ◆ *Knowledge management:* Developing and implementing systems for creating, managing, and distributing knowledge ◆ *Organization development theory and application:* Understanding the theories, techniques, and appropriate applications of organization development interventions as they are used for performance improvement ◆ *Performance gap analysis:* Performing front-end analysis by comparing actual and ideal performance levels in the workplace; identifying opportunities and strategies for performance improvement ◆ *Performance theory:* Recognizing the implications, outcomes, and consequences of performance interventions to distinguish between activities and results ◆ *Quality implications:* Identifying the relationships and implications among quality programs and performance ◆ *Reward system theory and application:* Understanding the theories, techniques, and appropriate applications of reward system interventions used for performance improvement ◆ *Staff selection theory and application:* Understanding the theories, techniques, and appropriate applications of staff selection interventions used for performance improvement ◆ *Training theory and application:* Understanding the theories, techniques, and appropriate applications of training interventions for performance improvement

(continued on next page)

*Some competencies are used in more than one step of the model.

Table 3.1: Relationship Between Intervention Selection and the Competencies of the Intervention Selector (continued)

Model of Intervention Selection	Competencies of the Intervention Selector Role
Identify constraints or limitations on the choice of the interventions	♦ *Adult learning:* Understanding how adults learn and how they use knowledge, skills, and attitudes ♦ *Analyzing performance data:* Interpreting performance data and determining the effect of interventions on customers, suppliers, and employees ♦ *Consulting:* Understanding the results that stakeholders desire from a process and providing insight into how they can best use their resources to achieve goals ♦ *Cost-benefit analysis:* Accurately assessing the relative value of performance improvement interventions ♦ *Knowledge management:* Developing and implementing systems for creating, managing, and distributing knowledge ♦ *Quality implications:* Identifying the relationships and implications among quality programs and performance ♦ *Systems thinking:* Recognizing the interrelationship among events by determining the driving forces that connect seemingly isolated incidents within the organization; taking a holistic view of performance problems in order to find root causes
Identify possible changes in the performance problem that may influence the interventions	♦ *Adult learning:* Understanding how adults learn and how they use knowledge, skills, and attitudes ♦ *Consulting:* Understanding the results that stakeholders desire from a process and providing insight into how they can best use their resources to achieve goals ♦ *Cost-benefit analysis:* Accurately assessing the relative value of performance improvement interventions ♦ *Identification of critical business issues:* Determining key business issues and forces for change and applying that knowledge to performance improvement strategies ♦ *Industry awareness:* Understanding the current and future climate of the organization's industry ♦ *Quality implications:* Identifying the relationships and implications among quality programs and performance ♦ *Systems thinking:* Recognizing the interrelationship among events by determining the driving forces that connect seemingly isolated incidents within the organization; taking a holistic view of performance problems in order to find root causes

Model of Intervention Selection	Competencies of the Intervention Selector Role
Consider possible side effects of interventions if implemented and plan for addressing them	♦ *Adult learning:* Understanding how adults learn and how they use knowledge, skills, and attitudes ♦ *Consulting:* Understanding the results that stakeholders desire from a process and providing insight into how they can best use their resources to achieve goals ♦ *Cost-benefit analysis:* Accurately assessing the relative value of performance improvement interventions ♦ *Identification of critical business issues:* Determining key business issues and forces for change and applying that knowledge to performance improvement strategies ♦ *Industry awareness:* Understanding the current and future climate of the organization's industry ♦ *Quality implications:* Identifying the relationships and implications among quality programs and performance ♦ *Systems thinking:* Recognizing the interrelationship among events by determining the driving forces that connect seemingly isolated incidents within the organization; taking a holistic view of performance problems in order to find root causes
Determine necessary stakeholder support, involvement, and ownership	♦ *Buy-in advocacy:* Building ownership and support for workplace initiatives ♦ *Communication:* Applying effective verbal, nonverbal, and written communication methods to achieve desired results ♦ *Communication networks:* Understanding the various methods through which communication is achieved ♦ *Computer-mediated communication:* Understanding the implication of current and evolving computer-based electronic communication ♦ *Distance education:* Understanding the evolving trends in technology-supported delivery methods and the implications of separating instructors and learners in time and location ♦ *Diversity awareness:* Assessing the impact and appropriateness of interventions on individuals, groups, and organizations ♦ *Electronic performance support systems:* Understanding current and evolving performance support systems and their appropriate applications ♦ *Ethics modeling:* Modeling exemplary ethical behavior and understanding the implications of this responsibility ♦ *Interpersonal relationship building:* Effectively interacting with others in order to produce meaningful outcomes ♦ *Outsourcing management:* Ability to identify and select specialized resources outside of the organization; identifying, selecting, and managing technical specifications for these specialized resources ♦ *Technological literacy:* Understanding and appropriately applying existing, new, or emerging technology

(continued on next page)

Table 3.1: Relationship Between Intervention Selection and the Competencies of the Intervention Selector *(continued)*

Model of Intervention Selection	Competencies of the Intervention Selector Role
Select appropriate interventions to close the performance gap and thereby address the performance problem	♦ *Cost-benefit analysis:* Accurately assessing the relative value of performance improvement interventions ♦ *Intervention selection:* Selecting performance improvement strategies that address the root causes of performance gaps, rather than treat symptoms or side effects
Clarify the initial and eventual scope of the performance interventions	♦ *Consulting:* Understanding the results that stakeholders desire from a process and providing insight into how they can best use their resources to achieve goals ♦ *Knowledge management:* Developing and implementing systems for creating, managing, and distributing knowledge ♦ *Performance gap analysis:* Performing front-end analysis by comparing actual and ideal performance levels in the workplace; identifying opportunities and strategies for performance improvement ♦ *Systems thinking:* Recognizing the interrelationship among events by determining the driving forces that connect seemingly isolated incidents within the organization; taking a holistic view of performance problems in order to find root causes

Steps in the Intervention Selection Process

Step 1: Verify That the Root Causes of the Performance Problem Have Been Distinguished From the Symptoms or Consequences

The descriptions of each step of the intervention selection process follow a similar format. They begin with the definition and purpose of the step, follow with notes about implementing the step, and end with an example of the step that illustrates and dramatizes what it can mean in practice.

Definition and Purpose of Step 1

Begin intervention selection by verifying that the analysis has effectively distinguished the root causes of a performance problem from its symptoms or consequences. (See figure 3.2.) That means double-checking the results of analysis. The analysis is critically important because it will lead to an improper intervention selection if it has been done incorrectly.

Intervention selectors are like analysts in that they begin focusing attention on problem behaviors (see Hollands, 1997). The main reason for pinpointing root causes first is that all subsequent steps in selecting, designing and developing, and implementing interventions hinge on it. If the analysis was performed by someone who will not be making decisions about intervention selection, it is essential to double-check that the results of the analysis have been performed properly. If the WLP practitioners or someone else who will be making the decisions performed the analysis, it is still wise to double-check. After all, nobody is perfect. Mistakes could have been made. And the stakes are just too high to make the assumption that the results of the analysis are flawless. You cannot trust everything you hear—or that is done by other people. It would be dangerous and foolish to separate the roles when the work of one is so dependent on the results of another.

Indeed, a common mistake made by managers and inexperienced WLP practitioners is to confuse the symptoms—that is, the consequences or effects of performance problems—with the causes, and seasoned WLP practitioners will take care to avoid confusing them.

Take a simple example. Suppose an organization is experiencing high turnover. Managers may complain about it. But turnover is not the problem, and it is not the root cause. It is a symptom of other problems. Until an analysis is completed, it is not clear what that cause (or those causes) might be. Of course, there could be many reasons for high turnover. And an intervention to address turnover is not likely to be effective unless it addresses the causes of that turnover.

Consider the following statements, which represent complaints about symptoms:

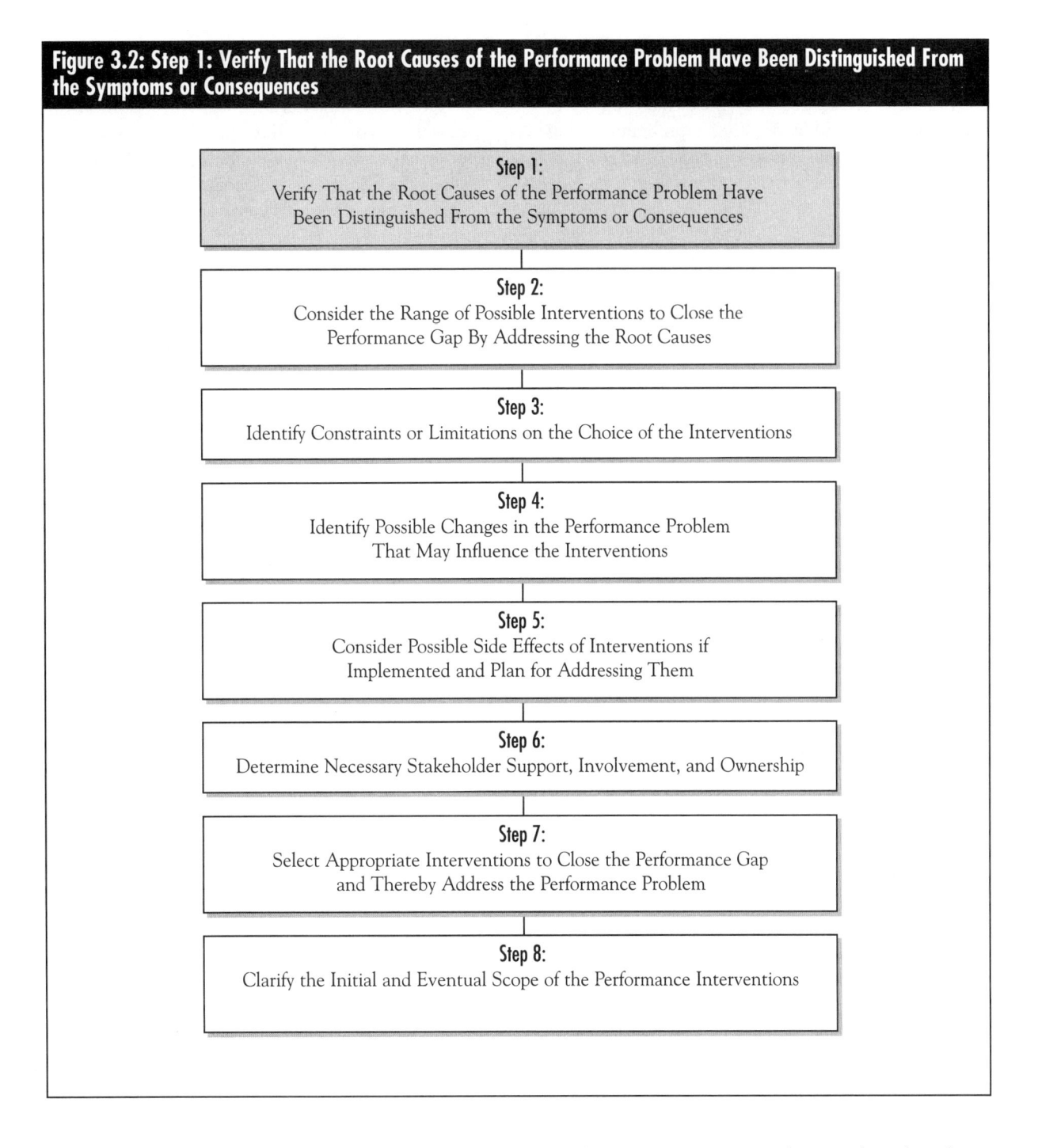

Figure 3.2: Step 1: Verify That the Root Causes of the Performance Problem Have Been Distinguished From the Symptoms or Consequences

```
┌─────────────────────────────────────────────────────────────┐
│ Step 1:                                                     │
│ Verify That the Root Causes of the Performance Problem Have │
│ Been Distinguished From the Symptoms or Consequences        │
└─────────────────────────────────────────────────────────────┘
                              │
┌─────────────────────────────────────────────────────────────┐
│ Step 2:                                                     │
│ Consider the Range of Possible Interventions to Close the   │
│ Performance Gap By Addressing the Root Causes               │
└─────────────────────────────────────────────────────────────┘
                              │
┌─────────────────────────────────────────────────────────────┐
│ Step 3:                                                     │
│ Identify Constraints or Limitations on the Choice of the Interventions │
└─────────────────────────────────────────────────────────────┘
                              │
┌─────────────────────────────────────────────────────────────┐
│ Step 4:                                                     │
│ Identify Possible Changes in the Performance Problem        │
│ That May Influence the Interventions                        │
└─────────────────────────────────────────────────────────────┘
                              │
┌─────────────────────────────────────────────────────────────┐
│ Step 5:                                                     │
│ Consider Possible Side Effects of Interventions if          │
│ Implemented and Plan for Addressing Them                    │
└─────────────────────────────────────────────────────────────┘
                              │
┌─────────────────────────────────────────────────────────────┐
│ Step 6:                                                     │
│ Determine Necessary Stakeholder Support, Involvement, and Ownership │
└─────────────────────────────────────────────────────────────┘
                              │
┌─────────────────────────────────────────────────────────────┐
│ Step 7:                                                     │
│ Select Appropriate Interventions to Close the Performance Gap │
│ and Thereby Address the Performance Problem                 │
└─────────────────────────────────────────────────────────────┘
                              │
┌─────────────────────────────────────────────────────────────┐
│ Step 8:                                                     │
│ Clarify the Initial and Eventual Scope of the Performance Interventions │
└─────────────────────────────────────────────────────────────┘
```

- "Our turnover is too high."
- "I never hear about a policy change until long after it has been made, and then I look foolish with customers when I tell them something that turns out to be wrong."
- "If you walk through our work areas, you get the impression that the people are working at a frenetic pace."
- "Our customers are complaining about how long it takes for us to fill orders."

In each statement, the speaker is describing the symptoms (consequences or symptoms) of a performance problem. But the reasons (causes) that account for those symptoms remain unknown.

The first step in selecting interventions, then, is to verify that the root causes of the problem have been isolated. (For one way to do that, see figure 3.3.) That must be done through analysis. But it is essential to double-check to ensure that the root causes have been isolated. When a preliminary diagnosis has been made, it is worth asking such follow-up questions as these:

- Could the problems be caused by reasons other than those pinpointed by analysis? If so, what are those other possible causes? How much influence are they exerting on the problem?
- Could there be more than one cause of the performance problem? If so, what are the other possible causes, and how could their influence on the performance gap be assessed?
- If action is taken to address the identified causes, will the performance problem be solved, or will the performance gap narrow? How can we tell?

Once these questions have been posed and their answers double-checked, the intervention selector is positioned to progress to other steps in the intervention selection process.

Implementing Step 1

Begin any intervention selection process by double-checking the identified causes and asking stakeholders for their opinions. Use Step 1 of the worksheet in figure 6.1 to answer the preceding questions to stakeholders. If you wish, poll stakeholders on these and related issues by using the survey questionnaire appearing in figure 3.4. However, remember that stakeholders may end up being the real culprits: They, not employees, may be to blame for most performance problems because managers often fail to establish and communicate clear work expectations (Manzoni and Barsoux, 1998).

Vignette: The director of WLP in the LMN Corporation, Marsha Kung, had been hearing widespread complaints about the company's performance appraisal system from workers and managers alike. Like directors of workplace learning in many companies, Kung reports to a vice president of human resources, in her case, Mike Santiago. Kung is new to her job, having accepted her current position only two months before Santiago asked her to chair a task force to improve the company's performance appraisal system. However, Kung is a seasoned WLP practitioner with 10 years of work experience in the industry of which LMN Corporation is part.

Kung hired an external consultant, Gordon Roswell, to conduct a third-party analysis of the performance appraisal system. She asked him to review the company's performance appraisal system by conducting interviews and focus groups with company managers and workers, identify and benchmark best practice performance management programs, and conduct a literature review of current practices and proven research in performance appraisal and performance management systems.

After conducting his analysis, Roswell presented a report to Kung in which he identified several major performance issues to be addressed:

1. Workers and managers alike perceived that no relationship existed between high performance, as measured by the company's performance appraisal system, and compensation practices. In fact, Roswell quoted several workers and managers who used the same joke: "If you do a good job at LMN, you get a 2 percent raise, and if you do a bad job at LMN, you get a 2 percent raise."

2. Workers and managers alike perceived that no relationship existed between promotion decisions and performance measured by the company's performance appraisal system. In focus groups facilitated by Roswell, workers repeatedly (and in almost a refrain) chanted, "It's who you know here, not what you know or how you perform, that counts in promotions."

3. Supervisors and managers noted that the appraisal was nothing more than a "check box activity." Some of them told Roswell candidly that they thought it was an enormous waste of time, since nothing was done with the results.

4. Supervisors and managers complained that they had not received training on how to complete performance appraisal forms and often had difficulty providing advice to workers whose performance was not acceptable.

5. Workers complained that performance appraisal interview sessions often turned into "gotcha sessions" in which even exemplary performers were told by their immediate

Figure 3.3: Assessment for Pinpointing the Causes of a Performance Problem

Directions: There are many possible causes of any human performance problem. Use this assessment to guide you in isolating the causes of the problem. First, describe the problem in the space below. Then, assess how much of the problem is a result of each of the possible criteria listed. Circle the number corresponding to the level of attribution you believe to be true. Use the following scale: 1 = The cause is not applicable; 2 = None of the problem is attributable to the cause listed; 3 = Some of the problem is attributable to the cause listed; 4 = Much of the problem is attributable to the cause listed; 5 = Most, and perhaps all, of the problem is attributable to the cause listed. When you finish, compare the results of your assessment with the results of assessments completed by others.

The problem:

	Possible Causes of the Problem	How Much of the Problem is Attributable to the Causes Listed?				
	Do Performers:	Not Applicable	None of the Problem Is Attributable to the Cause	Some of the Problem Is Attributable to the Cause	Much of the Problem Is Attributable to the Cause	Most, and Perhaps All, of the Problem Is Attributable to the Cause
1	Lack the knowledge that they must possess to perform	1	2	3	4	5
2	Lack the ability to perform (that is, the wrong person or people are in the job)	1	2	3	4	5
3	Lack motivation	1	2	3	4	5
4	Have insufficient opportunity to practice	1	2	3	4	5
5	Receive rewards for not performing	1	2	3	4	5
6	Receive no rewards for performing	1	2	3	4	5
7	Lack the tools or equipment for performing	1	2	3	4	5
8	Lack necessary information to perform	1	2	3	4	5
9	Not receive timely, specific feedback on what they do or how well they do it	1	2	3	4	5
10	Feel unsure about who is supposed to do what	1	2	3	4	5
11	Lack the knowledge that they must possess to perform	1	2	3	4	5
12	Face unclear organizational policies or procedures	1	2	3	4	5
13	Face unclear priorities for what they are to do	1	2	3	4	5
14	Other possible causes of the problem (List them):	1	2	3	4	5
15		1	2	3	4	5
16		1	2	3	4	5
17		1	2	3	4	5
18		1	2	3	4	5
19		1	2	3	4	5
20		1	2	3	4	5

Figure 3.4: Instrument for Assessing Stakeholder Agreement About the Causes of a Performance Problem

Directions: This instrument is designed to gauge your opinions about the causes of a performance problem. The problem and its possible causes are described below. Think about the stated causes and rate your opinion of each statement that follows. Circle the number corresponding to your level of agreement. Use the following scale:

1 = Strongly Disagree
2 = Disagree
3 = Agree
4 = Strongly Agree

When you finish scoring the instrument, hand it to the designated person. Your responses will help to clarify how much agreement exists on the causes of the performance problem.

The performance problem:

The causes of the performance problem:

Now, rate your agreement with each of the following statements as they apply to the identified causes of the performance problem described.	Strongly Disagree			Strongly Agree
How Much Do You Agree With Each Statement?	1	2	3	4
1	I think that the most important causes of the performance problem are listed above.	1	2	3	4
2	I think everyone I know agrees that the causes of the performance problem are listed above.	1	2	3	4
3	I think the facts and evidence are clear: The problem stems from the causes listed above.	1	2	3	4
4	I do not believe that additional analysis is necessary to pinpoint root causes of the performance problem listed above.	1	2	3	4
5	If additional analysis were to be conducted to pinpoint causes of the performance problem, I believe that such analysis should focus on the following possible causes, if any (List them below and tell why you believe they may be possible causes):				

organizational superiors that they had not done enough. In fact, it was considered rare for anyone to be told "you are doing a good job" in a performance appraisal interview.

Roswell completed the written report and turned it in. He also supplied Kung with an unsolicited proposal in which he offered to carry out a project to improve the company's performance appraisal system. Although company decision makers felt that Roswell had done an outstanding job in identifying the problems and pinpointing the gaps between what the appraisal should be and what it was, they declined his proposal and asked Kung to lead an internal task force team to improve the company's performance appraisal system.

With the help of Mike Santiago, Kung assembled a task force to improve the company's performance appraisal system. The group consisted of representatives from the following: top management (the vice president of management information systems [MIS]), human resources (Santiago and Kung), marketing (a manager), sales (a district supervisor), production (a plant supervisor), engineering (a newly hired engineer), and the shipping department (a shipping clerk). Each person named to the task force was personally invited to participate by the company's CEO and was selected because he or she had the potential for advancement in the company (as determined by the company's succession planning efforts). Being named to this task force was considered an honor, and it was treated accordingly. The CEO attended the first meeting and personally charged the task force with solving the problem with the company's appraisal system. He said, "We get what we measure. If we don't measure effectively, we have no idea what we get. Since the consultant's report shows that there is no link between our appraisal system and our rewards and our promotions, then it should come as no surprise that our managers and workers alike view the appraisal system as ineffective. It is your job to fix it. Decide for yourselves if the consultant is right. I won't presume to tell you. But if the consultant is right, it is your job to prepare a proposal to fix the problem, present the proposal to the senior managers, and (if that proposal is accepted) to oversee—as a group—the creation of a more effective performance appraisal system. You have my best wishes for success since the work of this task force is critical to establishing and maintaining effective performance in this company now and in the future."

With those words, the CEO left the meeting.

At that point, Kung stood up and walked to the front of the meeting room. She began by saying this: "The CEO has given us our charter. I believe that the first order of business is to verify that the consultant has determined the root causes of this problem and that we are not focusing our attention on symptoms. Let us begin by clarifying what the problem is and what we believe causes it. There may be many possible causes, of course."

Kung then facilitated the group as group members brainstormed ways to describe the problem and list its causes. (She arranged to have the consultant's descriptions available to the group members.)

By the end of the meeting, group members had defined the performance problem in this way: "The company's performance appraisal system is ineffective. It does not accurately measure individual performance. It is not in keeping with best practices in other companies. It is not linked, as the group members believe it should be linked, to rewards for performance."

Among the root causes for the problem identified by the group were these:

- The company has not defined performance expectations or targets and has not clarified work duties, responsibilities, activities, or accountabilities. It is difficult to measure results when desired results are unclear or capricious.
- The company has not established an effective way to measure results.
- The company has not trained managers in their responsibilities for completing appraisals and has not trained workers in how to clarify work expectations.

These root causes matched the consultant's findings, though Kung took pains to give the members of the task force ample opportunity to add, delete, combine, or otherwise modify the consultant's findings. Therefore, she was satisfied—as were others in the group, when they were polled—that they had adequately verified the root causes of the performance problem. The group agreed that it was not worthwhile to replicate the consultant's study to test the reliability of the results.

Step 2: Consider the Range of Possible Interventions to Close the Performance Gap By Addressing the Root Causes

Definition and Purpose of Step 2

This step has to do with matching up the possible interventions (solutions) to address the performance problems identified, as shown in figure 3.5. Many possible interventions exist, and numerous models have also been published to describe what should be done to select the appropriate interventions to address specific performance problems. For instance, Mager and Pipe (1997) have described how to distinguish problems that can be solved by training from problems that must be solved by management action and have then gone on to provide a short list of possible interventions to solve training problems and management problems. Gilbert (1978) has described another model to match solutions to identified causes. Many other models have been proposed as well (see, for instance, Harless, 1997; Dean, Dean, and Guman, 1992; Langdon, 1997 and 1999a; "Matrix of Interventions," 1999; Sugrue and Fuller, 1999).

Implementing Step 2

There are many ways to go about implementing this step. One approach might be called the analytical approach; a second might be called the creative approach; and a third, the group process approach. They are not mutually exclusive. They can be used separately, or they can be combined.

The *analytical approach* relies on tools and techniques drawn from systematic problem solving. Many such approaches are well known and have often been used in work process improvement. Examples include flow charts, histograms, Pareto charts, run charts, root cause analysis, Ishikawa (fishbone) diagrams, portfolio analysis, and many others (Rothwell, 1996). The analytical approach is simple, straightforward, and logical. It assumes that finding a solution is a straightforward process once the cause of a problem has been identified. If this approach is used, the analyst role and intervention selector role are closely aligned. The analyst pinpoints the problem, determines the performance gap associated with the problem, and isolates one or more causes. Once the causes have been identified, the intervention selector chooses an intervention designed to address them. The solution is logical. This approach casts the intervention selector in the role of technician, one who possesses specialized knowledge and skill in determining how to use the results of an objective diagnosis. It can be a fast approach if the intervention selector assumes all or most of the responsibility for checking the causes of the problem and recommending interventions to solve them.

The *creative approach* relies on tools and techniques drawn from creativity theory. Many such approaches have also been applied in problem solving. But the goal of creative problem solving is to go beyond a simple cause and a simple solution to find breakthrough solutions.

Creative thinking goes beyond simple logic to find new, and sometimes unusual, solutions to performance problems. Well-known techniques associated with creative problem solving include brainstorming, nominal group technique, and the delphi method.

The creative approach is not necessarily straightforward or logical because it may rely on *lateral thinking* in which ideas from one discipline are paired with ideas from an utterly unrelated discipline in an attempt to find new ways of dealing with old problems. The creative approach thus assumes that every problem has many obvious solutions as well as some that are not so obvious. In this approach, the intervention selector role sets out to unleash creative thinking at the time that the causes of a performance problem are identified. Although the analyst pinpoints the problem, determines the performance gap associated with the problem, and isolates the cause, the intervention selector encourages stakeholders of the problem to think of new ways to solve it or address it. The solution is not necessarily logical because the creative approach demands new thinking. This approach casts the intervention selector in the role of creativity facilitator, one who helps a group of stakeholders find new ways to deal with the problem. It is not necessarily a fast approach, but it can lead to quantum leaps in productivity or performance improvement. The intervention selector helps others identify appropriate interventions, thereby seeking to achieve increased ownership in the intervention as well as increased creativity stemming from group thinking.

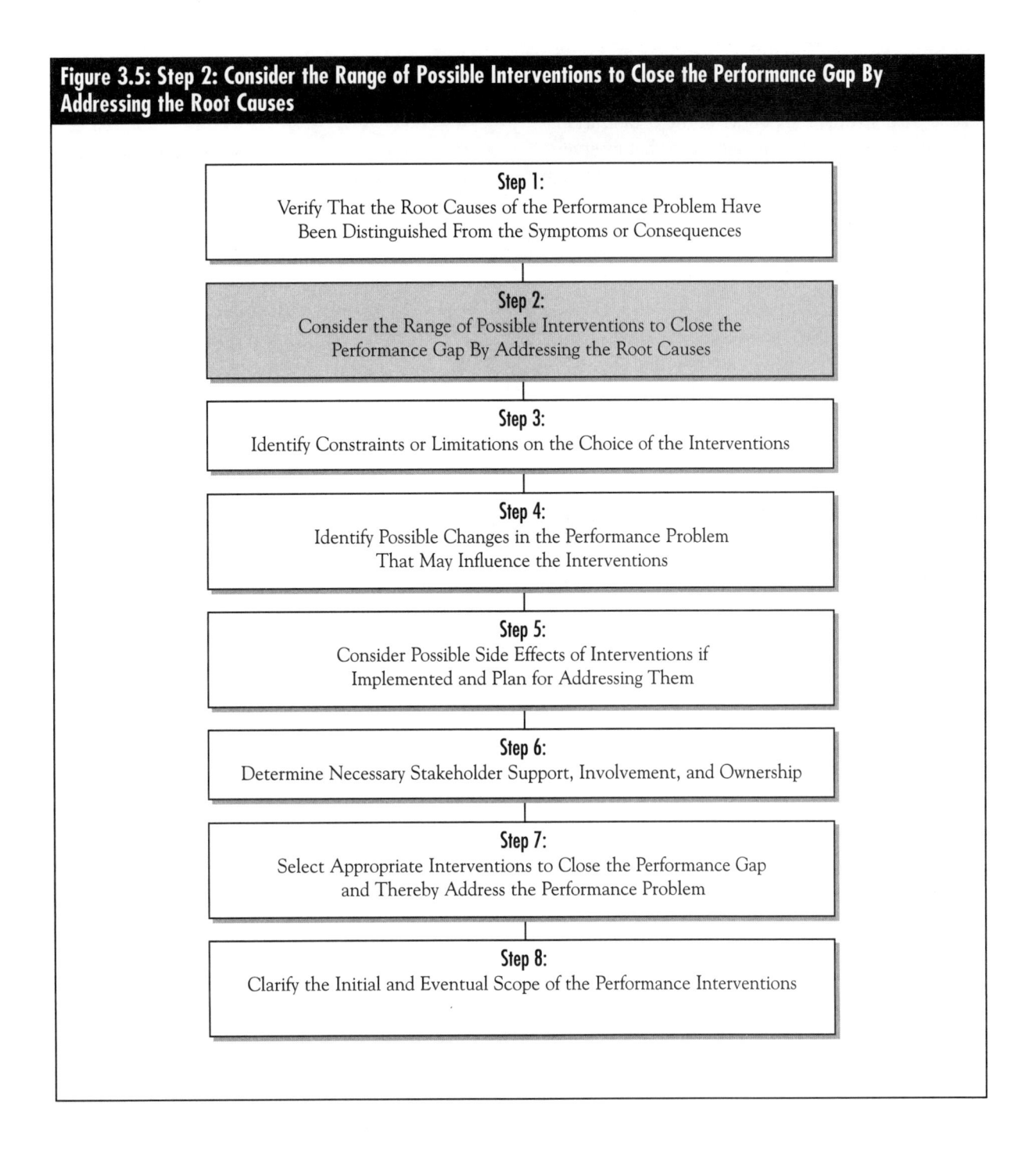

Figure 3.5: Step 2: Consider the Range of Possible Interventions to Close the Performance Gap By Addressing the Root Causes

Step 1:
Verify That the Root Causes of the Performance Problem Have Been Distinguished From the Symptoms or Consequences

Step 2:
Consider the Range of Possible Interventions to Close the Performance Gap By Addressing the Root Causes

Step 3:
Identify Constraints or Limitations on the Choice of the Interventions

Step 4:
Identify Possible Changes in the Performance Problem That May Influence the Interventions

Step 5:
Consider Possible Side Effects of Interventions if Implemented and Plan for Addressing Them

Step 6:
Determine Necessary Stakeholder Support, Involvement, and Ownership

Step 7:
Select Appropriate Interventions to Close the Performance Gap and Thereby Address the Performance Problem

Step 8:
Clarify the Initial and Eventual Scope of the Performance Interventions

The *group process approach* relies entirely on the power of groups, such as stakeholders, to find appropriate interventions to close performance gaps. For instance, force field analysis, depicted in figure 3.6, may be used to identify the factors preventing a solution from being applied and the factors encouraging a solution to be applied. The group process approach is neither entirely logical nor creative. Instead, it relies on a combination of analysis and creativity. Once the analyst pinpoints the problem, determines the performance gap associated with the problem, and isolates the cause, the intervention selector facilitates a process by which the stakeholders decide how best to address the problem. The solution is a function of the group process and is thus limited by issues associated with the expertise of the participants, the politics of the organization, and real or perceived constraints on what interventions to select. This approach casts the intervention selector in the role of facilitator who helps a group of stakeholders find any way to deal with the problem. While the approach may not always be particularly fast or effective, it gains in ownership and commitment of stakeholders what it loses in analytical rigor or creative ideas. (See figure 3.7 for an assessment instrument to help selection interventions.)

To carry out this step effectively, intervention selectors may wish to begin by posing several important questions:

- Considering the root causes of the performance problem, what are the most logical solutions to that problem? Why do we think so?
- Considering the root causes of the performance problem, how have other organizations solved the problem based on best-practice examples and benchmarking?
- Considering the root causes of the performance problem, what does available research on the topic, if any, suggest might be the most effective approaches to solving it and the least effective?
- What analytical, creative, or group process methods might be most helpful in identifying a range of possible interventions to solve the problem by closing the performance gap?

Figure 3.6: Summary of Force Field Analysis

Directions: Force field analysis is a technique invented by Kurt Lewin to help groups identify forces that drive change and forces that prevent change. To Lewin, conditions in organizations are always in stasis (the status quo). To move them from stasis to change, it is essential to weaken the forces (that is, factors) preventing change or strengthen the forces driving change, or do both. To conduct force field analysis and use it in intervention selection, call together a group of people who are knowledgeable about the problem and its possible causes. Explain Lewin's theory and ask them to identify as many forces as they can that would drive or encourage the solution to the performance problem and as many as they can that would prevent or discourage the solution to the performance problem. On a flipchart have the group list as many driving forces as possible and as many restraining forces as possible. Then, ask the group members what actions the organization should take to weaken the restraining forces or strengthen the driving forces. Those actions are components of an integrated performance improvement intervention to address the causes of the performance problem.

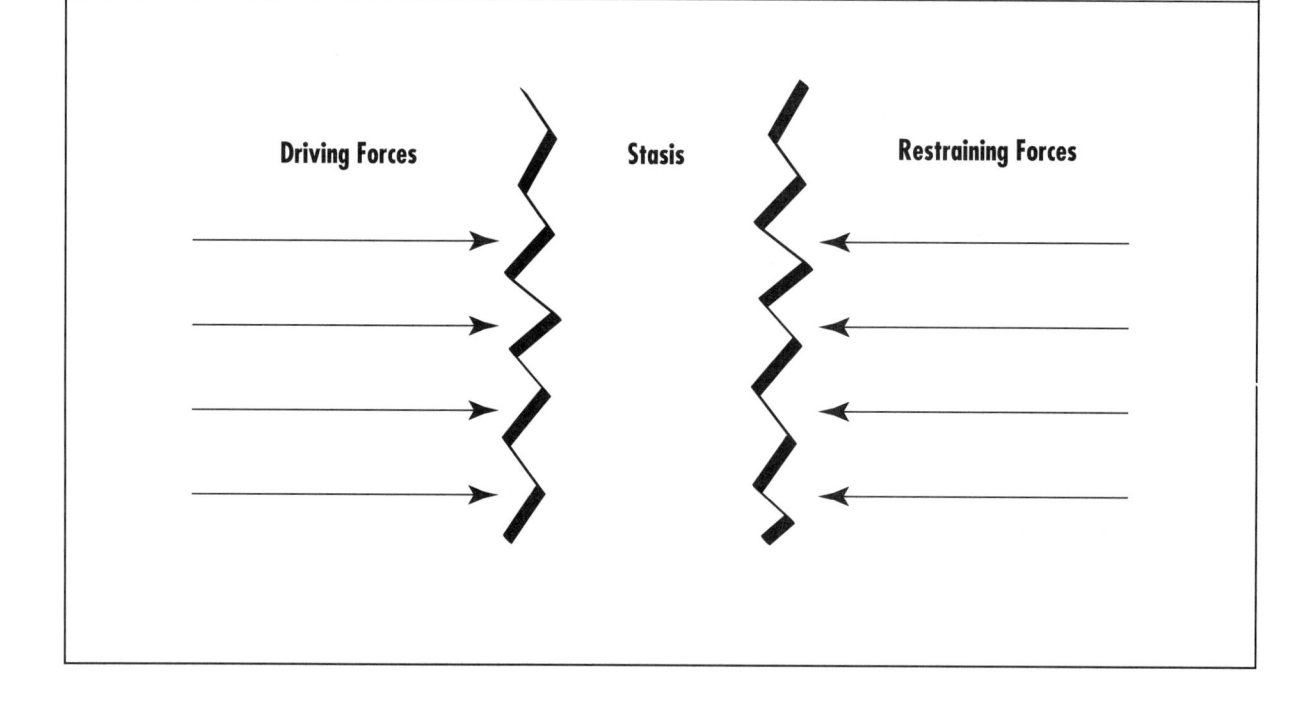

Driving Forces → ⟋⟍ **Stasis** ⟋⟍ ← **Restraining Forces**

Figure 3.7: Instrument for Assessing Possible Interventions to Solve a Performance Problem By Addressing Its Causes

Directions: An intervention should address the underlying causes of a performance problem. Use this instrument to guide you in selecting possible interventions to address the underlying causes of the problem. First, describe the problem and list the cause or causes in the spaces below. Then, for each of the 13 interventions listed, assess how well you believe it will solve the problem by addressing its causes. For each cause listed, circle a response in the middle column to indicate how much of the problem can be solved by choosing an intervention listed in column 1. Use the following scale: 1= The intervention is not applicable; 2 = None of the problem can be solved by the intervention; 3 = Some of the problem can be solved by the intervention; 4 = Much of the problem can be solved by the intervention; 5 = Most, and perhaps all, of the problem can be solved by the intervention. When you finish, compare the results of your assessment with the results of assessments completed by others.

The problem:

The cause or causes:

Possible Interventions to Solve the Problem by Addressing Its Causes		How Well Do You Believe That the Intervention Can Sove the Problem By Addressing Its Causes?				
		Not Applicable	None of the Problem Can Be Solved by the Intervention	Some of the Problem Can Be Solved by the Intervention	Much of the Problem Can Be Solved by the Intervention	Most, and Perhaps All, of the Problem Can Be Solved by the Intervention
1	Training	1	2	3	4	5
2	Improving recruitment and selection methods	1	2	3	4	5
3	Exciting enthusiasm and motivation by showing workers "what's in it for them"	1	2	3	4	5
4	Providing opportunity to practice	1	2	3	4	5
5	Providing incentives for performing	1	2	3	4	5
6	Providing rewards for performing	1	2	3	4	5
7	Providing the tools necessary to perform	1	2	3	4	5
8	Supplying the information that workers need to perform	1	2	3	4	5
9	Providing more timely, specific feedback	1	2	3	4	5
10	Allocating work responsibility	1	2	3	4	5
11	Clarifying work expectations	1	2	3	4	5
12	Clarifying organizational policies or procedures	1	2	3	4	5
13	Clarify priorities for what performers should do	1	2	3	4	5

(continued on next page)

Figure 3.7: Instrument for Assessing Possible Interventions to Solve a Performance Problem By Addressing Its Causes *(continued)*

Possible Interventions to Solve the Problem by Addressing Its Causes		How Well Do You Believe That the Intervention Can Save the Problem By Addressing Its Causes?				
		Not Applicable	None of the Problem Can Be Solved by the Intervention	Some of the Problem Can Be Solved by the Intervention	Much of the Problem Can Be Solved by the Intervention	Most, and Perhaps All, of the Problem Can Be Solved by the Intervention
14	Other possible causes of the problem (List them):	1	2	3	4	5
15		1	2	3	4	5
16		1	2	3	4	5
17		1	2	3	4	5
18		1	2	3	4	5
19		1	2	3	4	5
20		1	2	3	4	5

- How can those methods be used?
- Once those methods have been used, what range of possible performance interventions were identified? Was more than one necessary to address more than one root cause?
- Are there ways that the problem can be reframed so that the range of solutions might be different or the interventions proposed might avert the problem?

The important point to remember is that many performance interventions can be used in isolation or in combination (see, for example, Alden, 1999, and Rothwell, Hohne, and King, 2000; for further references on this topic, see Section 8).

Use Step 2 of the worksheet in figure 6.1 as you consider the possible interventions to close the performance gap by addressing the root causes.

Vignette: After Marsha Kung at LMN Corporation had verified the causes of the performance gap, she provided the task force members with some material about performance appraisal practices and the three approaches to solution finding. She then asked them to suggest next steps.

The young engineer in the group, Tom Lawson, offered the idea of starting a human factors study in LMN's industrial plant and using the results to create a pilot program for a new performance appraisal system that would provide daily feedback to workers about their own production, quality, and so on. The vice president of MIS suggested that the company's performance appraisal form could be placed online to expedite completion by managers. The marketing manager said group decision software (such as teamwave) could be useful for presenting online, anonymous conferencing in an effort to find solutions.

After listening to these ideas, Kung asked the participants if they would like to approach the task of solution finding in stages like classic brainstorming. In the first stage, many ideas would be proposed, but no criticism would be permitted. In the second stage, the ideas generated would be analyzed in terms of the causes. Group members agreed to this approach.

Following in no particular order is a summary of the ideas generated:

- Get rid of the performance appraisal system completely because it is not worth the trouble.
- Clarify performance expectations, make them measurable, and then find ways to document assessments of performance.
- Forget about a one-size-fits-all form of performance appraisal and focus instead on finding effective ways to define good performance, measure it, and provide rewards based on it.
- Redefine performance appraisal to include organizational responsibilities for supplying resources when needed as well as individual accomplishments.
- Get away from the notion of assuming that performance in the organization must always be charted on a bell curve and recognize that some groups would have skewed distributions with many high (or many low or mediocre) performers.
- Make rewards match results so that a performer who was 20 percent more productive would get a raise that was 20 percent better.
- Reconsider the system of linking rewards to performance so long as the company's decision makers are unwilling to pay for it. Be prepared to accept lower-than-desired performance because the company is unwilling to provide the resources to back up a true pay-for-performance system.
- Scrap the existing performance appraisal system and be prepared to reinvent it from scratch.

At the end of this brainstorming activity, Kung asked the group members to vote on the ideas they believed would be most effective in closing performance gaps. They voted overwhelmingly in favor of the ideas to forget about a one-size-fits-all form, to scrap the existing system, and to redefine performance appraisal. These ideas provided a possible list of performance interventions to address the root causes of the performance problem.

Step 3: Identify Constraints or Limitations on the Choice of the Interventions

Definition and Purpose of Step 3

Identification of constraints or limitations on the choice of interventions means the choice of an intervention is limited by the restrictions placed on the available time, money, people, or other requirements necessary to use the intervention. (See figure 3.8.) That is why we focus on selecting *appropriate* interventions instead of *optimal* interventions. *Appropriate* implies that the interventions are realistic and workable in the organization, whereas *optimal* or *best* implies that they would be the most effective, but might not be suitable for implementation because they require time, money, people, or other resources that are not readily available or cannot be made available.

Implementing Step 3

To implement this step, the intervention selector should pose the following questions:

♦ What interventions would be most effective—that is, optimal—to close the performance gap at present?

♦ How likely is it that the necessary resources to implement the optimal interventions can be obtained?

♦ What limitations or restrictions most likely influence the choice of an intervention or interventions? (Consider limitations on time, money, people, or other necessary resources, such as tools, equipment, and incentives.)

♦ What optimal interventions to solve the performance problem must be ruled out because they require resources that are not possible to secure?

♦ What interventions are the best fit or nearest fit in light of the existing limitations on resources?

♦ What are the trade-offs or consequences of using the best fit or nearest fit, rather than the optimal intervention? In other words, what benefits are sacrificed?

By posing these questions, intervention selectors can ground their selection decisions in reality rather than in fantasy. Optimal interventions are, of course, ideal, but not always practical. It is important to keep that distinction in mind. However, it is also worth emphasizing that quick wins or early successes may create rising expectations that will make stakeholders more willing to devote resources to interventions than they would have when interventions were under contemplation but not yet implemented. Small-scale pilot tests that demonstrate value can be most helpful in improving stakeholders' support and thereby improve decision makers' willingness to devote resources to optimal interventions.

Use Step 3 of the worksheet in figure 6.1 to answer those questions and identify constraints or limitations on the choice of the interventions.

Vignette: Marsha Kung facilitated her group to identify performance improvement interventions to address the root causes of the problem confronting LMN Corporation. The group identified the following three appropriate performance interventions:

• Forget about a one-size-fits-all form to performance appraisal and focus instead on finding effective ways to define good performance, measure it, and provide rewards based on it.

• Scrap the existing performance appraisal system and be prepared to reinvent it from scratch.

• Redefine performance appraisal to include organizational responsibilities for supplying resources when needed as well as individual accomplishments.

At a later meeting, Kung asked her task force to consider these performance interventions in light of the following questions:

• What limitations or restrictions most likely influence the choice of an intervention or interventions? (Consider limitations on time, money, people, or other necessary resources, such as tools, equipment, and incentives.)

• What optimal interventions to solve the performance problem must be ruled out because they require resources that are not possible to secure?

After much discussion, Kung's task force narrowed down the list of possible performance interventions to forgetting about a one-size-fits-all form and scrapping the existing performance appraisal system. Task force members felt that senior executives would not accept the third idea.

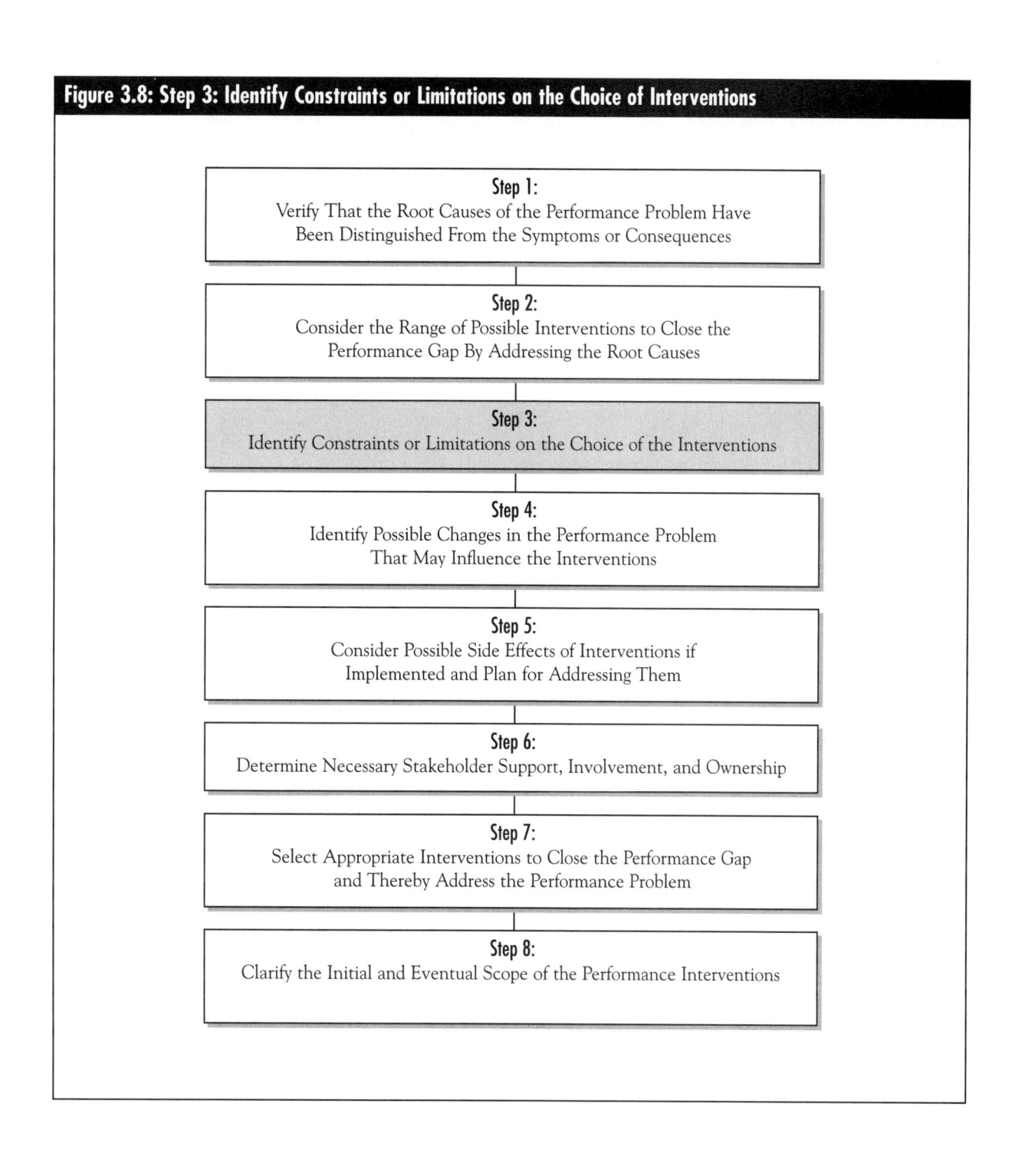

Figure 3.8: Step 3: Identify Constraints or Limitations on the Choice of Interventions

Step 1:
Verify That the Root Causes of the Performance Problem Have Been Distinguished From the Symptoms or Consequences

Step 2:
Consider the Range of Possible Interventions to Close the Performance Gap By Addressing the Root Causes

Step 3:
Identify Constraints or Limitations on the Choice of the Interventions

Step 4:
Identify Possible Changes in the Performance Problem That May Influence the Interventions

Step 5:
Consider Possible Side Effects of Interventions if Implemented and Plan for Addressing Them

Step 6:
Determine Necessary Stakeholder Support, Involvement, and Ownership

Step 7:
Select Appropriate Interventions to Close the Performance Gap and Thereby Address the Performance Problem

Step 8:
Clarify the Initial and Eventual Scope of the Performance Interventions

Step 4: Identify Possible Changes in the Performance Problem That May Influence the Interventions

Definition and Purpose of Step 4

The fourth step in intervention selection is to identify possible changes in performance problems over time. (See figure 3.9.) Just as analysts must be concerned about leading the target—that is, taking changes in the organization and its environment into account when examining performance problems—so too should intervention selectors take into account possible changes in the performance problem. The world does not stay the same. Neither do performance problems. Sometimes, when left alone, problems solve themselves. Changing conditions require planning, and they can also influence the selection of appropriate interventions.

Implementing Step 4

To implement this step, the intervention selector should pose the following questions:

- What will happen if no corrective is taken to address the performance problem or to narrow or close the performance gap?
- What changes in the future are likely to affect the organization, the industry, the performance problem, and performance interventions identified to solve the problem?
- How will those changes influence the problem and the intervention?
- When will the likely impact of those changes be felt?
- Who (what groups) in the organization is most likely to be affected by these trends, and in what ways will they be affected?
- Where in the organization will those changes have the most impact?

Use Step 4 of the worksheet in figure 6.1 to answer these questions and to identify possible changes in the performance problem that may influence the interventions over time.

Vignette: Kung asked the task force members, through online methods, to brainstorm on what would happen in the future to the problem. Task force members speculated that the following consequences would occur if no corrective action were taken:

- Turnover would increase.
- The organization would experience more difficulty in recruiting talent as word spread in the industry that LMN did not reward people on the basis of what they did.
- More people would be needed because the organization was not effectively managing the human resources that it already possessed.
- The succession planning program, key to providing a pipeline for future leaders, would not be effective because individuals would continue to be promoted on the basis of relationships, not results.

Task force members did not feel that trends pointed toward any significant changes that would affect performance appraisal soon. However, they did feel that the company's inability to measure performance would lead to mistakes in reward and incentive systems.

Step 5: Consider Possible Side Effects of Interventions if Implemented and Plan for Addressing Them

Definition and Purpose of Step 5

Just as medicine prescribed by doctors is likely to have side effects, so too do performance interventions selected for an organization. (See figure 3.10.) Organizations are open systems in which changes in any part of the system affect all the parts. Called the spider web principle, this linkage means that a tug on one part of the web causes the whole web to vibrate.

Performance interventions are "tugs" on the organization's "web" that can have both beneficial and detrimental side effects. It is important to make an effort to predict what those side effects will be

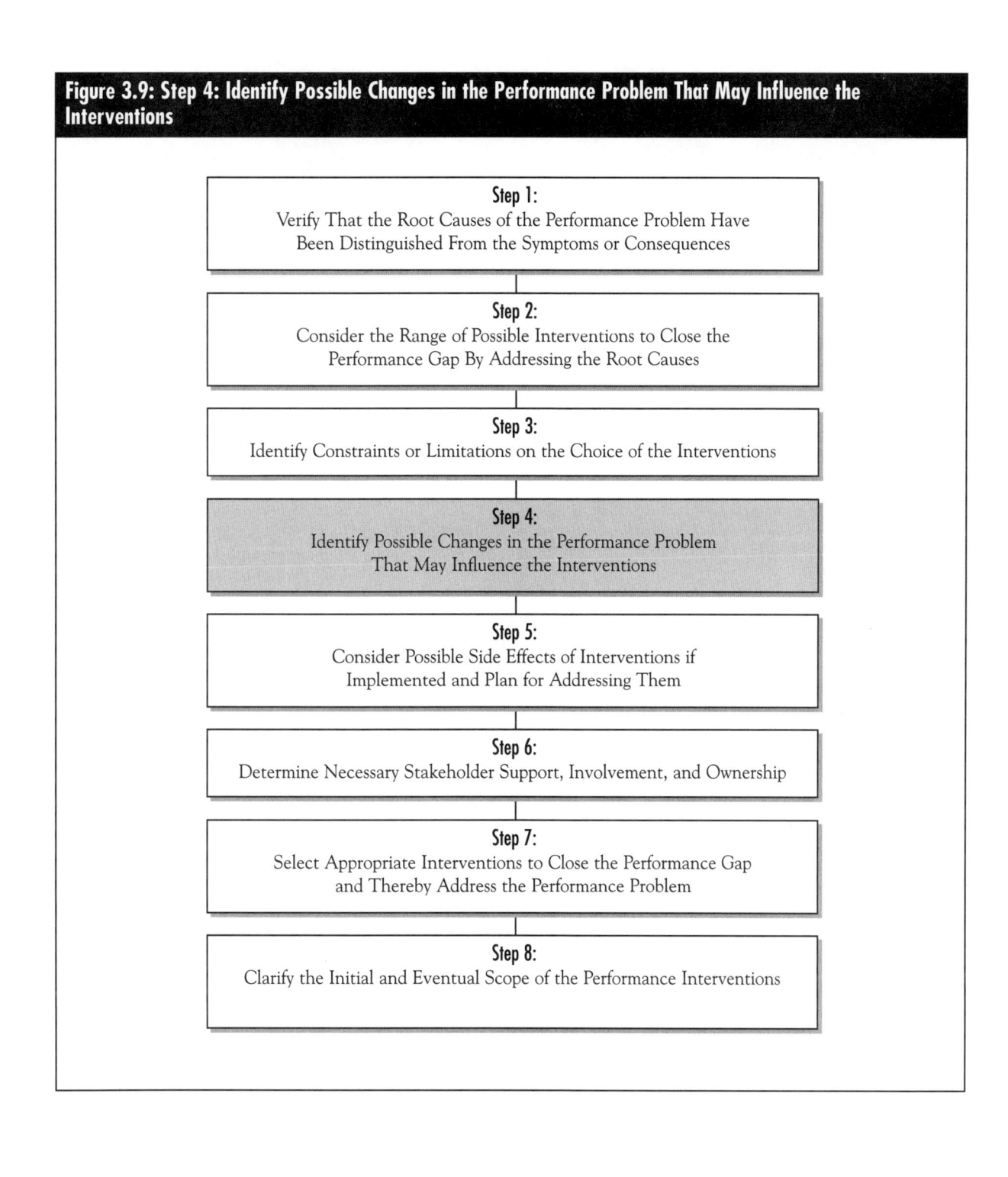

Figure 3.9: Step 4: Identify Possible Changes in the Performance Problem That May Influence the Interventions

Step 1:
Verify That the Root Causes of the Performance Problem Have Been Distinguished From the Symptoms or Consequences

Step 2:
Consider the Range of Possible Interventions to Close the Performance Gap By Addressing the Root Causes

Step 3:
Identify Constraints or Limitations on the Choice of the Interventions

Step 4:
Identify Possible Changes in the Performance Problem That May Influence the Interventions

Step 5:
Consider Possible Side Effects of Interventions if Implemented and Plan for Addressing Them

Step 6:
Determine Necessary Stakeholder Support, Involvement, and Ownership

Step 7:
Select Appropriate Interventions to Close the Performance Gap and Thereby Address the Performance Problem

Step 8:
Clarify the Initial and Eventual Scope of the Performance Interventions

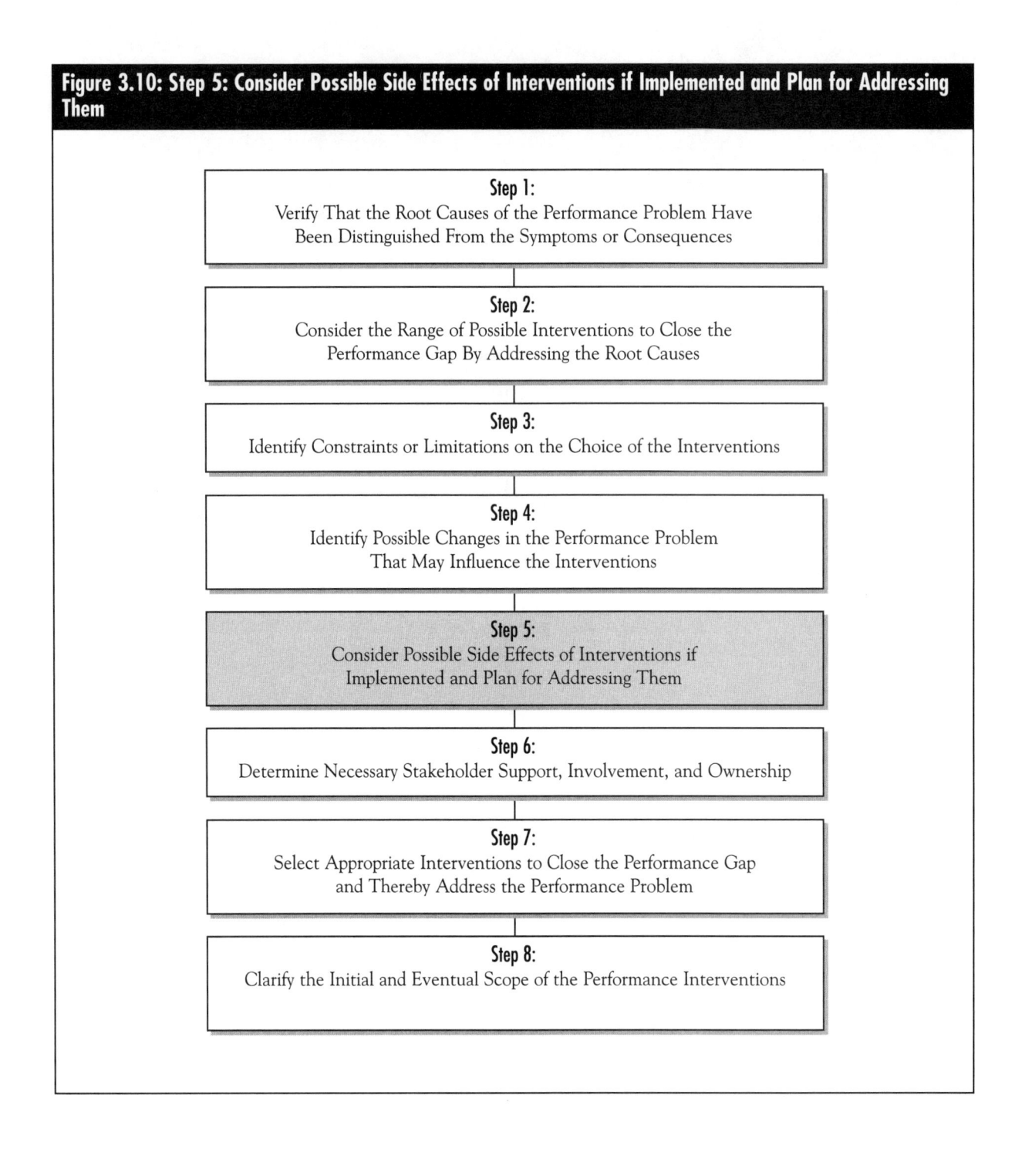

Figure 3.10: Step 5: Consider Possible Side Effects of Interventions if Implemented and Plan for Addressing Them

Step 1:
Verify That the Root Causes of the Performance Problem Have Been Distinguished From the Symptoms or Consequences

Step 2:
Consider the Range of Possible Interventions to Close the Performance Gap By Addressing the Root Causes

Step 3:
Identify Constraints or Limitations on the Choice of the Interventions

Step 4:
Identify Possible Changes in the Performance Problem That May Influence the Interventions

Step 5:
Consider Possible Side Effects of Interventions if Implemented and Plan for Addressing Them

Step 6:
Determine Necessary Stakeholder Support, Involvement, and Ownership

Step 7:
Select Appropriate Interventions to Close the Performance Gap and Thereby Address the Performance Problem

Step 8:
Clarify the Initial and Eventual Scope of the Performance Interventions

and to plan to address detrimental ones before the intervention is undertaken.

Implementing Step 5

To carry out this step effectively, intervention selectors should pose such questions as these:

- What will be the likely side effects of a performance intervention? What is likely to happen if the organization should implement the interventions?
- Who (what groups) is likely to be most affected by these side effects? Why?
- When will these side effects be felt—immediately or over the long term?
- Where will these side effects be felt? If the organization does business internationally, what impact will the intervention have on conditions in other parts of the organization around the globe? In different cultures?
- Why are these side effects likely? What is the probability that they will happen?
- How will these side effects influence the performance problem? How will they influence performance interventions?

Use Step 5 of the worksheet in figure 6.1 to answer these questions as you consider possible side effects of interventions if implemented and plan for addressing them.

Vignette: Marsha Kung's task force at LMN Corporation felt that continued inaction to fix the performance appraisal system would only lead to deteriorating conditions—higher turnover and misapplied rewards. Task force members believed that steps should be taken to create a new performance appraisal system.

Kung told them, "Every medicine has a side effect. If we change the performance appraisal system, we are going to have side effects. Let's spend a while thinking what those might be. Given what you know about the people and the conditions in this organization now, what bad things do you think will happen when we try to establish a new appraisal system?"

Kung facilitated additional brainstorming as group members answered that question. They concluded that, if performance appraisal was reinvented and launched, it would produce the following side effects:

- Some people who were promoted but whose performance did not measure up would leave the organization.
- Workers would complain that their salaries were too low because many workers associate compensation decisions with performance appraisals.
- Managers who were unwilling to take disciplinary action with poor performers would be forced to do so if performance appraisals actually measured performance.
- The morale of managers might suffer if they felt that they lost the power to promote their favorites to key positions and had to abide by measurable performance results instead.
- Managers and workers alike would be confused about the new system and would need extensive training to understand it and use it.
- The organization's decision makers would have to do a better job of communicating what results the organization needed for it to be successful, and they would have to help translate those result into performance measures at all levels and functions. The decision maker's failure to do so would render the interventions useless.

Step 6: Determine Necessary Stakeholder Support, Involvement, and Ownership

Definition and Purpose of Step 6

The sixth step in intervention selection is to determine how much and what kind of stakeholder support, involvement, and ownership is necessary for the performance interventions to be successful. (See figure 3.11.)

Figure 3.11: Step 6: Determine Necessary Stakeholder Support, Involvement, and Ownership

Step 1:
Verify That the Root Causes of the Performance Problem Have Been Distinguished From the Symptoms or Consequences

Step 2:
Consider the Range of Possible Interventions to Close the Performance Gap By Addressing the Root Causes

Step 3:
Identify Constraints or Limitations on the Choice of the Interventions

Step 4:
Identify Possible Changes in the Performance Problem That May Influence the Interventions

Step 5:
Consider Possible Side Effects of Interventions if Implemented and Plan for Addressing Them

Step 6:
Determine Necessary Stakeholder Support, Involvement, and Ownership

Step 7:
Select Appropriate Interventions to Close the Performance Gap and Thereby Address the Performance Problem

Step 8:
Clarify the Initial and Eventual Scope of the Performance Interventions

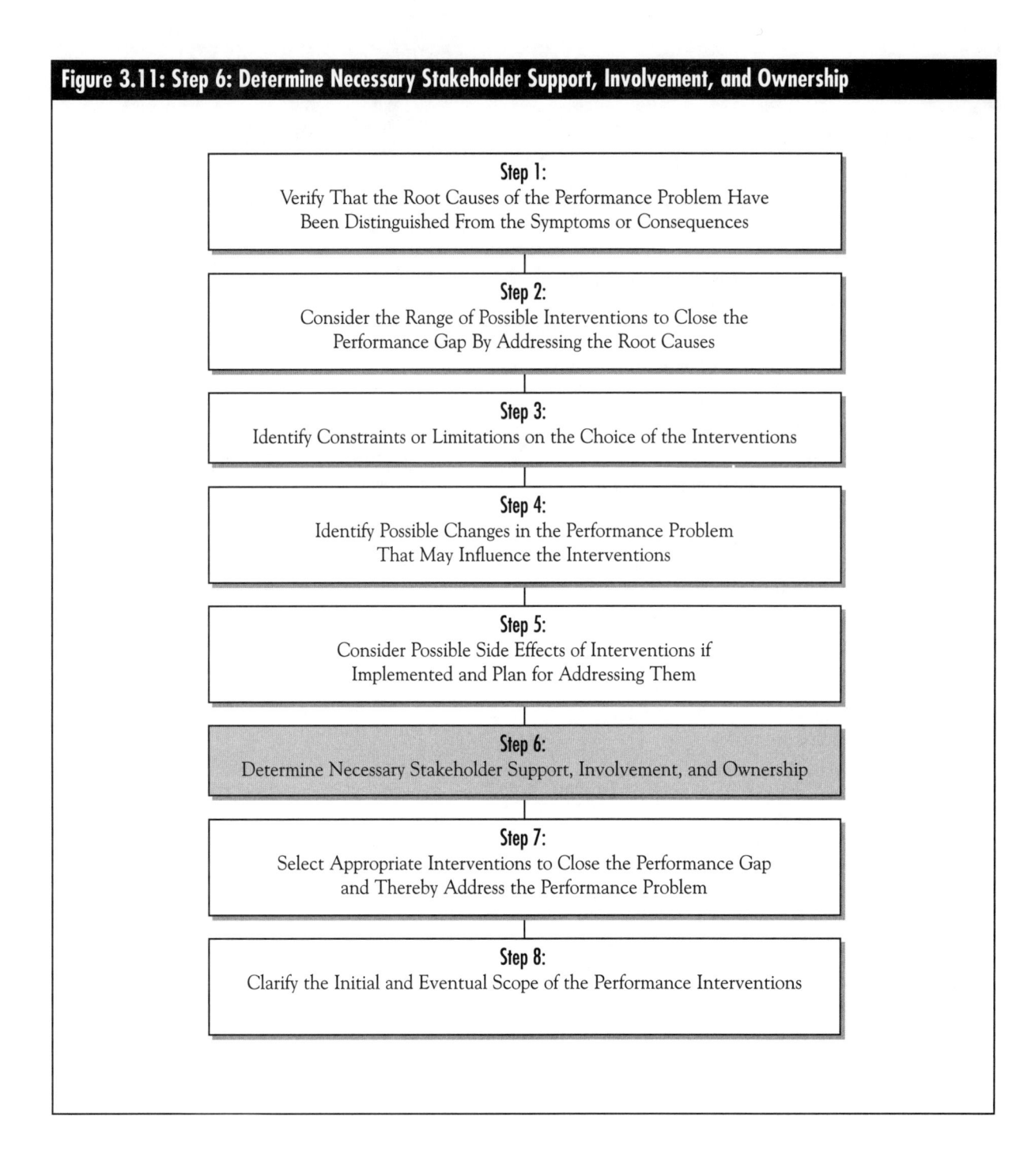

Generally speaking some stakeholder support is necessary for any intervention to be successful. If stakeholders withhold financial or human resources, then they do not support corrective action on a performance problem, no matter what they may say to the contrary. Actions always speak louder than words.

At the lowest level of Step 6 is *approval for action.* That occurs when stakeholders and decision makers admit that a performance problem exists and give approval for one or more interventions to address it. At times, such approval amounts to nothing more than paying lip service to corrective action. In that case, decision makers simply give approval for action, but do not supply additional (or necessary) resources to implement it successfully. At the next level is *approval for action coupled with the proposed resources necessary to implement the interventions successfully.* In that case, a proposal for an intervention is approved with a budget, staff, and other devoted resources.

That approval indicates some commitment. At the highest level is *approval for action coupled with the resources and the decision makers' willingness to take personal action (and devote personal time) to the effort.* In the latter case, decision makers are signaling wholehearted support and are willing to demonstrate that support by personal involvement in the effort.

Implementing Step 6

Not all performance interventions require the same amount of support, involvement, or ownership. Generally speaking, the larger the scope of the proposed intervention, the more stakeholder support, involvement, or ownership is necessary. Similarly, when the intervention will lead to radical change, the more stakeholder support, involvement, or ownership is necessary. Conversely, small-scale interventions require support, involvement, and ownership only from the stakeholders who will benefit from the change effort and those affected by it. In short, the CEO need not be involved personally when an individual or small group will be the focus of the intervention. However, the CEO's support, involvement, and ownership may be essential if the scope of the intervention is the total organization or if the amount of change is radically different from existing norms of the corporate culture.

To carry out this step effectively, intervention selectors should pose such questions as these:

♦ What is the scope of the intended interventions? Will the total organization be affected, or will only part of the organization be affected? Will that scope change over time?

♦ Who are the stakeholders and decision makers who stand to gain most by the interventions? Where are they located? What are their attitudes about the interventions?

♦ Who (what groups) is most influenced by the interventions, and what are their attitudes about the interventions?

♦ Who (what groups) can most influence the interventions, and what are their attitudes about them? (For instance, to select a performance intervention requiring a change of reward systems, it may be essential to have support from the vice president of human resources or the compensation manager.)

Use Step 6 of the worksheet in figure 6.1 to answer those questions to determine how much and what kind of stakeholder support, involvement, and ownership is necessary. Generally speaking, interventions cannot be successful until key stakeholders are convinced that they will meet their needs and help them achieve the results for which they are rewarded.

Vignette: Marsha Kung asked her task force members to consider the proposed performance interventions in light of the preceding questions. The members answered these questions by indicating that they believed the whole organization would be involved in the performance appraisal improvement intervention. Consequently, the CEO and the CEO's direct reports would have to be highly visible, supportive, and involved in the effort. Task force members also focused attention on Kung and Santiago, indicating that they would have to devote much time to personal oversight and facilitation of a new performance appraisal effort.

Step 7: Select Appropriate Interventions to Close the Performance Gap and Thereby Address the Performance Problem

Definition and Purpose of Step 7

The seventh step is to choose the interventions that will close the performance gap and thereby address the performance problem. (See figure 3.12.)

This is the most important step in the intervention selection process because it is at this point that WLP practitioners, working by themselves or with others, decide what to do to solve a performance problem. This decision is made after considering the issues described in steps 1 through 6. The decision may be based on an analytical approach, a creative approach, or a group process approach.

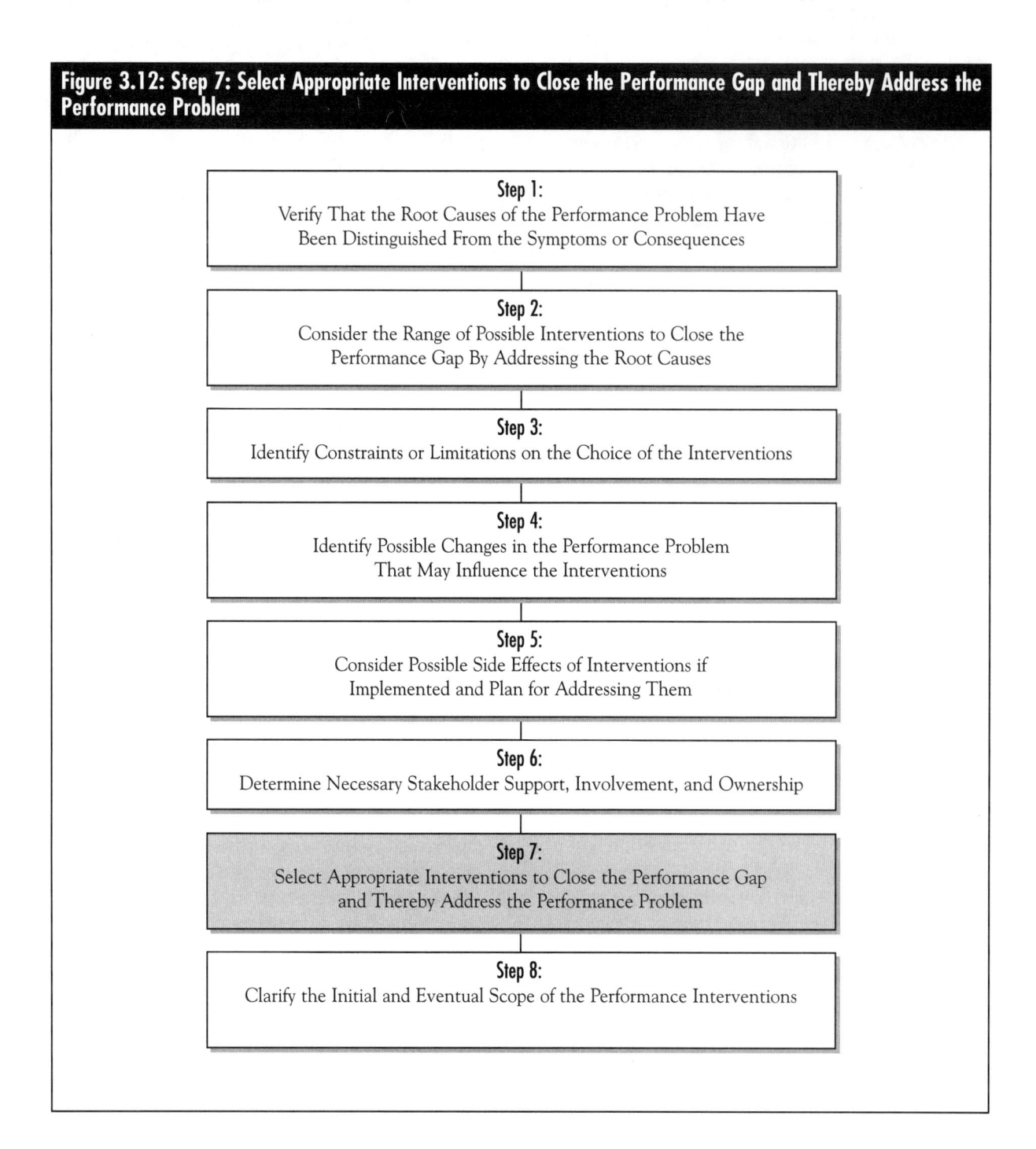

Figure 3.12: Step 7: Select Appropriate Interventions to Close the Performance Gap and Thereby Address the Performance Problem

Step 1:
Verify That the Root Causes of the Performance Problem Have Been Distinguished From the Symptoms or Consequences

Step 2:
Consider the Range of Possible Interventions to Close the Performance Gap By Addressing the Root Causes

Step 3:
Identify Constraints or Limitations on the Choice of the Interventions

Step 4:
Identify Possible Changes in the Performance Problem That May Influence the Interventions

Step 5:
Consider Possible Side Effects of Interventions if Implemented and Plan for Addressing Them

Step 6:
Determine Necessary Stakeholder Support, Involvement, and Ownership

Step 7:
Select Appropriate Interventions to Close the Performance Gap and Thereby Address the Performance Problem

Step 8:
Clarify the Initial and Eventual Scope of the Performance Interventions

Implementing Step 7

To carry out this step effectively, intervention selectors should pose such questions as these:

♦ Who should make the decisions about the interventions?

♦ What performance interventions will appropriately close performance gaps by addressing the root causes of performance problems?

♦ When should the decisions about the interventions be made?

♦ How should the decision be justified? On what basis will the decision be made?

♦ What are the relative costs and benefits of the performance interventions, and how were they estimated?

♦ How are the constraints or limitations on the interventions to be managed?

♦ How will the performance interventions address possible changes in the performance problem over time?

♦ How will possible side effects of the interventions be planned for, and what steps will be taken to avert side effects or minimize their detrimental effects?

♦ What stakeholder and participant support, involvement, and ownership is assumed, and how will it be recognized and (when possible) rewarded?

♦ What alternative interventions might achieve the same results at the same or lower cost?

Use Step 7 of the worksheet in figure 6.1 to answer the preceding questions and select the interventions most appropriate to close the performance gap and thereby address the performance problem.

A different, and perhaps more straightforward, way to think about this step is to ask several specific questions, as shown in figure 3.13. First, is the problem clearly defined? If not, clarify the problem. If it is clearly defined, then ask, Is there only one likely cause of the problem? If not, determine how many likely causes there are. If there is one likely cause, then ask, Is it clear how the problem can be solved by addressing the causes? If it is not clear, then what are the possible ideas for ways to solve the problem by addressing the causes? Once those questions are addressed, then select one or more tentative intervention strategies to address the causes of the problem.

Vignette: To carry out this step, Marsha Kung at LMN Corporation asked her task force members to consider the preceding questions. In discussing the answers, the task force members concluded the following:

• The task force had been given the charter by the CEO to propose a solution and intervention to address the problem.

• The task force should propose a new performance appraisal system, but that system should be linked closely to measurable performance expectations and not use a one-size-fits-all approach.

• The task force would need to prepare a proposal to convince top managers to create a budget and provide the resources for the performance appraisal redesign intervention.

• Decisions should be made as soon as possible.

• A step-by-step project plan would first have to be drafted to provide the basis for a budget, and that budget would have to be compared to expected costs of doing nothing.

• Possible side effects should be addressed in the proposal for the intervention, and they should be managed or averted.

• Personal support and participation by the CEO was key and the proposal should state that and explain why.

• No alternative interventions could achieve the same or similar results at the same or lower cost.

Figure 3.13: Another Way to Think About the Intervention Selection Process

Start here

Is the problem clearly defined? —*No*→ Clarify the problem.

↓ *Yes*

Is there only one likely cause of the problem? —*No*→ How many likely causes are there? → Identify the number of likely causes.

↓ *Yes*

Is it clear how the problem can be solved by addressing the causes? —*No*→ What are the possible ideas—based on analysis, creativity, or group process—for ways to solve the problem by addressing its causes?

↓ *Yes*

Select tentative intervention strategy (or strategies) to address the causes of the problem

→ Consider possible intervention strategies to address the causes of the problem.

Examples of possible interventions:

- Improve recruitment methods.
- Improve selection methods.
- Improve tools and equipment used.
- Improve incentive and reward systems.
- Clarify work duties and expectations.
- Improve feedback given to performers.
- Allocate work responsibilities.
- Provide training.
- Improve worker and job match.
- Give workers a chance to practice.
- Supply job aids.
- Establish clear policies and procedures.

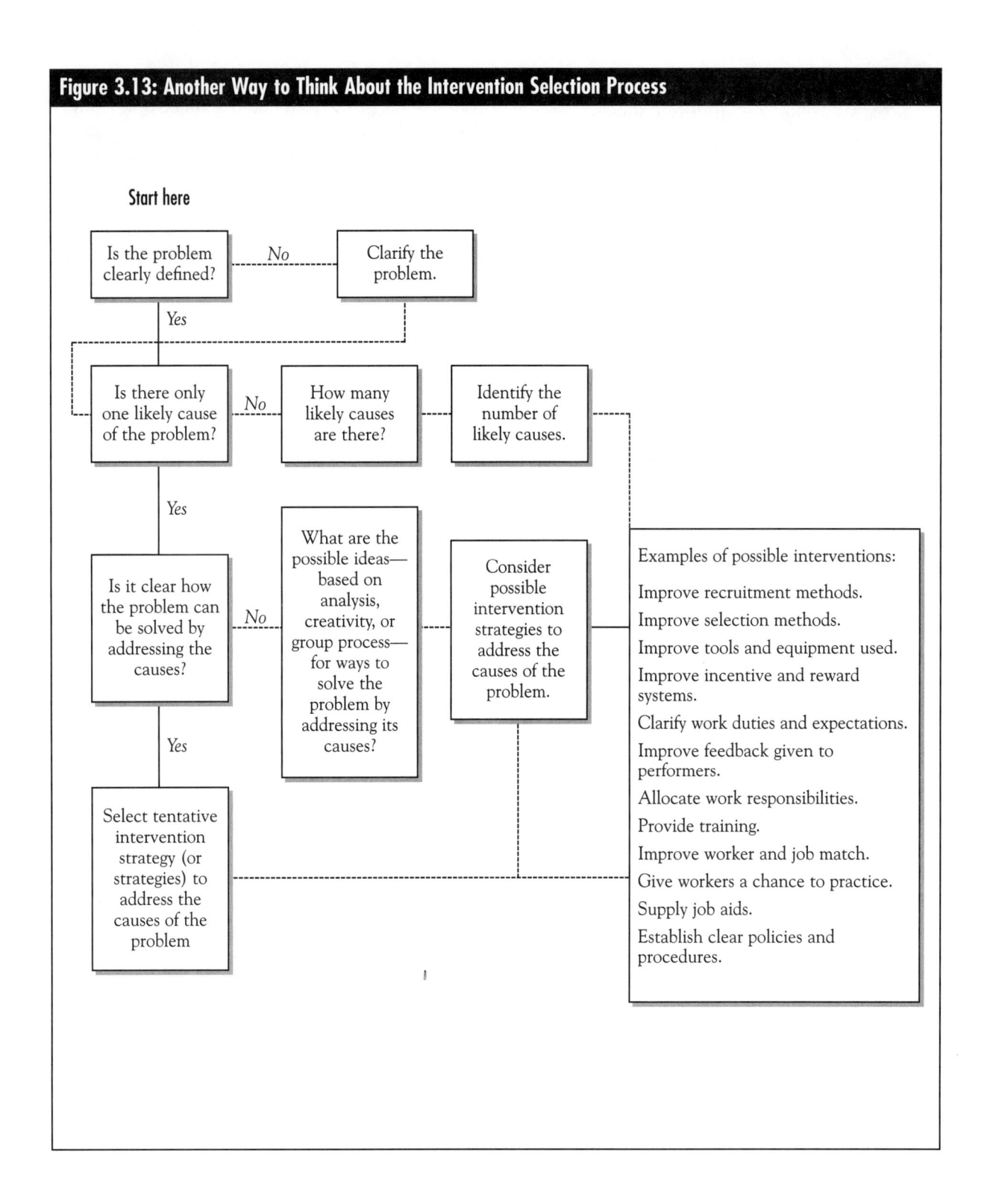

Step 8: Clarify the Initial and Eventual Scope of the Performance Interventions

Definition and Purpose of Step 8

The eighth and final step in intervention selection is to clarify the initial—and eventual—scope of the performance intervention. (See figure 3.14.) It is possible to select performance interventions initially for a small-scale pilot test in a small group or in one geographical location. In training, a small-scale pilot test is called a *formative evaluation*. In other interventions, the terms *pilot test, beta test,* or *rehearsal* are sometimes used. Eventually, however, the intention may be to roll out the performance interventions on

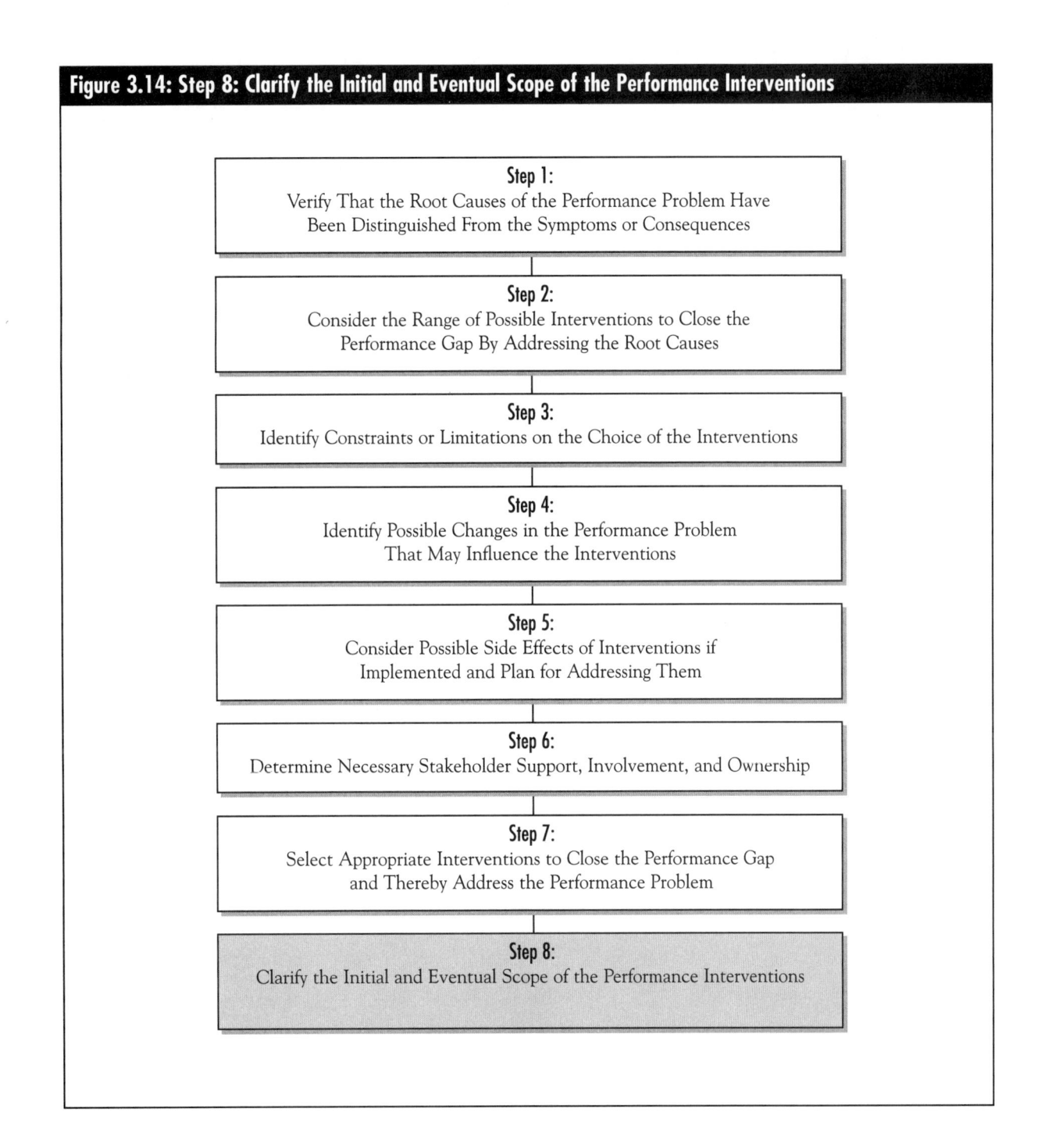

Figure 3.14: Step 8: Clarify the Initial and Eventual Scope of the Performance Interventions

Step 1:
Verify That the Root Causes of the Performance Problem Have Been Distinguished From the Symptoms or Consequences

Step 2:
Consider the Range of Possible Interventions to Close the Performance Gap By Addressing the Root Causes

Step 3:
Identify Constraints or Limitations on the Choice of the Interventions

Step 4:
Identify Possible Changes in the Performance Problem That May Influence the Interventions

Step 5:
Consider Possible Side Effects of Interventions if Implemented and Plan for Addressing Them

Step 6:
Determine Necessary Stakeholder Support, Involvement, and Ownership

Step 7:
Select Appropriate Interventions to Close the Performance Gap and Thereby Address the Performance Problem

Step 8:
Clarify the Initial and Eventual Scope of the Performance Interventions

a larger scale, perhaps encompassing the total organization. This step is thus about the long-term plans for rolling out the interventions.

Implementing Step 8

To carry out this step effectively, intervention selectors should pose such questions as these:

- How will the performance interventions, once selected, be designed and developed?
- Who (what groups) will be the focus of the performance interventions initially? Eventually?
- What groups might improve the most in a short time if the performance interventions are focused on them?
- Where will the performance interventions likely enjoy the most stakeholder support, involvement, and ownership?
- How much time should be permitted for the performance interventions to be successful, and how will results be tracked and measured?

Use Step 8 of the worksheet in figure 6.1 to answer these questions and thus to clarify the initial and eventual scope of the performance intervention.

Vignette: As a next step, the task force unanimously agreed to draft a detailed proposal for presentation to top managers to implement the performance intervention. The task force members decided not to propose enactment of a pilot performance appraisal effort. They believed that any effort to pilot test a new performance appraisal system would lead to an active and ill-toned rumor mill that would intensify worker dissatisfaction and potentially increase turnover. They based that decision on the belief that workers closely associate performance appraisal with compensation and rewards, and so any effort to pilot test a new appraisal system would lead some workers to believe that one work group was benefiting at the expense of others.

Section Summary

This section described how to enact the role of intervention selector, the role that "chooses appropriate interventions to address root causes of human performance gaps" (Rothwell, Sanders, and Soper, 1999, p. 43). When WLP practitioners or others enact this role, they make the switch from focusing on performance problems and their causes to solutions and their implementation. When carrying out this role, intervention selectors:

1. Verify that the root causes of the performance problem have been distinguished from the symptoms or consequences.
2. Consider the range of possible interventions appropriate to close the performance gap by addressing the root causes.
3. Identify constraints or limitations on the choice of the interventions.
4. Identify possible changes in the performance problem that may influence the interventions.
5. Consider possible side effects of interventions if implemented and plan for addressing them.
6. Determine necessary stakeholder support, involvement, and ownership.
7. Select appropriate interventions to close the performance gap and thereby address the performance problem.
8. Clarify the initial and eventual scope of the performance interventions.

The intervention selector's role is logically related to the intervention designer and developer's role, which is described in the next section.

SECTION 1	**GETTING STARTED**

SECTION 2	**DEFINING THE ROLES**

SECTION 3	**ENACTING THE ROLE OF INTERVENTION SELECTOR**

SECTION 4	**ENACTING THE ROLE OF INTERVENTION DESIGNER AND DEVELOPER**

- ♦ A Model of the Intervention Design and Development Process
- ♦ Steps in the Intervention Design and Development Process
  - — *Step 1:* Examine the Characteristics of the Participants in the Intervention
  - — *Step 2:* Examine the Competencies Necessary for Successful Achievement
  - — *Step 3:* Examine the Characteristics of the Work Environment
  - — *Step 4:* Formulate Performance Objectives to Guide the Intervention
  - — *Step 5:* Formulate Specific Methods by Which to Measure Performance Objectives
  - — *Step 6:* Create a Detailed Project Plan
  - — *Step 7:* Create a Detailed Communication and Marketing Plan to Clarify What Is Happening, Has Happened, and Will Happen
  - — *Step 8:* Make, Buy, or Buy and Modify Materials and Media to Support the Implementation of the Intervention
- ♦ Section Summary

SECTION 5	**ENACTING THE ROLE OF INTERVENTION IMPLEMENTOR**

SECTION 6	**TOOLS FOR CONDUCTING INTERVENTION SELECTION, DESIGN AND DEVELOPMENT, AND IMPLEMENTATION**

SECTION 7	**AFTERWORD**

SECTION 8	**BIBLIOGRAHY**

SECTION 4 ENACTING THE ROLE OF INTERVENTION DESIGNER AND DEVELOPER

Section 2 introduced the role of intervention designer and developer. That role "creates learning and other interventions that help to address the specific root causes of human performance gaps. Some examples of the work of the intervention designer and developer include serving as instructional designer, media specialist, materials developer, process engineer, ergonomics engineer, instructional writer, and compensation analyst" (Rothwell, Sanders, and Soper, 1999, p. 43).

The instructional designer and developer takes the results of the intervention selector's decisions about interventions and finds or creates plans, materials, and media by which to transform that intervention selection decision into reality. It is the instructional designer and developer's responsibility to make, buy, or buy and modify the intervention's content materials (that is, what will be used) and media applications (that is, how the intervention will be delivered). If *instructional* designers and developers work with a learning intervention, they will make, buy, or buy and modify training materials (such as leader guides, participant guides, tests, and overhead masters) and will choose the media by which training is delivered (such as classroom, on the job, and online). If *intervention* designers and developers work with a nonlearning intervention, they will make, buy, or buy and modify other materials appropriate to the specific intervention and will prepare media applications to support the use of those materials. For instance, if they are involved in a reward system intervention, they may undertake the preparation of wage and salary studies, innovative alternative reward strategies, and materials and media to support the implementation of that intervention (for instance, presentations delivered in print, on kiosks, and on the Web).

It is worth noting that there is a difference between design and development. *Design* is the process of transforming desired results (an output of the intervention selection process) into detailed intervention performance objectives, detailed project plans, and detailed metrics by which to track successful accomplishment or change to assess how well and how much a performance gap is being closed. *Development* is the process of transforming desired intervention performance objectives (an output of the design process) into materials, media, marketing and communication methods, and other tangible products or services necessary to transform an intervention design into a reality. Perhaps it is simplest to think of it this way: Design is what architects do when they draw blueprints; development is akin to what contractors do when they construct a house from those blueprints (Rothwell, Hohne, and King, 2000).

Just as a model can be helpful in describing how other WLP roles are enacted, so can one be useful in describing how intervention design and development is carried out. An intervention design and development process model helps WLP practitioners and other people carry out effective intervention design and development. As with other models of WLP roles, each step in the intervention design and development process model requires WLP practitioners (or others) to take action.

Much has been written about the instructional systems design model as a guide to help instructional designers navigate training course preparation (Rothwell and Kazanas, 1998). To be effective in WLP, however, the instructional systems design model must be broadened to become the intervention systems design model. After all, WLP practitioners do more than simply design and develop learning interventions. They also design and develop nonlearning interventions, including (but not limited to) making improvements in recruitment methods, selection methods, feedback systems, reward systems, and the use of tools and equipment.

A Model of the Intervention Design and Development Process

Think of the intervention design and development process as a series of general steps as follows:

1. Examine the characteristics of the participants in the intervention.
2. Examine the competencies necessary for successful achievement.
3. Examine the characteristics of the work environment.
4. Formulate performance objectives to guide the intervention.
5. Formulate specific methods by which to measure performance objectives.
6. Create a detailed project plan.

7. Create a detailed communication and marketing plan to clarify what is happening, has happened, and will happen.
8. Make, buy, or buy and modify materials and media to support the implementation of the intervention.

These steps are depicted in figure 4.1, and their relationship to the intervention designer and developer's competencies are depicted in table 4.1. This section addresses these steps and provides guidance for applying them. As you think about designing and developing an intervention, use figure 6.2,

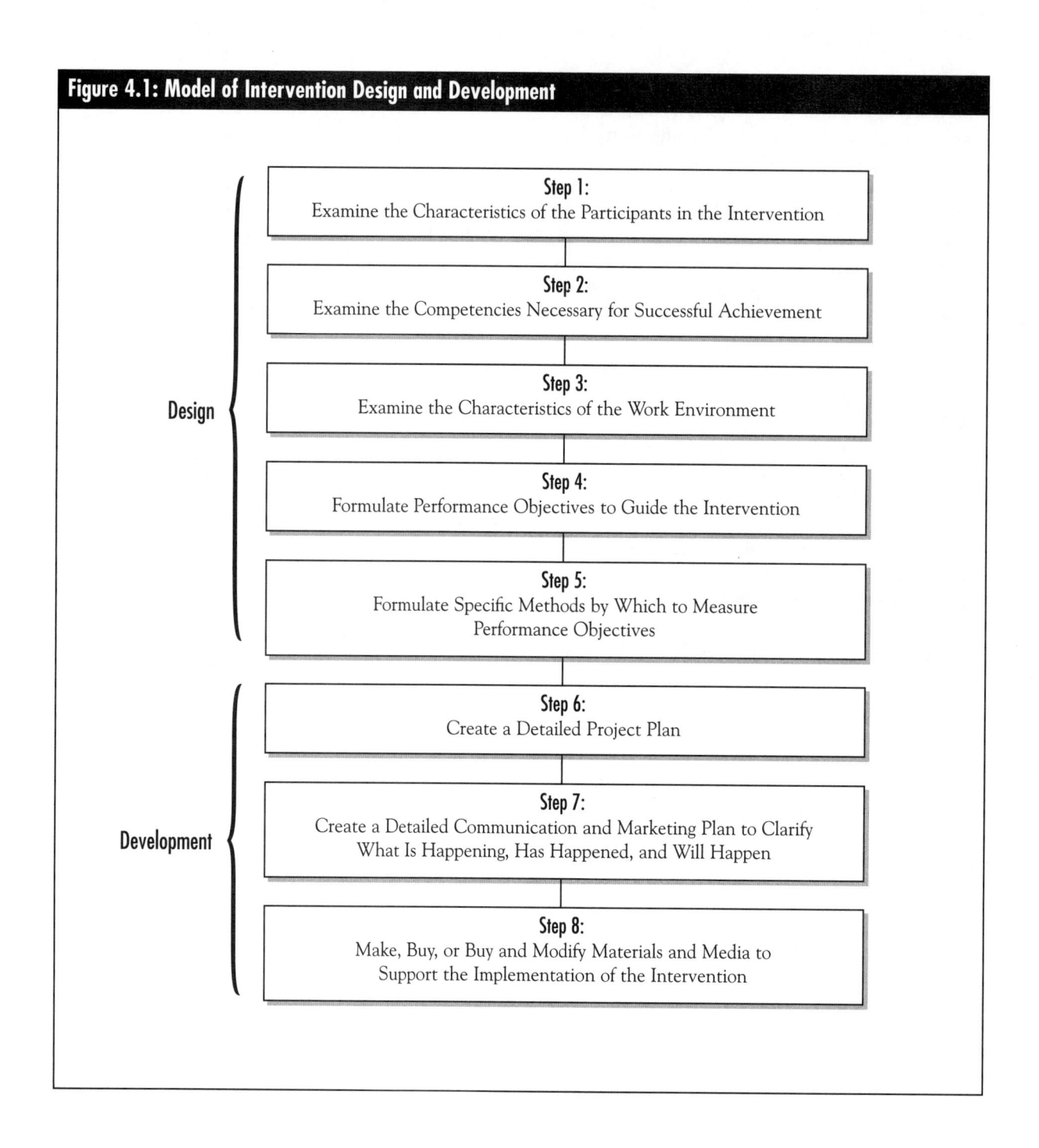

Figure 4.1: Model of Intervention Design and Development

Design
- **Step 1:** Examine the Characteristics of the Participants in the Intervention
- **Step 2:** Examine the Competencies Necessary for Successful Achievement
- **Step 3:** Examine the Characteristics of the Work Environment
- **Step 4:** Formulate Performance Objectives to Guide the Intervention
- **Step 5:** Formulate Specific Methods by Which to Measure Performance Objectives

Development
- **Step 6:** Create a Detailed Project Plan
- **Step 7:** Create a Detailed Communication and Marketing Plan to Clarify What Is Happening, Has Happened, and Will Happen
- **Step 8:** Make, Buy, or Buy and Modify Materials and Media to Support the Implementation of the Intervention

Table 4.1: Relationship Between Intervention Design and Development and the Competencies of the Intervention Designer and Developer*

Model of Intervention Design and Development	Competencies of the Intervention Designer and Developer
Examine the characteristics of the participants in the intervention	◆ *Analyzing performance data:* Interpreting performance data and determining the effect of interventions on customers, suppliers, and employees. ◆ *Career development theory and application:* Understanding the theories, techniques, and appropriate applications of career development interventions used for performance improvement. ◆ *Intervention selection:* Selecting performance improvement strategies that address the root causes of performance gaps, rather than treat symptoms or side effects.
Examine the competencies necessary for successful achievement	◆ *Adult learning:* Understanding how adults learn and how they use knowledge, skills, and attitudes. ◆ *Knowledge management:* Developing and implementing systems for creating, managing, and distributing knowledge. ◆ *Model building:* Conceptualizing and developing theoretical and practical frameworks that describe complex ideas. ◆ *Performance theory:* Recognizing the implications, outcomes, and consequences of performance interventions to distinguish between activities and results. ◆ *Standards identification:* Determining what constitutes success for individuals, organizations, and processes. ◆ *Systems thinking:* Recognizing the interrelationship among events by determining the driving forces that connect seemingly isolated incidents within the organization; taking a holistic view of performance problems in order to find root causes. ◆ *Training theory and application:* Understanding the theories, techniques, and appropriate applications of training interventions for performance improvement.
Examine the characteristics of the work environment	◆ *Industry awareness:* Understanding the current and future climate of the organization's industry and formulating strategies that respond to that climate. ◆ *Organization development theory and application:* Understanding the theories, techniques, and appropriate applications of organization development interventions as they are used for performance improvement. ◆ *Reward system theory and application:* Understanding the theories, techniques, and appropriate applications of reward system interventions used for performance improvement. ◆ *Workplace performance, learning strategies, and intervention evaluation:* Continually evaluating and improving interventions before and during implementation.
Formulate performance objectives to guide the intervention	◆ *Project management:* Planning, organizing, and monitoring work. ◆ *Standards identification:* Determining what constitutes success for individuals, organizations, and processes.

(continued on next page)

*Some competencies are used in more than one step of the model.

Table 4.1: Relationship Between Intervention Design and Development and the Competencies of the Intervention Designer and Developer (continued)

Model of Intervention Design and Development	Competencies of the Intervention Designer and Developer
Formulate specific methods by which to measure performance objectives	♦ *Standards identification:* Determining what constitutes success for individuals, organizations, and processes.
Create a detailed project plan	♦ *Project management:* Planning, organizing, and monitoring work.
Create a detailed communication and marketing plan to clarify what is happening, has happened, and will happen	♦ *Communication:* Applying effective verbal, nonverbal, and written communication methods to achieve desired results. ♦ *Communication networks:* Understanding the various methods through which communication is achieved. ♦ *Computer-mediated communication:* Understanding the implication of current and evolving computer-based electronic communication. ♦ *Diversity awareness:* Assessing the impact and appropriateness of interventions on individuals, groups, and organizations. ♦ *Ethics modeling:* Modeling exemplary ethical behavior and understanding the implications of this responsibility. ♦ *Interpersonal relationship building:* Effectively interacting with others in order to produce meaningful outcomes. ♦ *Survey design and development:* Creating survey approaches that use open-ended (essay) and closed-style questions (multiple choice and Likert items) for collecting data; preparing instruments in written, verbal, or electronic formats.
Make, buy, or buy and modify materials and media to support the implementation of the intervention	♦ *Distance education:* Understanding the evolving trends in technology-supported delivery methods and the implications of separating instructors and learners in time and location. ♦ *Electronic performance support systems:* Understanding current and evolving performance support systems and their appropriate applications. ♦ *Technological literacy:* Understanding and appropriately applying existing, new, or emerging technology.

"Worksheet to Guide Intervention Design and Development," on page 121 to help pose questions related to each step of the model.

Steps in the Intervention Design and Development Process

The descriptions of each step of the intervention design and development process follow a similar format. They begin with the definition and purpose of the step, follow with notes about implementing the step, and end with an example of the step that illustrates and dramatizes what it can mean in practice.

Step 1: Examine the Characteristics of the Participants in the Intervention

Definition and Purpose of Step 1

Begin intervention design and development by examining the characteristics of the participants in the intervention. (See figure 4.2.) This is an essential step in instructional design (Rothwell and Kazanas, 1998), and it is also an essential step in designing and developing nonlearning interventions. After all, the characteristics of the participants influence what changes can be made and how successful they will be.

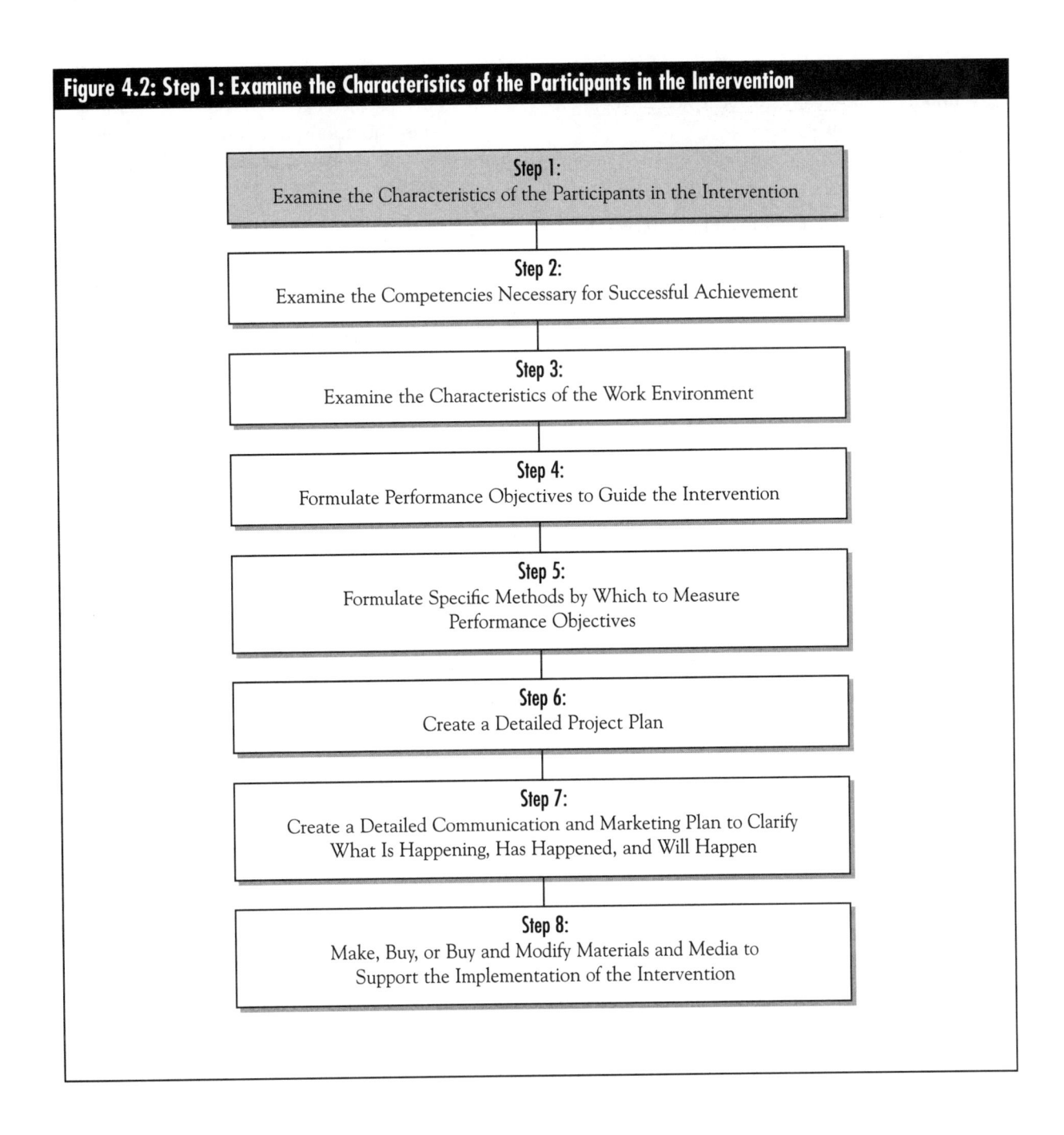

Figure 4.2: Step 1: Examine the Characteristics of the Participants in the Intervention

```
Step 1:
Examine the Characteristics of the Participants in the Intervention
         |
Step 2:
Examine the Competencies Necessary for Successful Achievement
         |
Step 3:
Examine the Characteristics of the Work Environment
         |
Step 4:
Formulate Performance Objectives to Guide the Intervention
         |
Step 5:
Formulate Specific Methods by Which to Measure
Performance Objectives
         |
Step 6:
Create a Detailed Project Plan
         |
Step 7:
Create a Detailed Communication and Marketing Plan to Clarify
What Is Happening, Has Happened, and Will Happen
         |
Step 8:
Make, Buy, or Buy and Modify Materials and Media to
Support the Implementation of the Intervention
```

Implementing Step 1

Begin any intervention design and development process by posing at least the following questions:

- Who (specifically) will participate?
- To whom do the participants report?
- What (specifically) are the participants expected to do during the intervention?
- What do the participants think and feel about the performance problem and the intervention intended to address it? Do they believe that the problem *is* a problem? Do they support the intervention? Are they motivated to participate in it?
- How will the participants be involved in designing and developing the intervention and in designing and developing the materials and media to implement it?

- What disabilities, if any, might affect the intervention, and how can reasonable accommodation be made for them?
- What physical, mental, and emotional demands will the intervention require of participants?
- How much time and effort will the intervention require, and are participants able to devote that time and effort to the intervention? Do their immediate organizational superiors support it? Do their superiors' superiors support it?

Implementing Step 1

Use Step 1 of the worksheet in figure 6.2 to pose the preceding questions to examine the characteristics of the participants in the intervention.

Vignette: Section 3 introduced the example of Marsha Kung, the director of WLP at LMN Corporation, who was working with a task force to solve a performance problem. That problem stemmed from a performance appraisal system that was perceived not to be effective. At the end of Section 3, Kung and the task force decided to propose full-scale implementation of an intervention intended to improve the performance appraisal system.

The top managers of LMN accepted the proposal with minor modifications. They signaled their complete support for the intervention by approving the resources needed to make it successful and by agreeing to be involved personally in formulating and implementing the intervention. The CEO, in particular, was most supportive.

As a next step, Kung called the task force members together to clarify the specific people to be targeted for change in the intervention. A widespread implementation was planned in which the entire organization was to be the target for change. However, as Kung said, "we cannot assume that all groups in our company know the same things about this intervention, value its importance equally, or will be equally supportive. This change will be like the introduction of a new product to consumers: Some people will buy it early, others will buy it later when it is more established and accepted, and some will never buy it. Our task is to improve the adoption rate and reduce the errors so that the results are successful."

She then asked the task force members the questions specified earlier in this step. As Kung asked these questions, task force members pinpointed supervisors and managers as key participants in the intervention because they have the most people directly reporting to them and therefore conduct the most performance appraisals.

Step 2: Examine the Competencies Necessary for Successful Achievement

Definition and Purpose of Step 2

This step has to do with examining what people must know, do, or feel to succeed in performing in the context of the intervention. (See figure 4.3.) This step is useful because many performance interventions may require a learning intervention to help participants build their competencies (Dubois and Rothwell, 2000). For instance, if selection methods are to be improved, then participants may have to be trained to apply those methods. The same principle applies to other interventions.

Implementing Step 2

Intervention designers and developers involved in this step should pose the following questions:

- What competencies do participants already possess that are relevant to addressing the performance problem and designing and developing the intervention?
- What competencies do participants need that are relevant to addressing the performance problem and designing and developing the intervention?
- How can the organization build the competencies participants require to be successful in the intervention?
- How can the organization build the competencies required of participants' immediate organizational superiors in the intervention?
- What experience, if any, have the participants had with a similar intervention, and how did they feel about that experience? Was the intervention successful or unsuccessful? Why?

By answering these questions, intervention designers and developers clarify what competencies are necessary for participants if they are to perform

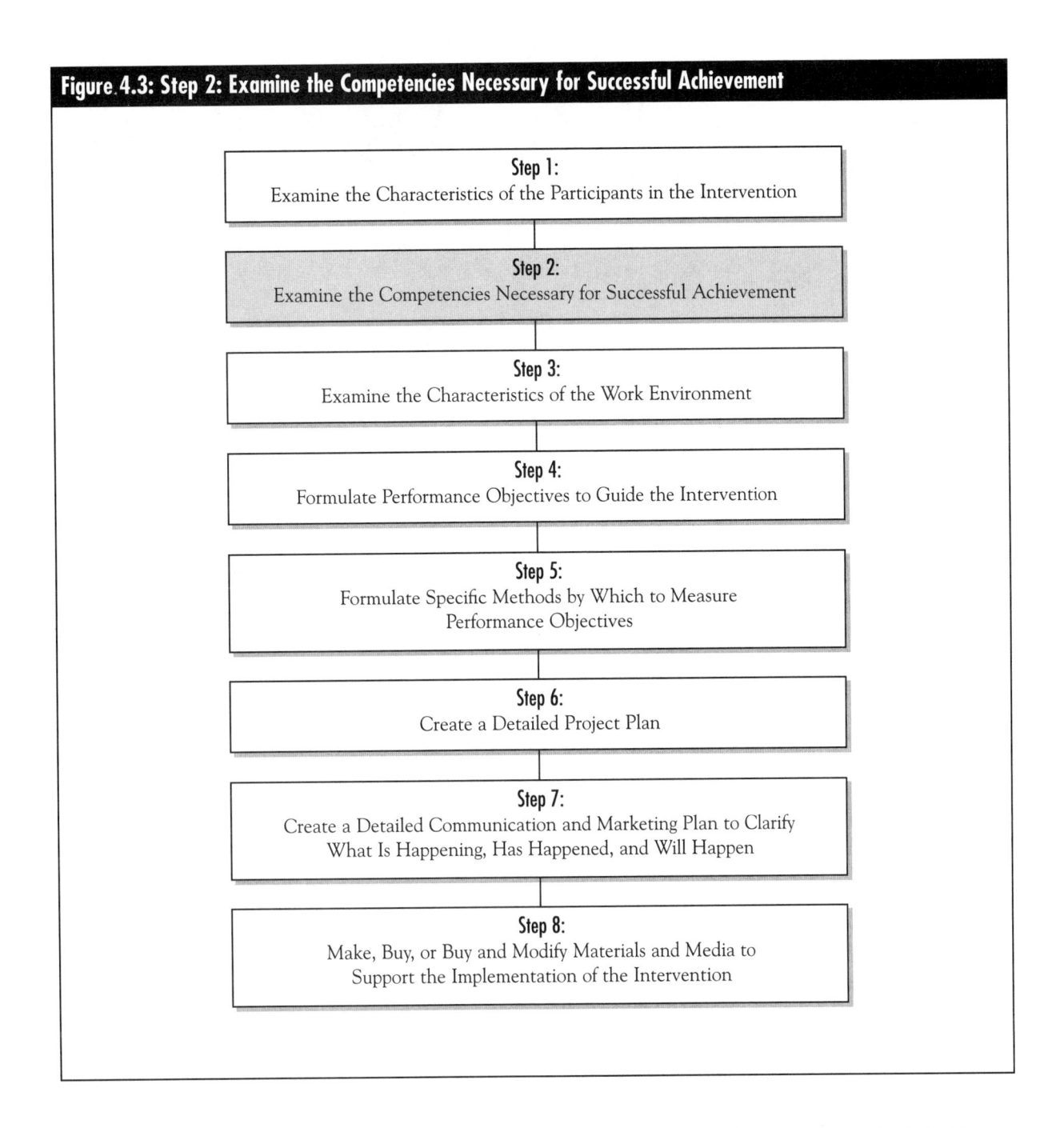

Figure 4.3: Step 2: Examine the Competencies Necessary for Successful Achievement

Step 1: Examine the Characteristics of the Participants in the Intervention

Step 2: Examine the Competencies Necessary for Successful Achievement

Step 3: Examine the Characteristics of the Work Environment

Step 4: Formulate Performance Objectives to Guide the Intervention

Step 5: Formulate Specific Methods by Which to Measure Performance Objectives

Step 6: Create a Detailed Project Plan

Step 7: Create a Detailed Communication and Marketing Plan to Clarify What Is Happening, Has Happened, and Will Happen

Step 8: Make, Buy, or Buy and Modify Materials and Media to Support the Implementation of the Intervention

---

in the intervention. That information is useful because building competencies may require materials suited to that purpose.

Use Step 2 of the worksheet in figure 6.2 to examine the competencies necessary for successful achievement of the intervention.

Vignette: Based on the definition of intervention participants, Kung and the task force described what competencies would be necessary for each targeted group of participants and stakeholders to perform their roles in the intervention successfully. To that end, they devised a "competency profile" that described what people should know, do, and feel at each hierarchical level of the organization during each intervention phase. Kung formed a subcommittee of the task force (consisting of herself; Mike Santiago, the vice president of human resources; and Tom Lawson, the engineer) to prepare draft proposals of these competency profiles for each group. These profiles were then to be reviewed, modified, and approved by the task force and top managers of LMN. They could then be used to devise training to support the performance appraisal system improvement intervention.

Step 3: Examine the Characteristics of the Work Environment

Definition and Purpose of Step 3

The third step in the intervention design and development process is to examine the characteristics of the work environment in which the performance will be achieved and in which the intervention will be implemented. (See figure 4.4.) This step thus involves investigating how supportive the work environment will be of the intervention and what factors or conditions in the work environment will influence implementation.

Implementing Step 3

To be successful in this step, intervention designers and developers should pose the following questions:

- What conditions in the work environment will influence the preparation and planning of the intervention? What conditions in the work environment will influence the preparation and planning of its implementation? What conditions in the work environment will influence its success in changing attitudes, behaviors, or results?
- What conditions in the work environment are most likely to support the intervention?
- What conditions in the work environment are most likely to pose barriers to the intervention?
- How can the conditions supporting the intervention be intensified, and how can barriers to the intervention be surmounted?

By posing these questions, intervention designers and developers can assess the work environment that will influence the intervention. The information yielded by researching these questions can be useful to intervention designers and developers in making, buying, or buying and modifying materials and media to support the intervention's implementation.

Use Step 3 of the worksheet in figure 6.2 to answer the questions in this section and examine the characteristics of the work environment in which the intervention will be implemented.

Vignette: Marsha Kung next asked her task force members, this time by an online query, to list the conditions in the work environment that they believed would influence the performance appraisal intervention. What forces or conditions in the work environment of the appraisers, she asked them, might stand in the way of success? What forces or conditions would be most likely to contribute to success?

The members were quick to respond. Nearly all of them indicated that the most important barriers in the work environment would be "lack of time to do appraisals thoroughly and thoughtfully," "lack of skill in conducting appraisal interviews," "the belief that performance appraisal is a paperwork exercise of low priority," and "no sense that doing a good job on performance appraisal will yield rewards or benefits to the appraiser." Their comments about conditions favoring performance appraisal were more nebulous. For instance, they said that "doing appraisals properly is like being on the side of the angels, motherhood, and apple pie" and "good appraisals will improve employee performance somehow—through feedback, if no other way."

Once these characteristics were identified, Kung led the task force members through an activity in which they brainstormed ways to strengthen the conditions supporting the intervention and weaken the barriers affecting the intervention. Based on the results of that activity, task force members formed subcommittees to strengthen or weaken the barriers.

Step 4: Formulate Performance Objectives to Guide the Intervention

Definition and Purpose of Step 4

The fourth step in the intervention design and development process is to formulate the performance objectives to guide the intervention. (See figure 4.5.)

A performance objective is a description of the results desired from an intervention (Rothwell, 1996b). While an instructional objective describes

Figure 4.4: Step 3: Examine the Characteristics of the Work Environment

- **Step 1:** Examine the Characteristics of the Participants in the Intervention
- **Step 2:** Examine the Competencies Necessary for Successful Achievement
- **Step 3:** Examine the Characteristics of the Work Environment
- **Step 4:** Formulate Performance Objectives to Guide the Intervention
- **Step 5:** Formulate Specific Methods by Which to Measure Performance Objectives
- **Step 6:** Create a Detailed Project Plan
- **Step 7:** Create a Detailed Communication and Marketing Plan to Clarify What Is Happening, Has Happened, and Will Happen
- **Step 8:** Make, Buy, or Buy and Modify Materials and Media to Support the Implementation of the Intervention

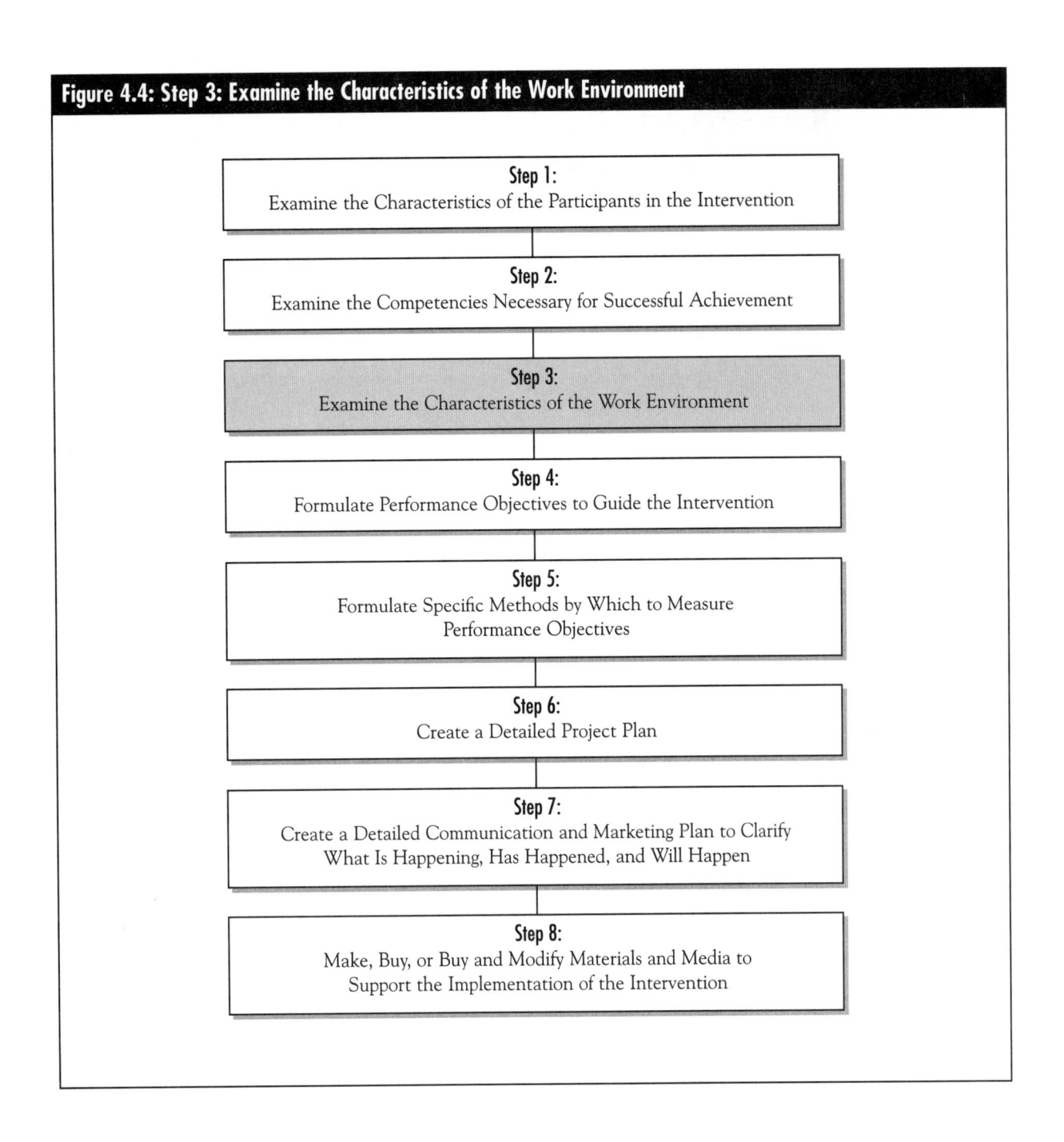

the results intended from a planned learning experience, a performance objective describes the final outcomes desired or planned from any performance intervention. Good instructional objectives have three components (Mager, 1997b): behaviors (what learners are supposed to do upon completion of instruction), conditions (what resources learners must possess to demonstrate the objective), and criteria (how much or how well learners must be able to perform or demonstrate knowledge of what they have learned).

Good performance objectives also have three components: results (what will be happening and what results will have been achieved upon completion of the intervention), conditions (what resources performers must possess to achieve the objective), and criteria (how much or how well performance should be demonstrated in on-the-job results). The

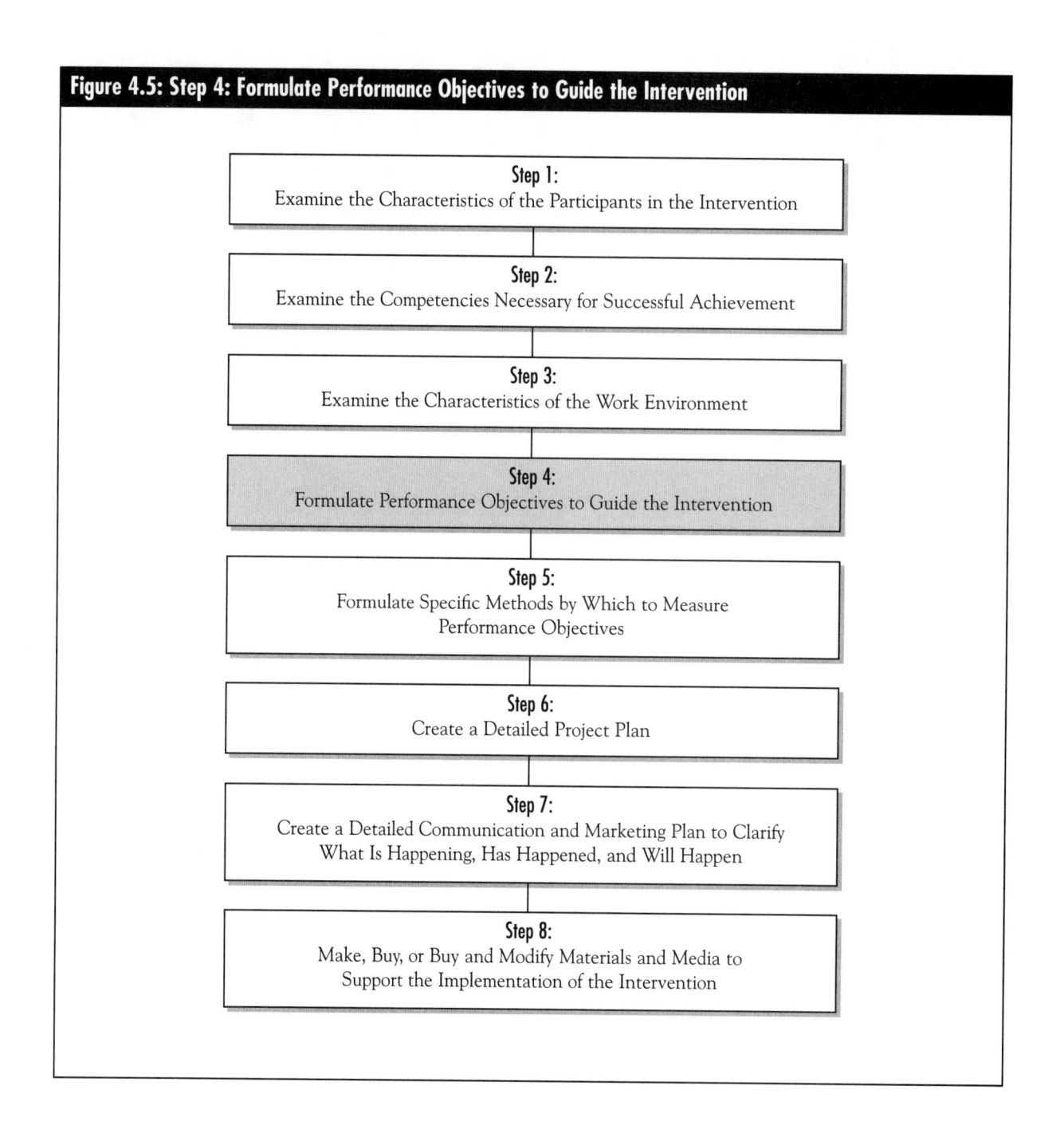

Figure 4.5: Step 4: Formulate Performance Objectives to Guide the Intervention

Step 1:
Examine the Characteristics of the Participants in the Intervention

Step 2:
Examine the Competencies Necessary for Successful Achievement

Step 3:
Examine the Characteristics of the Work Environment

**Step 4:
Formulate Performance Objectives to Guide the Intervention**

Step 5:
Formulate Specific Methods by Which to Measure Performance Objectives

Step 6:
Create a Detailed Project Plan

Step 7:
Create a Detailed Communication and Marketing Plan to Clarify What Is Happening, Has Happened, and Will Happen

Step 8:
Make, Buy, or Buy and Modify Materials and Media to Support the Implementation of the Intervention

---

relationship between instructional objectives and performance objectives is depicted in figure 4.6, and a worksheet for creating performance objectives is depicted in figure 4.7.

Implementing Step 4

To implement this step, intervention designers and developers should pose the following questions:

- What specific performance problems are to be addressed by the intervention?
- What performance gap is to be closed by the intervention?
- What final results or outcomes can be described that, taken together, will fully describe the final outcomes desired on completion of the intervention? (When these results are achieved, the

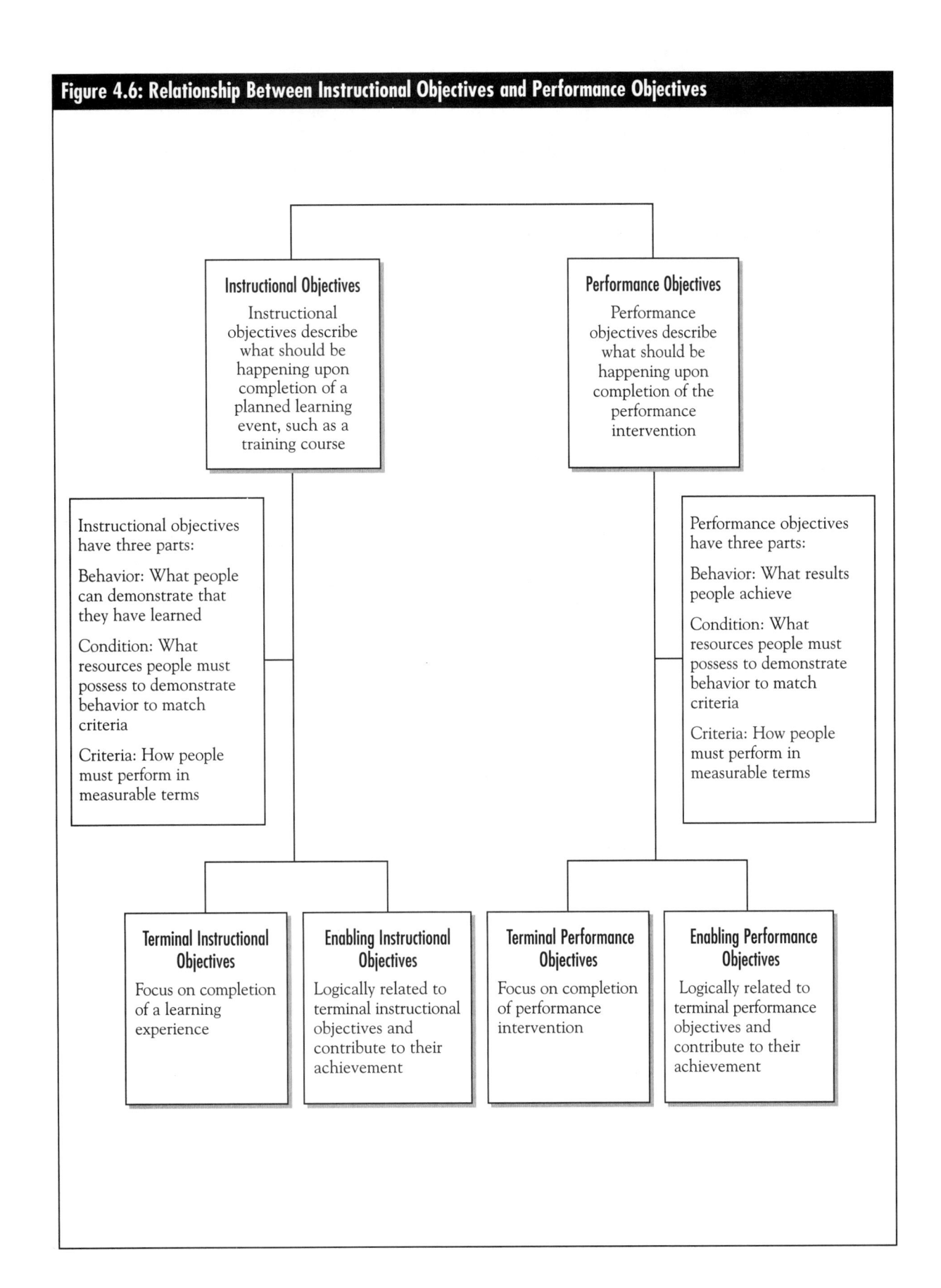

Figure 4.6: Relationship Between Instructional Objectives and Performance Objectives

Instructional Objectives

Instructional objectives describe what should be happening upon completion of a planned learning event, such as a training course

Performance Objectives

Performance objectives describe what should be happening upon completion of the performance intervention

Instructional objectives have three parts:

Behavior: What people can demonstrate that they have learned

Condition: What resources people must possess to demonstrate behavior to match criteria

Criteria: How people must perform in measurable terms

Performance objectives have three parts:

Behavior: What results people achieve

Condition: What resources people must possess to demonstrate behavior to match criteria

Criteria: How people must perform in measurable terms

Terminal Instructional Objectives

Focus on completion of a learning experience

Enabling Instructional Objectives

Logically related to terminal instructional objectives and contribute to their achievement

Terminal Performance Objectives

Focus on completion of performance intervention

Enabling Performance Objectives

Logically related to terminal performance objectives and contribute to their achievement

Figure 4.7: Worksheet for Preparing Performance Objectives for an Intervention

Directions: Use this worksheet in preparing performance objectives to guide a performance intervention. Describe the performance problem to be solved by the intervention below. Then, in column 1, lists its causes. In column 2, describe what results are needed by the end of the performance intervention to close the performance gap by addressing the causes of the performance problem. In column 3, for each result listed in column 2, indicate what behaviors and results will be observable upon completion of the performance intervention; what resources or conditions are necessary for those behaviors and results to be demonstrated; and how the behaviors and results will be measured in terms of quantity, quality, cost, time, or customer satisfaction. There are no "right" or "wrong" answers to these questions in any absolute sense. However, by clarifying what results are to be achieved upon completion of the performance intervention, stakeholders should be able to track results during the intervention against desired outcomes.

Describe the performance problem clearly and succinctly:

	Column 1 Causes of the Performance Problem	Column 2 What results are needed by the end of the performance intervention to close the performance gap by addressing the causes of the performance problem?	Column 3 For each result listed under column 2, indicate what behaviors and results will be observable upon completion of the performance intervention. What resources or conditions are necessary for those behaviors and results to be demonstrated? How will the behaviors and results be measured in terms of quantity, quality, cost, time, or customer satisfaction?
1			*Behaviors and results:*
			Resources:
			Measurements:
2			*Behaviors and results:*
			Resources:
			Measurements:
3			*Behaviors and results:*
			Resources:
			Measurements:
4			*Behaviors and results:*
			Resources:
			Measurements:

performance gap will be closed or its effects at least minimized.)

- What interim results or outcomes are desired at various milestones during the implementation of the intervention?
- What results or outcomes will performers achieve on completion of the intervention?
- What conditions or resources will be necessary for the performers if they are to demonstrate the desired results or outcomes?
- How can the conditions or resources be measured?

Use Step 4 of the worksheet in figure 6.2 to formulate performance objectives to guide the intervention.

Vignette: Marsha Kung explained to the task force members that an important next step in preparing for the performance appraisal improvement intervention was to clarify the desired results. As she explained to them, "If we don't know where we are going, we have no idea where we will go with this. Our destination must be as clear as possible at the outset. For that reason, we must establish intervention performance objectives that will describe exactly what results the intervention will achieve. We may also want to establish project milestones and enabling performance objectives." To that end, she said they needed to answer the foregoing questions.

The answers were reviewed by top managers at LMN Corporation. These performance objectives clarified exactly what outcomes would be sought from the intervention.

Step 5: Formulate Specific Methods by Which to Measure Performance Objectives

Definition and Purpose of Step 5

The fifth step in intervention design and develop is to formulate specific methods by which to measure performance objectives. (See figure 4.8.) Of course, during learning interventions, it is typical to measure achievement of instructional objectives by criterion-based testing (Mager, 1997a, 1997b). Criterion-based testing is, by definition, testing that is based on how well learners achieve the measurable criteria described in the instructional objectives. In non-learning interventions, it is necessary to go beyond criterion-based testing to performance-based measurement. The goal is to measure how well performance objectives were achieved on the job and how much the organization or its people changed as a direct result of the intervention. That is the result desired from this step.

Implementing Step 5

To carry out this step effectively, intervention designers and developers should pose such questions as these:

- What should be happening (and what should be the final measurable performance levels) upon completion of the intervention?
- How should results be measured?
- When should results be measured? When do the milestones occur, and what results should have been achieved by each milestone?
- Who will conduct the measurements of the interventions?
- Where will results be measured? Will comparison groups (such as pretest and posttest groups or experimental and control groups) be established? If so, where and how?

Use Step 5 of the worksheet in figure 6.2 to answer the foregoing questions and formulate specific methods by which to measure performance objectives.

Vignette: As a next step in the performance appraisal improvement intervention, Marsha Kung asked the task force members how achievement of the performance objectives of the intervention could be measured. She provided them with a briefing about approaches to measuring performance objectives. Task force members recommended that several focus groups take place with the key performance appraisal intervention participants—executives, managers, and supervisors—so they would take ownership of the measurement methods associated with performance objectives.

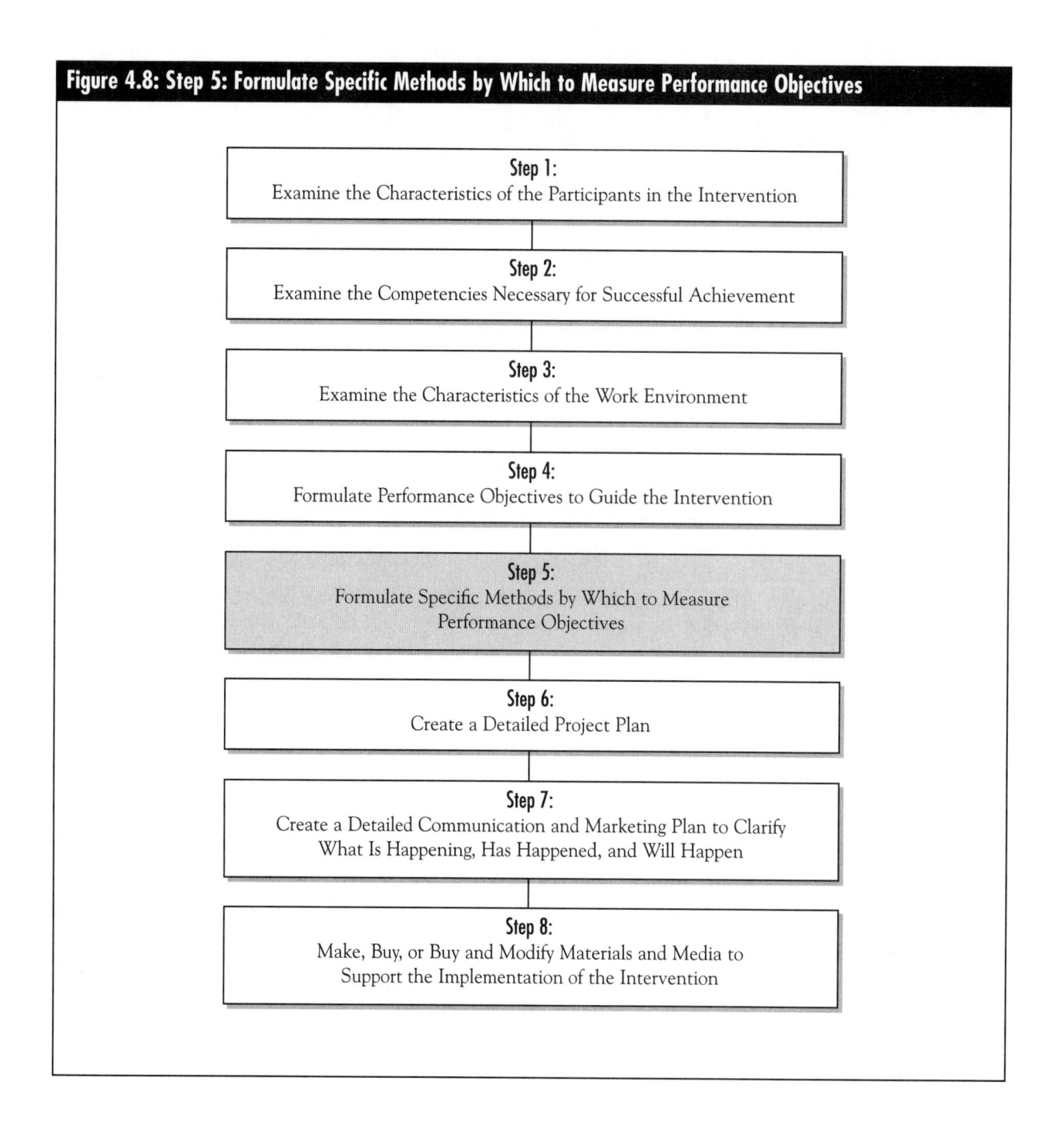

Figure 4.8: Step 5: Formulate Specific Methods by Which to Measure Performance Objectives

Step 1:
Examine the Characteristics of the Participants in the Intervention

Step 2:
Examine the Competencies Necessary for Successful Achievement

Step 3:
Examine the Characteristics of the Work Environment

Step 4:
Formulate Performance Objectives to Guide the Intervention

Step 5:
Formulate Specific Methods by Which to Measure Performance Objectives

Step 6:
Create a Detailed Project Plan

Step 7:
Create a Detailed Communication and Marketing Plan to Clarify What Is Happening, Has Happened, and Will Happen

Step 8:
Make, Buy, or Buy and Modify Materials and Media to Support the Implementation of the Intervention

Step 6: Create a Detailed Project Plan

Definition and Purpose of Step 6

The sixth step is to create a detailed project plan to guide the implementation of the intervention. (See figure 4.9.) This project plan should be more detailed than the action plan that was prepared during intervention selection. This plan should effectively establish accountabilities and clarify who should do what and when, with what resources, and with what results. It is not enough to establish a project plan to guide the actions of WLP practitioners. Instead, the project plan should also stipulate the roles and responsibilities of decision makers and participants.

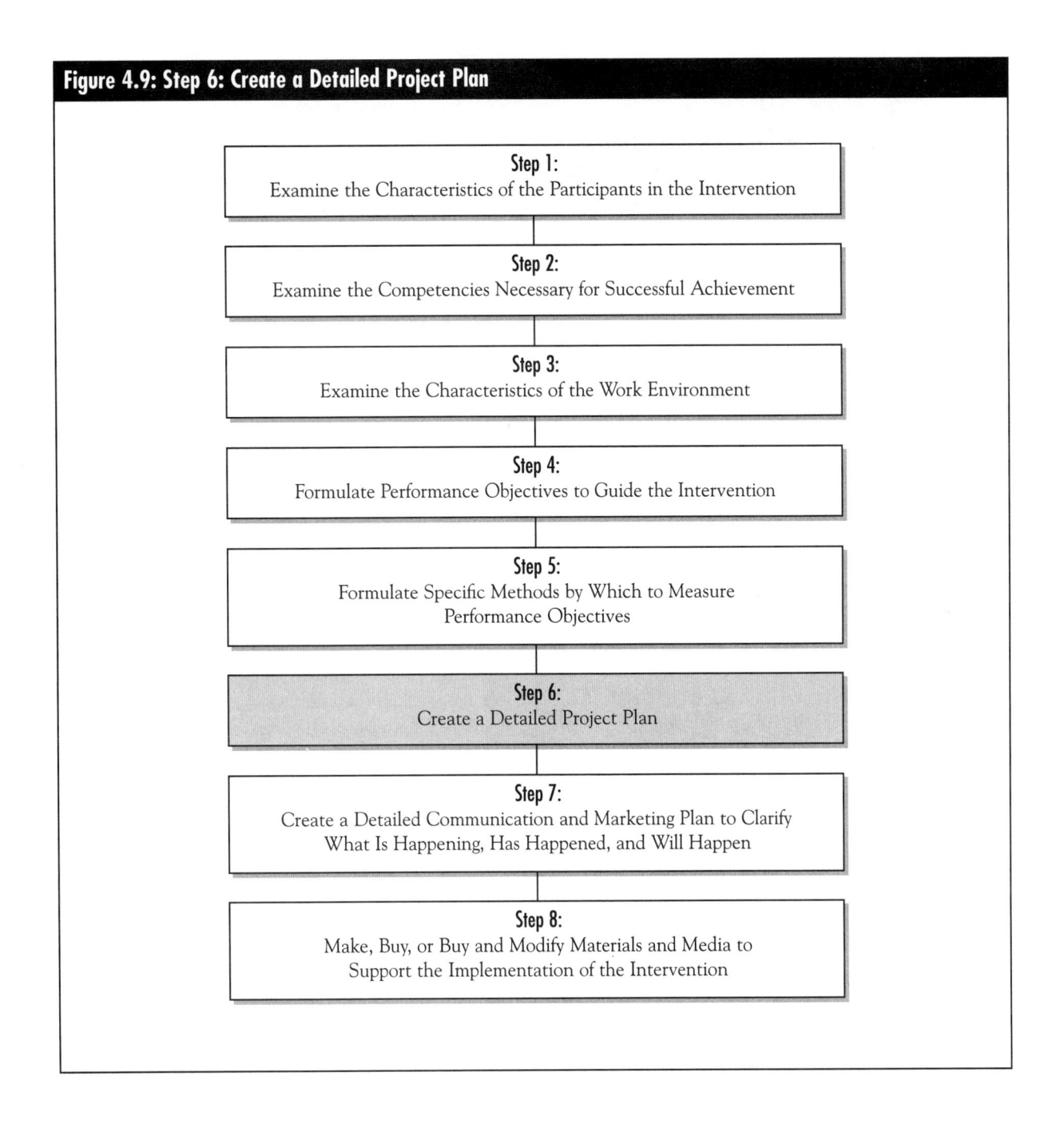

Figure 4.9: Step 6: Create a Detailed Project Plan

Step 1:
Examine the Characteristics of the Participants in the Intervention

Step 2:
Examine the Competencies Necessary for Successful Achievement

Step 3:
Examine the Characteristics of the Work Environment

Step 4:
Formulate Performance Objectives to Guide the Intervention

Step 5:
Formulate Specific Methods by Which to Measure Performance Objectives

Step 6:
Create a Detailed Project Plan

Step 7:
Create a Detailed Communication and Marketing Plan to Clarify What Is Happening, Has Happened, and Will Happen

Step 8:
Make, Buy, or Buy and Modify Materials and Media to Support the Implementation of the Intervention

Implementing Step 6

To carry out this step effectively, whether working alone or in a team with stakeholders and participants, intervention designers and developers should pose the following questions:

- Who will take action during each part of the intervention?
- What tasks should they carry out, and what measurable results are they expected to achieve?
- What are the deadlines for achievement?
- What is the budget, and what other resources are available during the intervention?

Use Step 6 of the worksheet in figure 6.2 to answer the foregoing questions and create a detailed project plan to guide implementation of the intervention.

Vignette: During a full-day retreat, Kung and the task force members developed a project plan that was much more detailed than the earlier one the top managers had approved. When the action plan was completed, task force members broke up into subcommittees (called design teams) to oversee specific facets of the performance appraisal improvement intervention. One project team focused on establishing performance expectations in the organization, working with specific divisions and departments; a second team focused on developing policies, procedures, forms, and other materials to support the performance appraisal process; a third team focused on linking rewards to performance measures; and a fourth focused on developing training by hierarchical level to support the intervention and build the competencies necessary for executives, managers, and supervisors to use the appraisal process.

Step 7: Create a Detailed Communication and Marketing Plan to Clarify What Is Happening, Has Happened, and Will Happen

Definition and Purpose of Step 7

The seventh step is to create a detailed communication and marketing plan to clarify what is happening, what has happened, and what will happen in the intervention. (See figure 4.10.) It is at this point that WLP practitioners, working by themselves or with others, decide what to do to solve a performance problem.

This decision is made after considering the issues described in steps 1 through 6. The decision may be based on an analytical approach, a creative approach, or a group process approach.

Implementing Step 7

To carry out this step effectively, intervention designers and developers should pose such questions as these:

♦ What are the phases, steps, tasks, or events of the intervention?

♦ Who has a need to know about each step?

♦ What do they need to know at each step, and when do they need to know it?

♦ What are the most effective ways to communicate about the intervention to participants and other stakeholders for introducing each phase, step, task, or event of the intervention?

♦ How should the communication plan be prepared, approved, tested, and evaluated?

♦ How many details should be provided about the interventions?

♦ What should be communicated about what is happening in the intervention, what has happened (progress to date) in the intervention, and what is expected or planned to happen in the intervention?

Use Step 7 of the worksheet in figure 6.2 to answer these questions and create a detailed communication and marketing plan to clarify what is happening, what has happened, and what will happen in the intervention.

Vignette: At the same retreat at which the task force worked on a detailed project plan to guide implementation of the intervention, Marsha Kung facilitated the team's formulation of a communication and marketing plan to support the implementation of the intervention. One task force member volunteered to serve as chairwoman of an action team to provide communication about the intervention to key stakeholders. The team decided to use the company's in-house newsletter as part of an integrated communication plan and to list progress reports toward achievement of the performance objectives as an agenda item at top management meetings.

Step 8: Make, Buy, or Buy and Modify Materials and Media to Support the Implementation of the Intervention

Definition and Purpose of Step 8

The eighth and final step in the intervention design and development process is to make, buy, or buy and modify materials and media to support the implementation of the intervention. (See figure 4.11.) This step is about finding the materials and media to support the intervention. Much has been written about

Figure 4.10: Step 7: Create a Detailed Communication and Marketing Plan to Clarify What Is Happening, Has Happened, and Will Happen

```
Step 1:
Examine the Characteristics of the Participants in the Intervention
           |
Step 2:
Examine the Competencies Necessary for Successful Achievement
           |
Step 3:
Examine the Characteristics of the Work Environment
           |
Step 4:
Formulate Performance Objectives to Guide the Intervention
           |
Step 5:
Formulate Specific Methods by Which to Measure Performance Objectives
           |
Step 6:
Create a Detailed Project Plan
           |
Step 7:
Create a Detailed Communication and Marketing Plan to Clarify What Is Happening, Has Happened, and Will Happen
           |
Step 8:
Make, Buy, or Buy and Modify Materials and Media to Support the Implementation of the Intervention
```

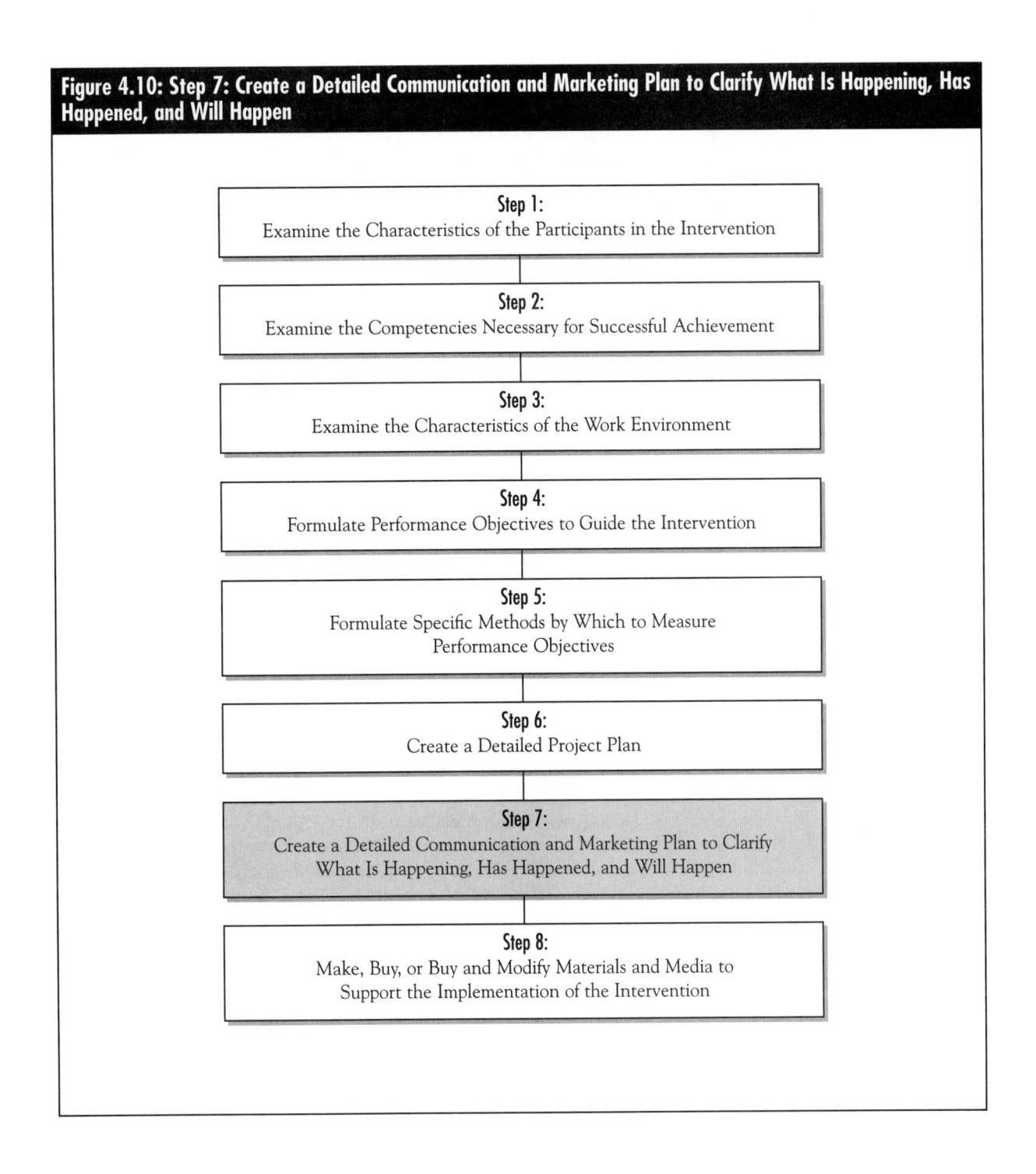

materials selection and media selection (see, for instance, Rothwell and Kazanas, 1998; Marx, 1999).

Making materials or media means preparing the content or delivery methods so that they are customized to the people, places, and events of the intervention.

Buying materials or media means purchasing the content or delivery methods from other sources. These sources may include external contractors or vendors, internal groups of the organization, or temporary employees who assist in creating materials or media for the intervention.

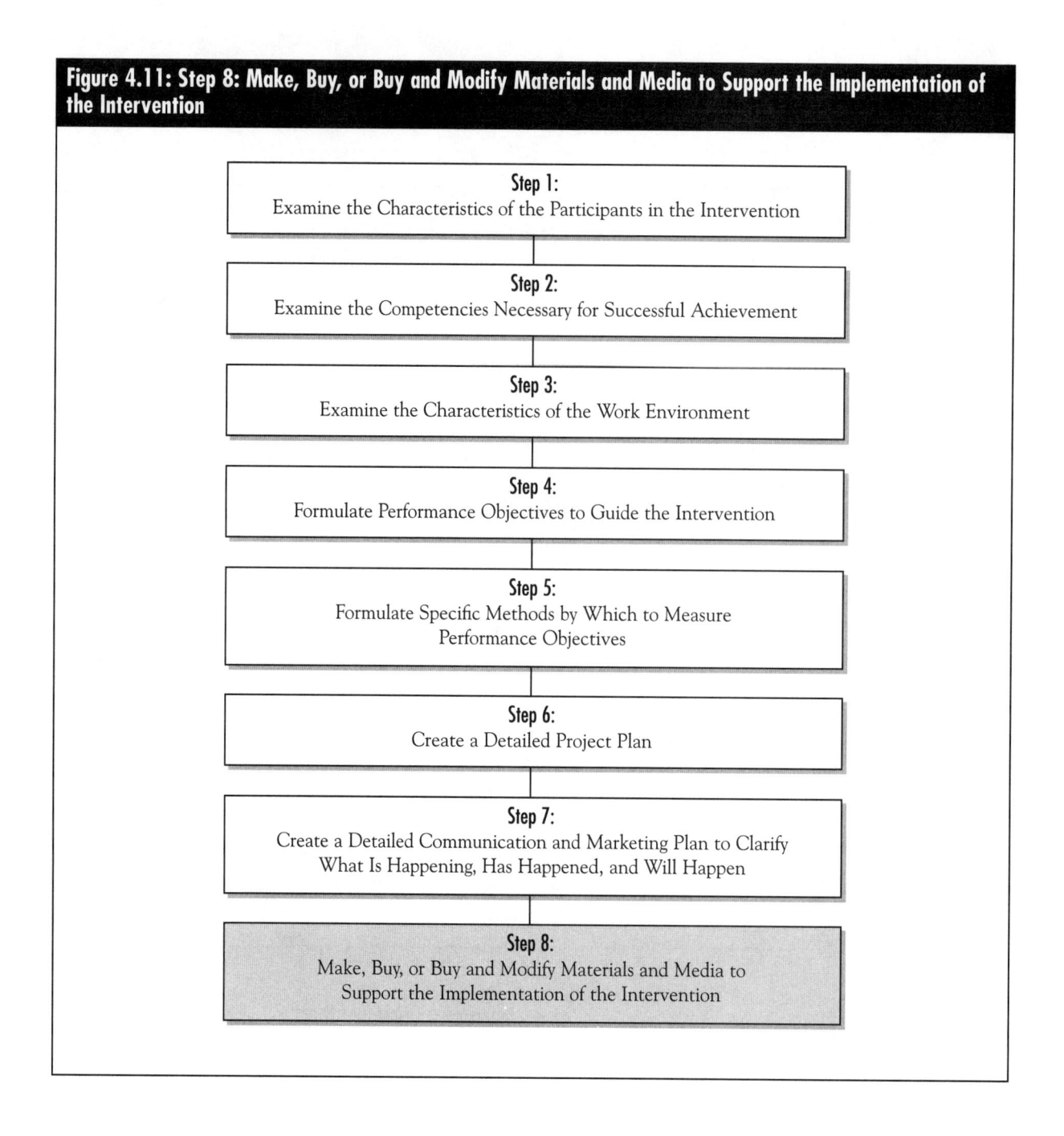

Figure 4.11: Step 8: Make, Buy, or Buy and Modify Materials and Media to Support the Implementation of the Intervention

- Step 1: Examine the Characteristics of the Participants in the Intervention
- Step 2: Examine the Competencies Necessary for Successful Achievement
- Step 3: Examine the Characteristics of the Work Environment
- Step 4: Formulate Performance Objectives to Guide the Intervention
- Step 5: Formulate Specific Methods by Which to Measure Performance Objectives
- Step 6: Create a Detailed Project Plan
- Step 7: Create a Detailed Communication and Marketing Plan to Clarify What Is Happening, Has Happened, and Will Happen
- **Step 8: Make, Buy, or Buy and Modify Materials and Media to Support the Implementation of the Intervention**

Buying and modifying materials and media means purchasing materials or media from external sources and then modifying them so that they are better suited to the unique needs, issues, problems, and desired results of the intervention.

Implementing This Step

To carry out this step effectively, intervention designers and developers should pose such questions as these:

- What materials are necessary for use in the intervention to help meet the performance objectives?
- Where can the materials be obtained? Should they be made, bought, or bought and modified? If bought, from where or from whom?
- How should the materials be most cost-effectively delivered to participants and other groups to support achievement of the performance objectives?

- Where can media support, if required, be obtained?

Use Step 8 of the worksheet in figure 6.2 to answer these questions and figure out where to obtain the materials needed to support the implementation of the intervention.

Vignette: At the same retreat at which Marsha Kung and the task force formulated a detailed project plan and a communication and marketing plan to guide implementation of the intervention, she asked for a volunteer to spearhead a design team to scope the materials and media that would be required to support the intervention. One member of the team volunteered to chair that group and identified people from the organization who would be approached to help with that effort. Kung volunteered to brief the design team on various models that could be helpful. At that time, she handed out the model in figure 4.12 and explained how it could be useful in identifying the appropriate materials and media to support each step of the performance appraisal improvement intervention. She advised the chair of the design team to use consultant assistance, provided for in the project budget, to help with this effort.

Section Summary

This section described how to enact the role of intervention designer and developer, defined as the role that "creates learning and other interventions that help to address the specific root causes of human performance gaps. Some examples of the work of the intervention designer and developer include serving as instructional designer, media specialist, materials developer, process engineer, ergonomics engineer, instructional writer, and compensation analyst" (Rothwell, Sanders, and Soper, 1999, p. 43). The instructional designer and developer takes the results of the intervention selector's decisions about interventions and finds or creates plans, materials, and media by which to transform that intervention selection decision into reality. Key steps in carrying out intervention design and development process are

1. Examine the characteristics of the participants in the intervention.
2. Examine the competencies necessary for successful achievement.
3. Examine the characteristics of the work environment.
4. Formulate performance objectives to guide the intervention.
5. Formulate specific methods by which to measure performance objectives.
6. Create a detailed project plan.
7. Create a detailed communication and marketing plan to clarify what is happening, has happened, and will happen.
8. Make, buy, or buy and modify materials and media to support the implementation of the intervention.

The intervention designer and developer's role is logically related to the intervention implementor's role, which is described in section 5.

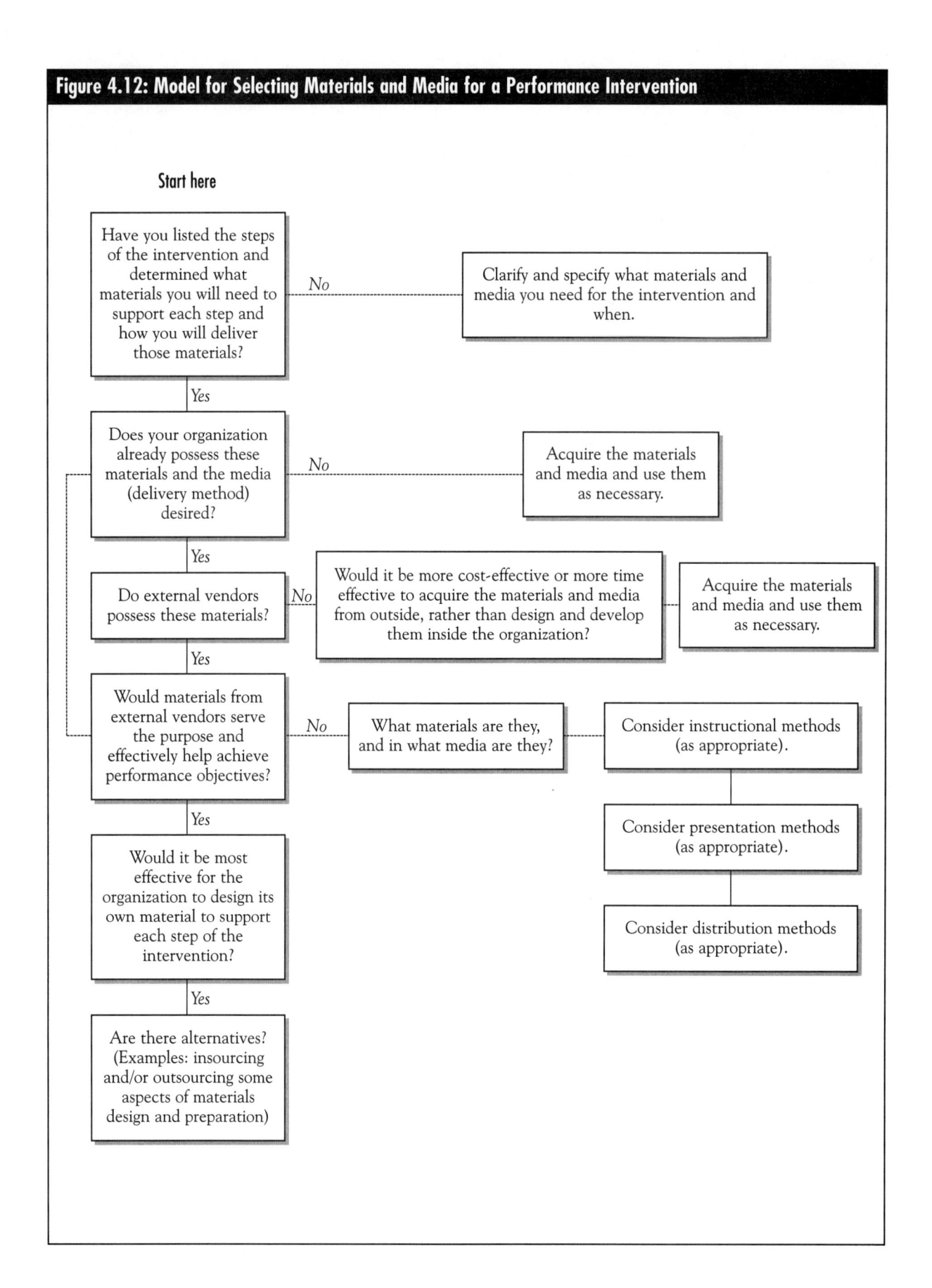

Figure 4.12: Model for Selecting Materials and Media for a Performance Intervention

Start here

- Have you listed the steps of the intervention and determined what materials you will need to support each step and how you will deliver those materials?
  - **No** → Clarify and specify what materials and media you need for the intervention and when.
  - **Yes** ↓
- Does your organization already possess these materials and the media (delivery method) desired?
  - **No** → Acquire the materials and media and use them as necessary.
  - **Yes** ↓
- Do external vendors possess these materials?
  - **No** → Would it be more cost-effective or more time effective to acquire the materials and media from outside, rather than design and develop them inside the organization? → Acquire the materials and media and use them as necessary.
  - **Yes** ↓
- Would materials from external vendors serve the purpose and effectively help achieve performance objectives?
  - **No** → What materials are they, and in what media are they? → Consider instructional methods (as appropriate). → Consider presentation methods (as appropriate). → Consider distribution methods (as appropriate).
  - **Yes** ↓
- Would it be most effective for the organization to design its own material to support each step of the intervention?
  - **Yes** ↓
- Are there alternatives? (Examples: insourcing and/or outsourcing some aspects of materials design and preparation)

SECTION 1   GETTING STARTED

SECTION 2   DEFINING THE ROLES

SECTION 3   ENACTING THE ROLE OF INTERVENTION SELECTOR

SECTION 4   ENACTING THE ROLE OF INTERVENTION DESIGNER AND DEVELOPER

SECTION 5   ENACTING THE ROLE OF INTERVENTION IMPLEMENTOR

- ◆ A Model of the Intervention Implementation Process
- ◆ Steps in the Intervention Implementation Process
  - — *Step 1:* Work With Participants and Stakeholders on a Daily Basis to Implement the Action Plan
  - — *Step 2:* Use Materials and Media Supplied by the Intervention Designers and Developers and Provide Feedback to Them About Ways to Improve Their Use
  - — *Step 3:* Deliver, or Facilitate Delivery of, the Intervention to Targeted Participants
  - — *Step 4:* Ensure That Communication about the Intervention Is Carried out Effectively
  - — *Step 5:* Track Short-Term Results Against the Intervention Performance Objectives
  - — *Step 6:* Surmount Barriers to Implementation and Ensure That the Intervention Is Implemented as Planned
  - — *Step 7:* Provide Clear, Specific, and Continuing Feedback to Stakeholders about the Results of the Intervention
- ◆ Section Summary

SECTION 6   TOOLS FOR CONDUCTING INTERVENTION SELECTION, DESIGN AND DEVELOPMENT, AND IMPLEMENTATION

SECTION 7   AFTERWORD

SECTION 8   BIBLIOGRAPHY

SECTION 5   ENACTING THE ROLE OF INTERVENTION IMPLEMENTOR

The intervention implementor "ensures the appropriate and effective implementation of desired interventions that address the specific root causes of human performance gaps. Some examples of the work of the intervention implementor include serving as administrator, instructor, organization development practitioner, career development specialist, process re-design consultant, workspace designer, compensation specialists, and facilitator" (Rothwell, Sanders, and Soper, 1999, p. 43). The intervention implementor implements the intervention chosen by the intervention selector role and uses material and media prepared by the intervention designer and developer role. The day-to-day tactical operations of the intervention are guided by the intervention implementor, a role confronted by many challenges (Whiteside, 1997). Intervention implementors are most successful when they make sure to tie their interventions to organizational goals, choose an opportune time in the organization's work cycle to begin the intervention, build management support, gain employee ownership and involvement, align the intervention with other organizational initiatives, ensure that the results are evaluated, ensure continuous communication with participants and stakeholders, celebrate accomplishments, and demonstrate tenacity (Spitzer, 1996).

Just as a model can be helpful in describing how other WLP roles are enacted, so can it be useful in describing how intervention implementation is carried out. An intervention implementation process model helps WLP practitioners and other people carry out effective intervention implementation. As with other models of WLP roles, each step in the intervention implementation process model requires WLP practitioners (or others) to take action.

A Model of the Intervention Implementation Process

Think of the intervention implementation process as a series of general steps as follows:

1. Work with participants and stakeholders on a daily basis to implement the action plan.

2. Use materials and media supplied by intervention designers and developers and provide feedback to them about ways to improve their use.

3. Deliver, or facilitate delivery of, the intervention to targeted participants.

4. Ensure that communication about the intervention is carried out effectively.

5. Track short-term results against the intervention performance objectives.

6. Surmount barriers to implementation and ensure that the intervention is implemented as planned.

7. Provide clear, specific, and continuing feedback to stakeholders about the results of the intervention.

These steps are depicted in figure 5.1, and their relationship to the intervention implementor's competencies are depicted in table 5.1. This section addresses these steps and provides guidance for applying them. As you think about designing and developing an intervention, use figure 6.3, "Worksheet to Guide Intervention Implementation," on page 128 to help pose questions related to each step of the model.

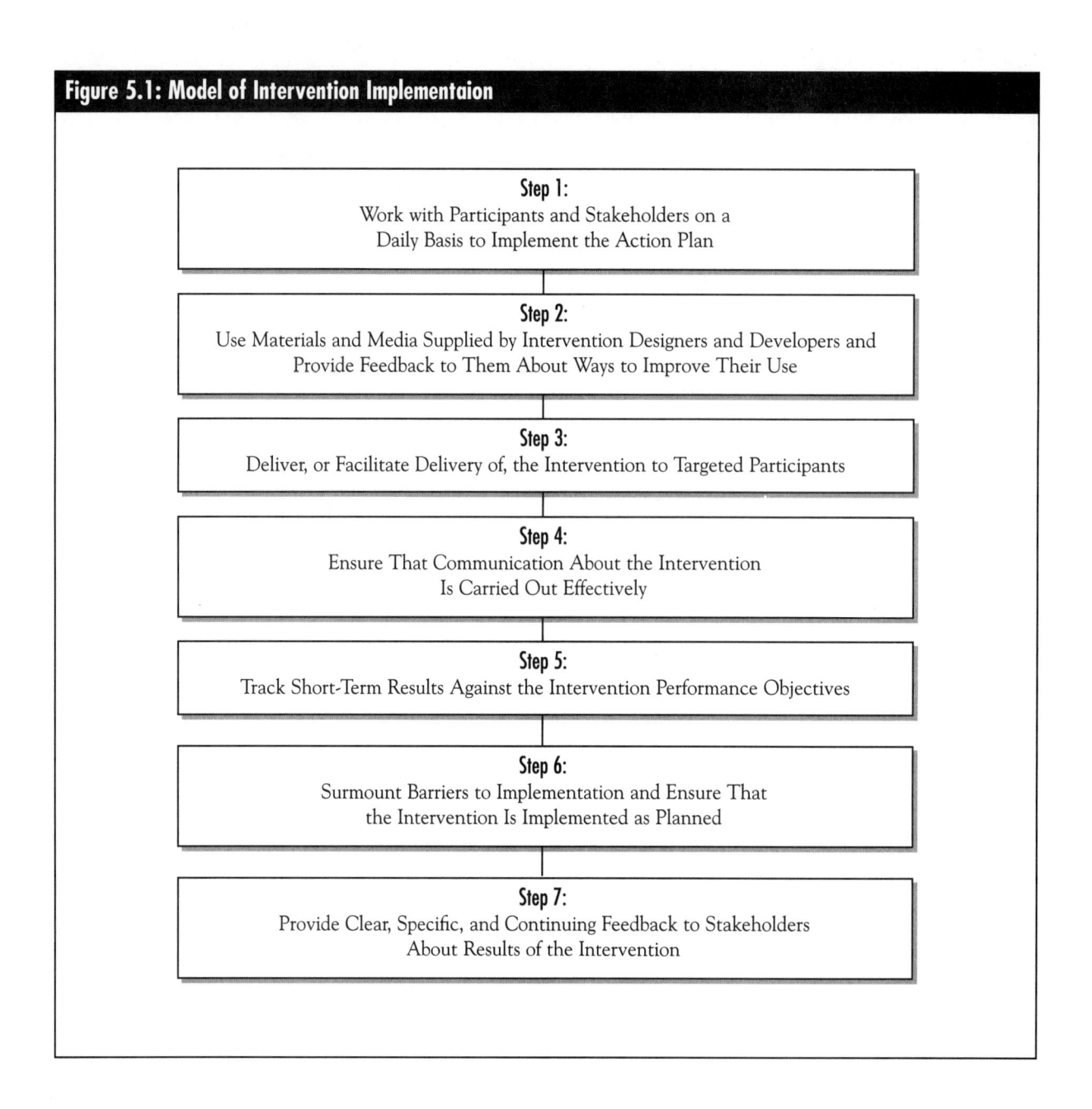

Figure 5.1: Model of Intervention Implementaion

Step 1:
Work with Participants and Stakeholders on a
Daily Basis to Implement the Action Plan

Step 2:
Use Materials and Media Supplied by Intervention Designers and Developers and
Provide Feedback to Them About Ways to Improve Their Use

Step 3:
Deliver, or Facilitate Delivery of, the Intervention to Targeted Participants

Step 4:
Ensure That Communication About the Intervention
Is Carried Out Effectively

Step 5:
Track Short-Term Results Against the Intervention Performance Objectives

Step 6:
Surmount Barriers to Implementation and Ensure That
the Intervention Is Implemented as Planned

Step 7:
Provide Clear, Specific, and Continuing Feedback to Stakeholders
About Results of the Intervention

Table 5.1: Relationship Between Intervention Implementation and the Competencies of the Intervention Implementor*

Model of Intervention Implementation	Competencies of the Intervention Implementor
Work with participants and stakeholders on a daily basis to implement the action plan	♦ *Buy-in advocacy:* Building ownership and support for workplace initiatives ♦ *Consulting:* Understanding the results that stakeholders desire from a process and providing insight into how they can best use their resources to achieve goals ♦ *Coping skills:* Dealing with ambiguity and stress resulting from conflicting information and goals; helping others deal with ambiguity and stress ♦ *Diversity awareness:* Assessing the impact and appropriateness of interventions on individuals, groups, and organizations ♦ *Facilitation:* Helping others discover new insights ♦ *Group dynamics:* Assessing how groups of people function and evolve as they seek to meet the needs of their members and of the organization ♦ *Interpersonal relationship building:* Effectively interacting with others in order to produce meaningful outcomes ♦ *Process consultation:* Using a monitoring and feedback method to continually improve the productivity of work groups ♦ *Workplace performance, learning strategies, and intervention evaluation:* Continually evaluating and improving interventions before and during implementation
Use materials and media supplied by intervention designers and developers and provide feedback to them about ways to improve their use	♦ *Adult learning:* Understanding how adults learn and how they use knowledge, skills, and attitudes ♦ *Communication:* Applying effective verbal, nonverbal, and written communication methods to achieve desired results ♦ *Communication networks:* Understanding the various methods through which communication is achieved ♦ *Computer-mediated communication:* Understanding the implication of current and evolving computer-based electronic communication ♦ *Intervention monitoring:* Tracking and coordinating interventions to assure consistency in implementation and alignment with organizational strategies ♦ *Training theory and application:* Understanding the theories, techniques, and appropriate applications of training interventions for performance improvement

(continued on next page)

*Some competencies are used in more than one step of the model.

Table 5.1: Relationship Between Intervention Implementation and the Competencies of the Intervention Implementor *(continued)*

Model of Intervention Implementation	Competencies of the Intervention Implementor
Deliver, or facilitate delivery of, the intervention to targeted participants	♦ *Adult learning:* Understanding how adults learn and how they use knowledge, skills, and attitudes ♦ *Buy-in advocacy:* Building ownership and support for workplace initiatives ♦ *Communication:* Applying effective verbal, nonverbal, and written communication methods to achieve desired results ♦ *Communication networks:* Understanding the various methods through which communication is achieved ♦ *Computer-mediated communication:* Understanding the implication of current and evolving computer-based electronic communication ♦ *Diversity awareness:* Assessing the impact and appropriateness of interventions on individuals, groups, and organizations ♦ *Electronic performance support systems:* Understanding current and evolving performance support systems and their appropriate applications ♦ *Facilitation:* Helping others discover new insights ♦ *Group dynamics:* Assessing how groups of people function and evolve as they seek to meet the needs of their members and of the organization ♦ *Intervention monitoring:* Tracking and coordinating interventions to assure consistency in implementation and alignment with organizational strategies
Ensure that communication about the intervention is carried out effectively	♦ *Communication:* Applying effective verbal, nonverbal, and written communication methods to achieve desired results ♦ *Communication networks:* Understanding the various methods through which communication is achieved ♦ *Computer-mediated communication:* Understanding the implication of current and evolving computer-based electronic communication ♦ *Intervention monitoring:* Tracking and coordinating interventions to assure consistency in implementation and alignment with organizational strategies ♦ *Process consultation:* Using a monitoring and feedback method to continually improve the productivity of work groups
Track short-term results against the intervention performance objectives	♦ *Intervention monitoring:* Tracking and coordinating interventions to assure consistency in implementation and alignment with organizational strategies

Model of Intervention Implementation	Competencies of the Intervention Implementor
Surmount barriers to implementation and ensure that the intervention is implemented as planned	♦ *Buy-in advocacy:* Building ownership and support for workplace initiatives ♦ *Consulting:* Understanding the results that stakeholders desire from a process and providing insight into how they can best use their resources to achieve goals ♦ *Coping skills:* Dealing with ambiguity and stress resulting from conflicting information and goals; helping others deal with ambiguity and stress ♦ *Interpersonal relationship building:* Effectively interacting with others in order to produce meaningful outcomes
Provide clear, specific, and continuing feedback to stakeholders about the results of the intervention	♦ *Communication:* Applying effective verbal, nonverbal, and written communication methods to achieve desired results ♦ *Communication networks:* Understanding the various methods through which communication is achieved ♦ *Computer-mediated communication:* Understanding the implication of current and evolving computer-based electronic communication ♦ *Intervention monitoring:* Tracking and coordinating interventions to assure consistency in implementation and alignment with organizational strategies ♦ *Process consultation:* Using a monitoring and feedback method to continually improve the productivity of work groups

Steps in the Intervention Implementation Process

The descriptions of each step of the implementation process follow a similar format. They begin with the definition and purpose of the step, follow with notes about implementing the step, and end with an example of the step that illustrates and dramatizes what it can mean in practice.

Step 1: Work With Participants and Stakeholders on a Daily Basis to Implement the Action Plan

Definition and Purpose of Step 1

Begin intervention implementation by establishing ways to work with participants and stakeholders on a daily basis to implement the action plan of the intervention. (See figure 5.2.)

Intervention implementors function in many possible interventions, requiring different kinds of interactions with participants and stakeholders. Instructors or facilitators may see participants only during a training session, a focus group, or another group gathering. Of course, advance work will be required, and that may call for visits to the immediate organizational superiors, peers of participants, or others. Intervention implementors may also work in such other roles as process redesign consultants to lead a work team through process improvement or as HR specialists to install new recruitment systems, selection systems, feedback systems, or reward systems.

Intervention implementors must establish ways to communicate with participants and stakeholders on a continuing basis to ensure effective follow-through on intervention plans. They may choose among all communication channels—in person, over the phone, by email, to name a few.

One way to stay in contact is to schedule regular meetings with intervention participants and their immediate stakeholders to check progress. Another way is to form a task force, council, ad hoc team, or other group that represents the constituencies of the intervention and a microcosm of the organization's key groups. The intervention implementor can then work with that group to ensure that the intervention

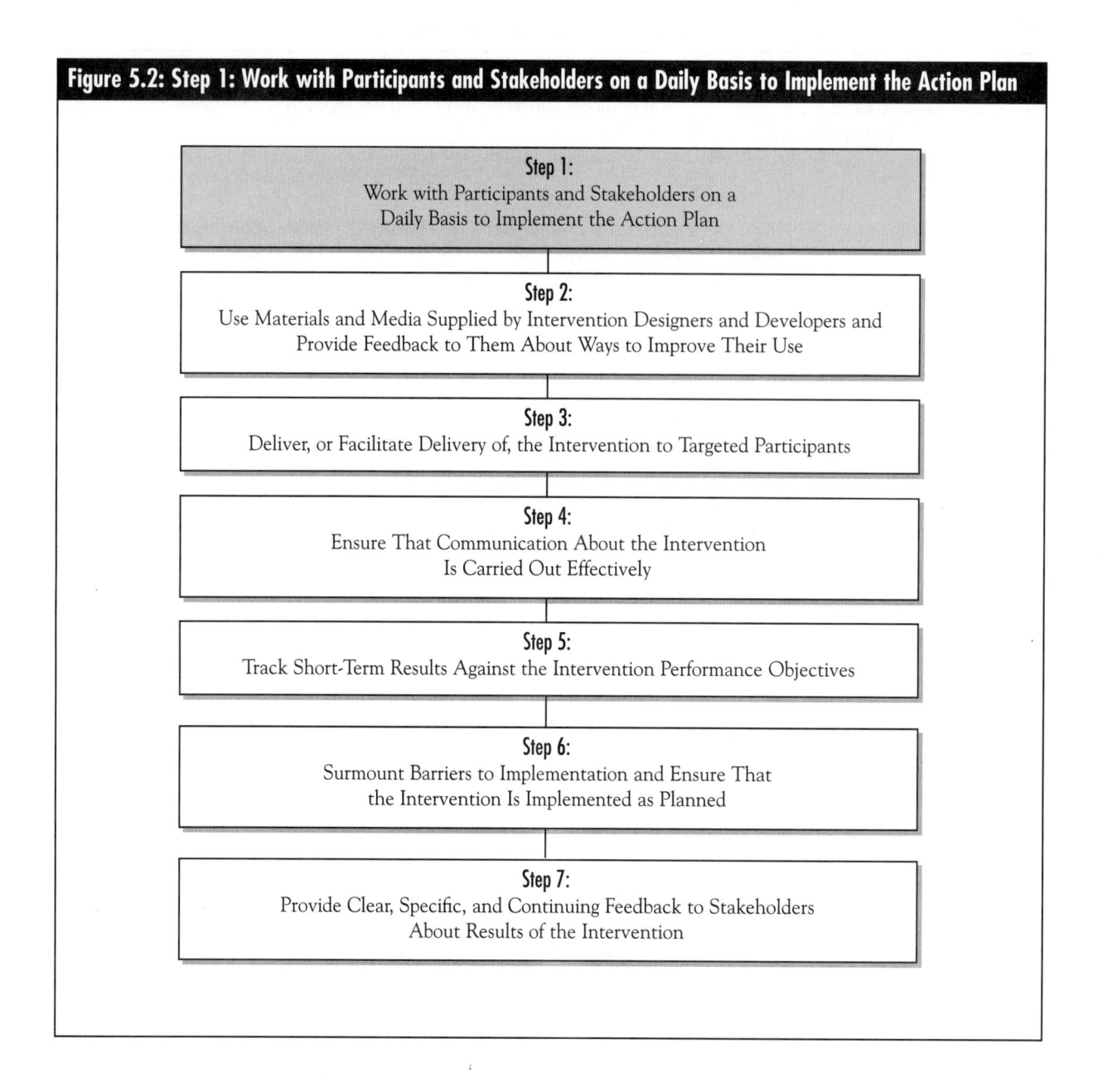

Figure 5.2: Step 1: Work with Participants and Stakeholders on a Daily Basis to Implement the Action Plan

Step 1:
Work with Participants and Stakeholders on a Daily Basis to Implement the Action Plan

Step 2:
Use Materials and Media Supplied by Intervention Designers and Developers and Provide Feedback to Them About Ways to Improve Their Use

Step 3:
Deliver, or Facilitate Delivery of, the Intervention to Targeted Participants

Step 4:
Ensure That Communication About the Intervention Is Carried Out Effectively

Step 5:
Track Short-Term Results Against the Intervention Performance Objectives

Step 6:
Surmount Barriers to Implementation and Ensure That the Intervention Is Implemented as Planned

Step 7:
Provide Clear, Specific, and Continuing Feedback to Stakeholders About Results of the Intervention

is installed as planned and that feedback is provided to key groups on a continuing basis.

Implementing Step 1

Begin any intervention implementation process by posing the following questions about how to work with participants and stakeholders on a daily basis to implement the action plan of the intervention:

- What work relationships are most important to the successful implementation of the intervention?
- How can those work relationships be identified?
- How can interpersonal relationships and rapport be established and maintained with key individuals and groups?
- How can the intervention implementor establish and maintain credibility with the key individuals and groups necessary for successful intervention implementation?
- How should conflict relevant to the implementation of the intervention be handled among key individuals and groups?

By posing these questions and answering them, WLP practitioners or others involved in intervention implementation can effectively plan for establishing and maintaining effective ways of working with intervention participants and stakeholders. Use Step 1 of the worksheet in figure 6.3 to pose the preceding questions about implementation of the action plan of the intervention.

Vignette: Section 3 introduced the example of Marsha Kung, LMN Corporation's WLP director, who was working with a task force to solve a performance problem. That problem stemmed from a performance appraisal system that was perceived not to be effective. By the end of Section 4, Kung and the task force had formed design teams to formulate a detailed project plan, create a communication and marketing plan, and make, buy, or buy and modify the materials and media necessary to support the intervention. The teams began their work and were successful in preparing the plans and identifying the material and media needed to implement them. A consulting company that specialized in performance appraisals was hired to help prepare the materials and media to support the intervention. (That company outsourced the preparation of training materials and media to a subcontractor with which the company had previously worked.)

As the plans were implemented, Kung became actively involved in two facets of the intervention. First, she worked with the design teams from the task force to create an approach to developing work expectations and measuring them. Second, she worked with the consulting company to prepare training materials related to the intervention because the WLP practitioners reporting to her were asked to spearhead companywide training of executives, managers, and supervisors on the new performance appraisal system.

Much of Kung's time each day was taken up with intervention-related activities. She interacted with the design team members as they worked on their projects. She interacted with the staff members as they prepared training to the targeted participants and stakeholders of the intervention and then began delivering it. She also kept in touch with key stakeholder groups, such as the CEO, who was taking a personal interest in the intervention and agreed to make cameo appearances in each training session delivered to company executives, managers, and supervisors.

When asked what she did, Kung said:

My job at this stage involved gluing all the pieces together. I worked with each design team, attending meetings and offering advice when I was asked. I also tried to keep teams updated on one another's progress when they were affected. Much of my time was also spent in fire fighting—that is, dealing with tactical problems that arose on a daily basis. One side effect of this intervention that we had not planned was that employees started to visit me when they had trouble with their bosses. At first, those visits were linked directly to the performance appraisal (as an excuse for them to talk to me as a third party, I think). But later, I turned into a sort of company ombudsman to deal with a broad array of problems between bosses and their workers. Later, even bosses started to visit me to ask for my advice about how to deal with specific performance problems of their subordinates. While this was time-consuming, I believe that much of it was really what WLP should be all about—that is, helping the company improve the performance of the workers, whatever the cause of the performance problem might be. You have to remember that I was meeting with people nonstop through this whole process, managing my staff, and seeing to a thousand details. But, clearly, this stage moved from the strategic to the tactical.

Step 2: Use Materials and Media Supplied by the Intervention Designers and Developers and Provide Feedback to Them About Ways to Improve Their Use

Definition and Purpose of Step 2

This step has to do with making use of the materials and media that were supplied by intervention designers and developers and providing feedback to them about ways to improve the materials and media. (See figure 5.3.)

Materials (content) and media (delivery methods) should be geared to the intervention. For instance, learning interventions may require participant materials, leader or instructor materials, tests, and job aids. Nonlearning interventions may require other material, such as updated policies and procedures, workflow diagrams or flow charts, descriptions, job aids, on-the-job coaching guides for users, and online

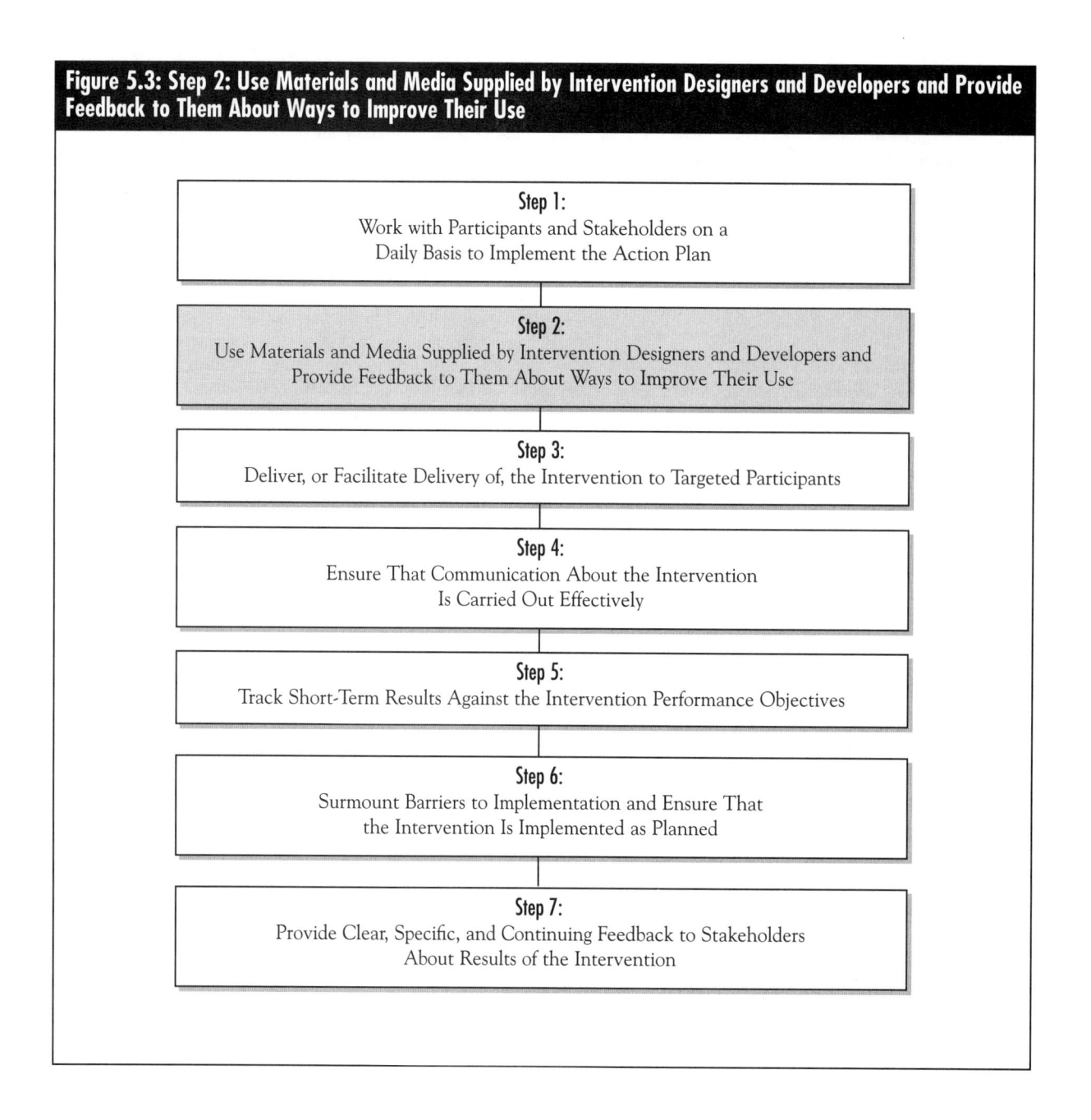

Figure 5.3: Step 2: Use Materials and Media Supplied by Intervention Designers and Developers and Provide Feedback to Them About Ways to Improve Their Use

Step 1:
Work with Participants and Stakeholders on a Daily Basis to Implement the Action Plan

Step 2:
Use Materials and Media Supplied by Intervention Designers and Developers and Provide Feedback to Them About Ways to Improve Their Use

Step 3:
Deliver, or Facilitate Delivery of, the Intervention to Targeted Participants

Step 4:
Ensure That Communication About the Intervention Is Carried Out Effectively

Step 5:
Track Short-Term Results Against the Intervention Performance Objectives

Step 6:
Surmount Barriers to Implementation and Ensure That the Intervention Is Implemented as Planned

Step 7:
Provide Clear, Specific, and Continuing Feedback to Stakeholders About Results of the Intervention

coaching guides or help sites. Intervention implementors use this material and these media, even though they did not prepare or select them. However, they are responsible for ensuring that they are effective, and they will catch the blame if materials are inappropriate or if media do not work effectively.

Implementing Step 2

During any intervention implementation process, pose the following questions about the materials and media supplied by intervention designers and developers:

- What materials and media are available for use in the intervention implementation process? Is everything available that is needed? Is everything available when needed? Do the media applications work as they are supposed to work to help meet performance objectives?
- What do intervention implementors need to know to make most effective use of the materials and media available to support the intervention? Have they been properly prepared through training, coaching, or other directions to use those materials and media?
- Who are the intervention designers and developers responsible for making modifications or revisions to materials and media devised for use in the implementation of the intervention?
- How should intervention implementors request modifications or revisions to materials and media? How will they recognize when such changes are necessary and appropriate?
- What processes or procedures should be established with the intervention designers and developers so that necessary modifications or revisions to materials and media can be identified and fed back, and so that corrections can be made on a timely and effective basis?
- How can participant and stakeholder feedback about materials and media be collected by intervention implementors on a continuing basis?
- How can the effectiveness of modifications or revisions be measured and feedback provided to intervention designers and developers?

The answers to these questions will enable intervention implementors to most effectively use the materials and media supplied by intervention designers and developers. They can also serve as an important conduit for feedback about necessary changes to those who prepared the material or chose the media. Use Step 2 of the worksheet in figure 6.3 to guide your thinking about how to use materials and media supplied by the intervention designers and developers and provide feedback to them about ways to improve the use of those materials and media.

Vignette: As the intervention at LMN Corporation was prepared for launch, Marsha Kung made a point of sending out emails to reinforce to all design teams the importance of tracking the progress of the intervention. She also emphasized to them the need to provide feedback to the contractors about the materials and media that had been designed and developed to support the intervention. She asked the task force members how they believed the company could solicit and use feedback from the intervention participants on the quality of the materials and media that had been developed to support the intervention. In response, the task force members suggested that a special company message board could be created on the company's Website to post feedback. The director of MIS agreed to set up a simple message board for that use. People began using it right away. That helped improve the quality of the materials and media almost immediately, and Kung visited the site regularly and flagged special items of attention to various groups.

Step 3: Deliver, or Facilitate Delivery of, the Intervention to Targeted Participants

Definition and Purpose of Step 3

The third step in the intervention implementation process is the most important one that intervention implementors perform: delivering, or facilitating the delivery of, the intervention. (See figure 5.4.)

The terms *delivery* and *facilitation* are sometimes associated closely with training and other learning interventions. Much has been written on those topics (for example, Hunter, Bailey, and Taylor, 1995; King, King, and Rothwell, 2000; Schwartz, 1994). Intervention implementors should be familiar with effective methods of delivering instruction and facilitating creative decision making and problem solving.

However, both delivery and facilitation have broader meanings than *group delivery* or *group facilitation*. Indeed, appropriate delivery and facilitation depend on the intervention. In a reward system implementation, for instance, delivery could involve making presentations to key decision makers about proposed changes, and facilitation could involve problem-solving discussions with key stakeholders to discover the desired results intended from the

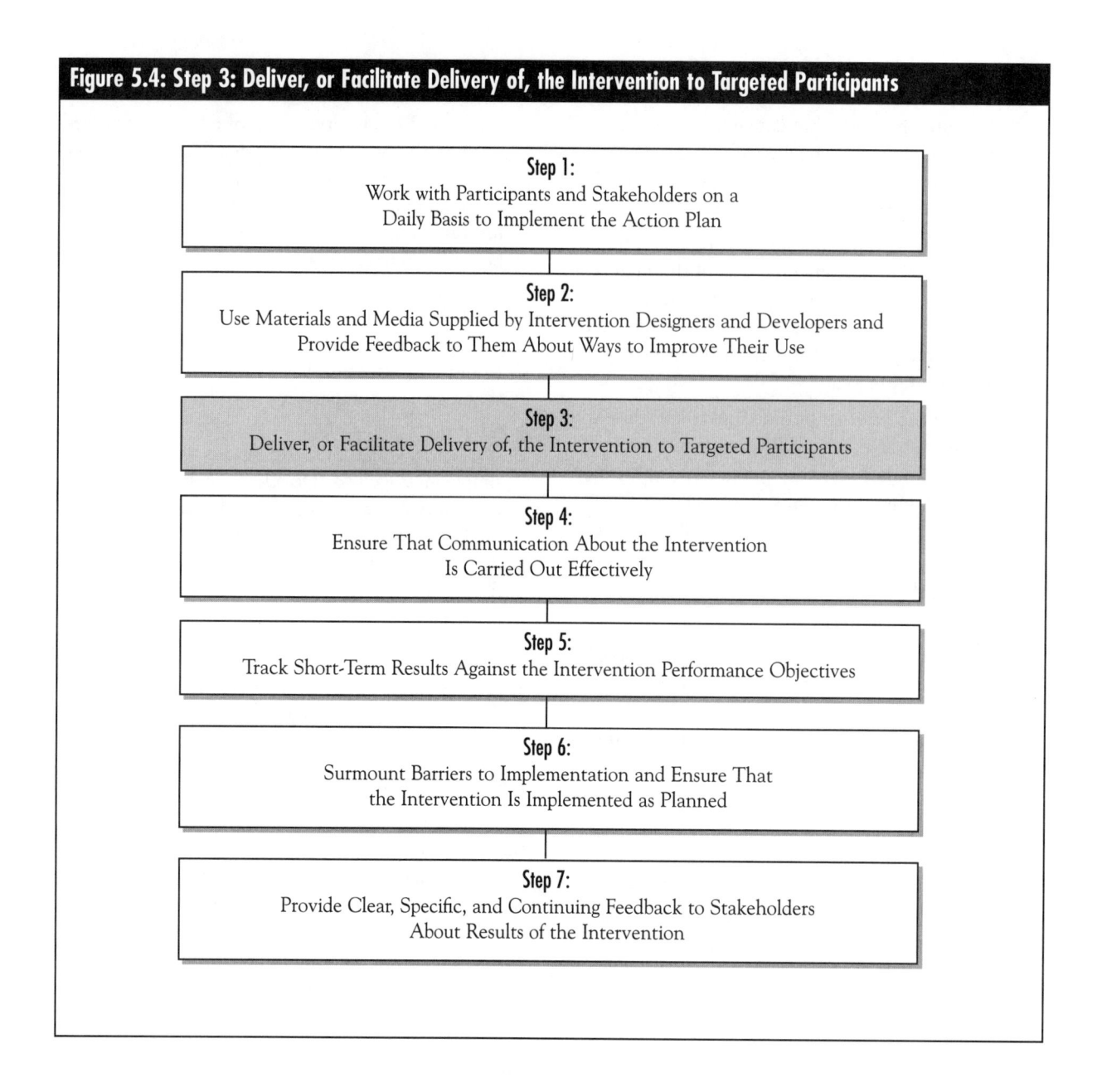

Figure 5.4: Step 3: Deliver, or Facilitate Delivery of, the Intervention to Targeted Participants

- **Step 1:** Work with Participants and Stakeholders on a Daily Basis to Implement the Action Plan
- **Step 2:** Use Materials and Media Supplied by Intervention Designers and Developers and Provide Feedback to Them About Ways to Improve Their Use
- **Step 3:** Deliver, or Facilitate Delivery of, the Intervention to Targeted Participants
- **Step 4:** Ensure That Communication About the Intervention Is Carried Out Effectively
- **Step 5:** Track Short-Term Results Against the Intervention Performance Objectives
- **Step 6:** Surmount Barriers to Implementation and Ensure That the Intervention Is Implemented as Planned
- **Step 7:** Provide Clear, Specific, and Continuing Feedback to Stakeholders About Results of the Intervention

reward system change and specific features of the intervention.

Implementing Step 3

To implement this step, intervention implementors should pose the following questions:

- What content should be delivered to participants and stakeholders during intervention implementation, and how can it be most effectively delivered?
- How should content be delivered to participants and stakeholders during intervention implementation?
- What methods of delivery or facilitation are appropriate for each phase of an intervention, and how can those methods be selected and used to help achieve performance objectives?
- How can the effectiveness of the delivery and facilitation methods be measured and, when necessary, improved?

Use Step 3 of the worksheet in figure 6.3 to answer these questions and guide your thinking as an intervention implementor about the most appropriate and effective ways to deliver, or facilitate delivery of, the intervention to targeted participants.

Vignette: After the design team working on the new appraisal system had completed its work and presented the task force and top managers with a new system for establishing work expectations and measuring performance, the company launched the intervention. At that point, delivery began. Briefing sessions were set up for workers by their level. Top managers attended the first briefings, and the intervention rollout and implementation cascaded down the organization from there. Executives attended sessions with managers to discuss implementation of the new system in each division; managers attended sessions with supervisors to discuss implementation of the new system in each department; and supervisors attended sessions with their workers to discuss implementation of the new system in each work team.

In each briefing session, participants learned the business reasons for the new system. They were then walked through the detailed process of establishing work expectations, measuring them, and recording them. They were also asked to participate in role plays in which their use of the appraisal system was practiced. (As Marsha Kung was overheard to say, "The research we did early in this process underscored to us the importance of the appraisal interview. We were surprised to learn that a poorly conducted performance appraisal interview, one where criticism was used more than other methods, could actually prompt a decline in worker performance.")

Step 4: Ensure That Communication About the Intervention Is Carried out Effectively

Definition and Purpose of Step 4

Ensuring that communication about the intervention is carried out effectively is the fourth step in the intervention implementation process. (See figure 5.5.)

Essential to any successful intervention implementation is a communication plan and a communication strategy. A *communication plan* describes who will receive communication about the intervention, what kind of communication they will receive, when they will receive it, how they will receive it, and how much time and money will be devoted to it. These issues may be considered for each stage of the intervention because the appropriate communication may not be the same for each stage.

A *communication strategy* is a description of the most effective ways to deliver that information. Communication plans are sufficiently important that some consultants even devise a communication plan that is separate from the intervention implementation plan but is integrated with it. The two plans are then implemented simultaneously.

Implementing Step 4

To implement this step successfully, intervention implementors should pose the following questions:

♦ Who will receive communication about the intervention's implementation?

♦ What kind of communication about the intervention should they receive? Is it necessary to describe activities (what is happening in the intervention) and results (what benefits were obtained)?

♦ When should participants and stakeholders receive information about the intervention implementation? Should they receive reports on a continuing basis, at specific milestones, upon completion, or on some other basis?

♦ How will intervention participants and stakeholders receive information? What media or methods should be used, and how should they be used?

♦ How much time and money will be devoted to communicating about the intervention?

♦ How might the targeted audience, level of information required, and other factors differ by stage of intervention implementation?

Use Step 4 of the worksheet in figure 6.3 to answer these questions. Use the answers to guide your thinking about ways to ensure that communication about intervention implementation is carried out effectively.

Vignette: As the intervention to improve performance appraisal at LMN Corporation was launched, Marsha Kung met regularly with the

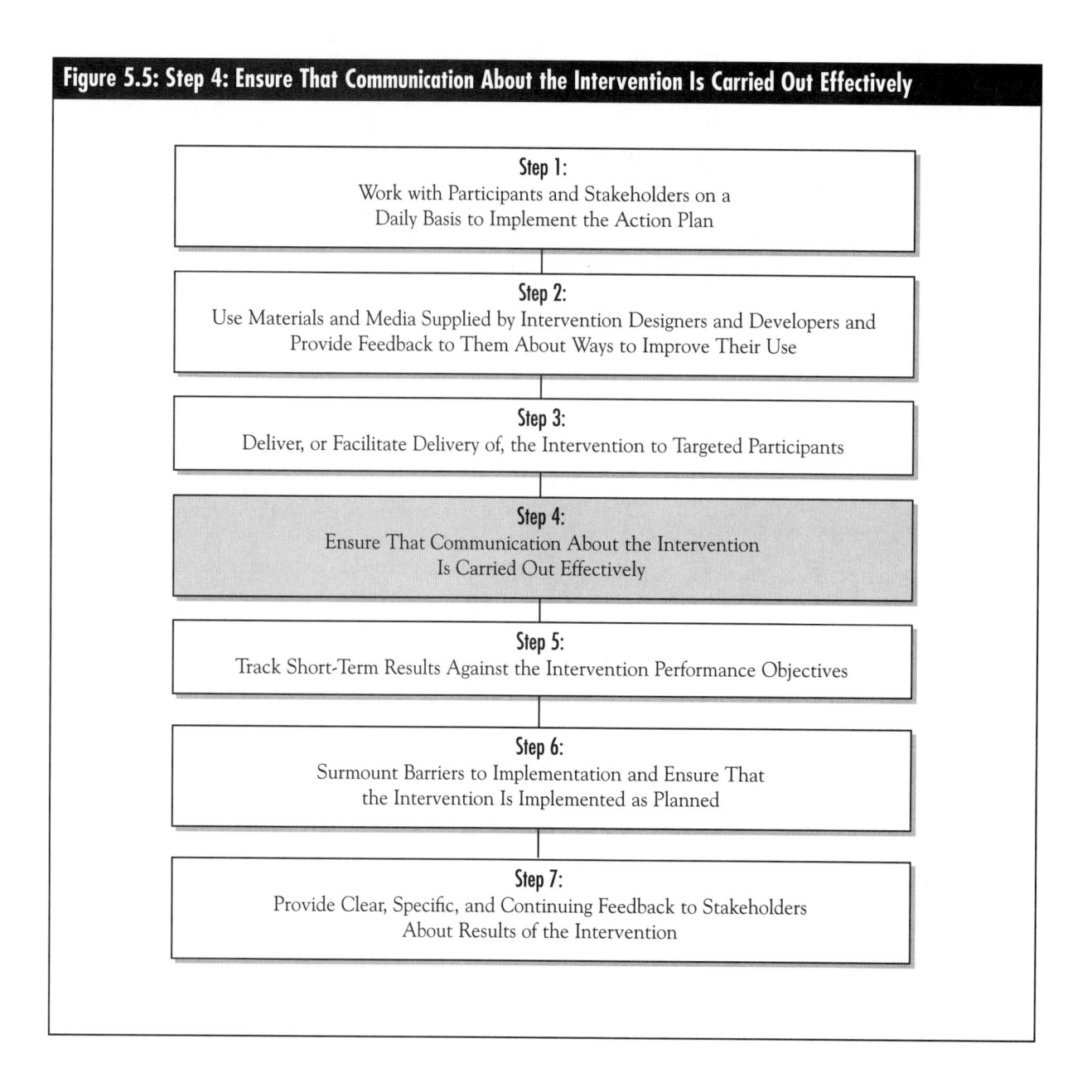

Figure 5.5: Step 4: Ensure That Communication About the Intervention Is Carried Out Effectively

Step 1:
Work with Participants and Stakeholders on a
Daily Basis to Implement the Action Plan

Step 2:
Use Materials and Media Supplied by Intervention Designers and Developers and
Provide Feedback to Them About Ways to Improve Their Use

Step 3:
Deliver, or Facilitate Delivery of, the Intervention to Targeted Participants

Step 4:
Ensure That Communication About the Intervention
Is Carried Out Effectively

Step 5:
Track Short-Term Results Against the Intervention Performance Objectives

Step 6:
Surmount Barriers to Implementation and Ensure That
the Intervention Is Implemented as Planned

Step 7:
Provide Clear, Specific, and Continuing Feedback to Stakeholders
About Results of the Intervention

---

design team for communication to ensure that communication about the intervention was being effectively handled. At the recommendation of the design team chairperson, the company installed a hot line to handle questions about the new appraisal system. Kung was also interviewed about the new system for the company newsletter several times, and she even wrote a Q and A column about it. After-hour receptions were held in several locations to help workers and their managers understand the system and to provide an informal atmosphere for providing updates and information.

Step 5: Track Short-Term Results Against the Intervention Performance Objectives

Definition and Purpose of Step 5

The fifth step in intervention implementation is tracking short-term results against the intervention performance objectives. (See figure 5.6.) This step is necessary because it is important for someone to assess the implementation of the intervention in light of the desired results. While participants and stakeholders may become so engrossed in daily activities that they lose this big picture focus, intervention implementors should remain attuned to how much and how well short-term results match up to the desired final results. In that way, deviations can be pinpointed and, when necessary, corrective action can be taken.

Implementing Step 5

To carry out this step effectively, intervention implementors should pose such questions as these:

♦ What are the short-term results of the intervention?

♦ How often and in what ways should short-term results of the intervention be measured?

♦ By whom should short-term results be measured?

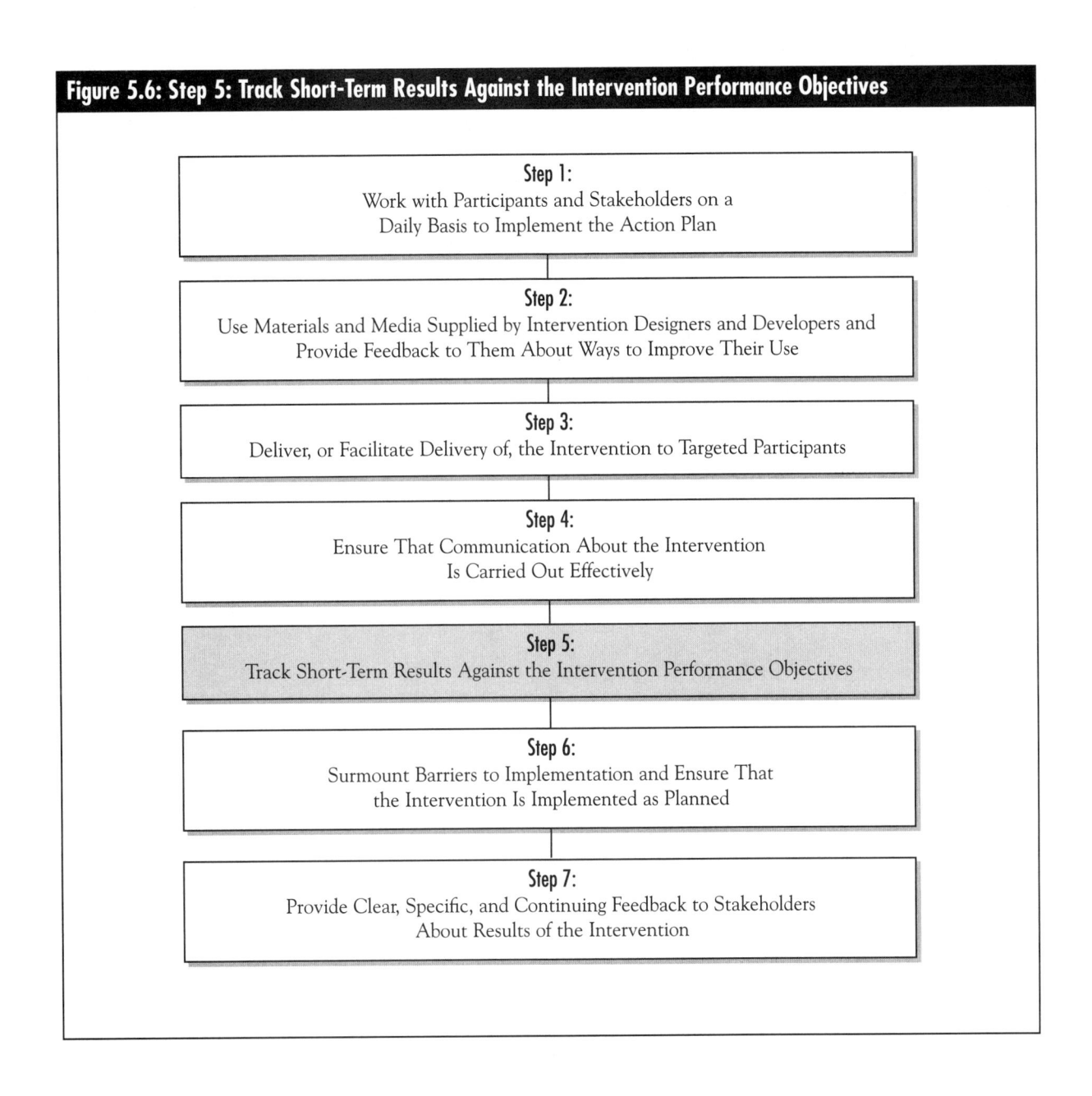

Figure 5.6: Step 5: Track Short-Term Results Against the Intervention Performance Objectives

Step 1:
Work with Participants and Stakeholders on a
Daily Basis to Implement the Action Plan

Step 2:
Use Materials and Media Supplied by Intervention Designers and Developers and
Provide Feedback to Them About Ways to Improve Their Use

Step 3:
Deliver, or Facilitate Delivery of, the Intervention to Targeted Participants

Step 4:
Ensure That Communication About the Intervention
Is Carried Out Effectively

Step 5:
Track Short-Term Results Against the Intervention Performance Objectives

Step 6:
Surmount Barriers to Implementation and Ensure That
the Intervention Is Implemented as Planned

Step 7:
Provide Clear, Specific, and Continuing Feedback to Stakeholders
About Results of the Intervention

- How should short-term results be reported, and to whom should they be reported?
- How should deviations from performance objectives be identified, and how should they be managed?

Use Step 5 of the worksheet in figure 6.3 to answer these questions and track short-term results against the intervention performance objectives.

Vignette: After the appraisal intervention had been launched, Marsha Kung reconvened the task force periodically to review reports about the intervention. At each task force meeting, the progress of the intervention was reported against the intervention performance objectives. This information was also routinely forwarded to top managers, who also discussed the intervention at their regular meetings. In this way, the short-term results of the intervention were tracked against its performance objectives.

Step 6: Surmount Barriers to Implementation and Ensure That the Intervention Is Implemented as Planned

Definition and Purpose of Step 6

The sixth step in intervention implementation involves working with participants and stakeholders to surmount barriers to implementation and ensure that the intervention is implemented as planned (or that unexpected problems in the implementation are solved). (See figure 5.7.)

It is not unusual to encounter barriers during any implementation effort. Typical examples of possible barriers might include changes in:

- the performance problem or its causes
- the environment or context in which the intervention is being implemented (such as changes in the organization, the organization's leadership, critical business issues)
- the desired timeline for implementation
- the availability of resources to implement the intervention.

Intervention implementors should monitor these changes, much as air traffic controllers monitor flight traffic on radar. When unexpected barriers arise, it is important to draw attention to them and formulate ways to manage them (or avert them) so that the intervention can remain on schedule. While some barriers are difficult to surmount—such as the loss of key stakeholders who back the intervention or sudden major problems confronting the organization such as a merger, acquisition, or layoff—intervention implementors must remain vigilant.

Implementing Step 6

To carry out this step effectively, intervention implementors should pose such questions as these:

- What barriers to the implementation of the intervention are expected or are being encountered?
- What are the most effective ways to surmount those barriers in the opinions of stakeholders, intervention participants, and others?
- How can contingency plans be formulated to manage barriers as they arise?
- How can the barriers be confronted and addressed without prompting skepticism about the intervention among participants and stakeholders?

Use Step 6 of the worksheet in figure 6.3 to answer these questions and work with participants and stakeholders to surmount barriers to implementation.

Vignette: As the performance appraisal improvement intervention at LMN Corporation progressed, Marsha Kung worked with participants and stakeholders to surmount barriers to implementation so that the intervention would be implemented as planned and any unexpected problems in the implementation would be solved. One approach Kung took was to ask the following questions on the company's participant training evaluations (and training on the new appraisal process was continuing):

- What barriers to the implementation of the intervention are you expecting, and what barriers have you so far encountered?
- What do you believe to be the most effective ways to surmount those barriers, and why do you think so?

Figure 5.7: Step 6: Surmount Barriers to Implementation and Ensure That the Intervention Is Implemented as Planned

```
Step 1:
Work with Participants and Stakeholders on a
Daily Basis to Implement the Action Plan
          │
Step 2:
Use Materials and Media Supplied by Intervention Designers and Developers and
Provide Feedback to Them About Ways to Improve Their Use
          │
Step 3:
Deliver, or Facilitate Delivery of, the Intervention to Targeted Participants
          │
Step 4:
Ensure That Communication About the Intervention
Is Carried Out Effectively
          │
Step 5:
Track Short-Term Results Against the Intervention Performance Objectives
          │
Step 6:
Surmount Barriers to Implementation and Ensure That
the Intervention Is Implemented as Planned
          │
Step 7:
Provide Clear, Specific, and Continuing Feedback to Stakeholders
About Results of the Intervention
```

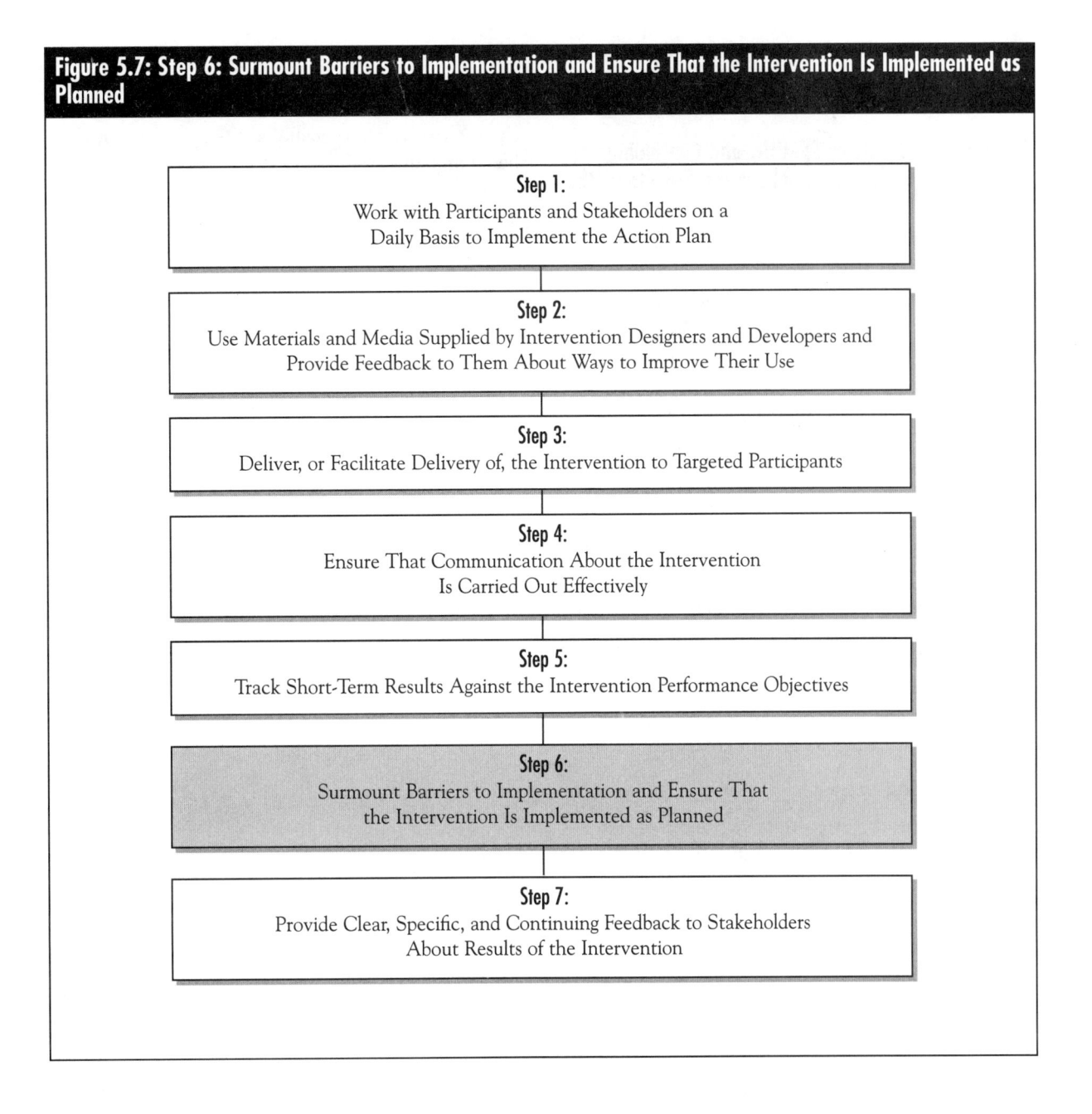

- What changes in the organization, your department or team, and your job may influence the implementation of this change effort, and how do you prepare contingency plans for them?
- What do you believe to be the best way to attack the barriers and communicate about them?

Another way was to solicit replies from appraisers by inserting the questions on the performance appraisal form. The responses to the questions were regularly compiled and described at task force meetings. Task force members worked to find strategies to address key barriers that arose during implementation. When their recommendations were completed, they forwarded a proposal for action to top managers, who often approved them.

Step 7: Provide Clear, Specific, and Continuing Feedback to Stakeholders about the Results of the Intervention

Definition and Purpose of Step 7

The seventh and final step in the intervention implementation process is to provide clear, specific, and continuing feedback to stakeholders about the results of the intervention. (See figure 5.8.) While this step is really part of maintaining effective communication, it is important enough to warrant separate attention. One reason is that intervention participants and stakeholders require continuing feedback about results if they are to remember why the intervention was undertaken, what value is being obtained from resources used in implementing the intervention, and how progress is being made in comparison to the performance objectives of the intervention. Without this step, stakeholders or intervention participants alike may weary of the intervention and question the reasons for its continuation—especially when the intervention requires a long-term implementation.

Implementing Step 7

To carry out this step effectively, intervention implementors should pose such questions as these:

♦ What feedback is necessary?

♦ To whom should that feedback be reported?

♦ When should that feedback be reported, and what form should the feedback take to make it most clear and specific?

♦ How should the feedback be communicated?

♦ What results are sought from providing the feedback? Do intervention implementors seek to increase awareness of the intervention, build continuing or additional support, demonstrate value received from the organization's investments, or achieve another end?

In these days of increasing accountability for workplace learning and performance professionals, intervention implementors will often have to show the impact of an intervention on the gap between what is happening and what should be happening. One way to do that is to increase feedback to the stakeholders about what benefits were received from the intervention, especially as the intervention is being implemented.

Use Step 7 of the worksheet in figure 6.3 to answer these questions and provide clear, specific, and continuing feedback to stakeholders about the results of the intervention.

Vignette: As the performance appraisal improvement intervention at LMN Corporation progressed, Marsha Kung provided clear, specific, and continuing feedback to stakeholders about the results of the intervention. She did that by issuing regular emails to all company executives, managers, and supervisors to report on the results of the intervention and to track progress against performance objectives. Through that communication, she maintained an impetus for change and provided stakeholders with a sense of the results they were getting from their investment in the intervention.

The results were impressive. Turnover declined. Employees reported in the company's annual attitude survey that the performance appraisal process had been dramatically improved. Anecdotal evidence from the HR function supported the view that the company was having an easier time recruiting talent.

Section Summary

This section described how to enact the role of intervention implementor. The intervention implementor "ensures the appropriate and effective implementation of desired interventions that address the specific root causes of human performance gaps. Some examples of the work of the intervention implementor include serving as administrator, instructor, organization development practitioner, career development specialist, process re-design consultant, workspace designer, compensation specialists, and facilitator" (Rothwell, Sanders, and Soper, 1999, p. 43). The intervention implementor thus implements the intervention chosen by the intervention selector role and uses material and media prepared by the intervention designer and developer role. Intervention implementors do the following:

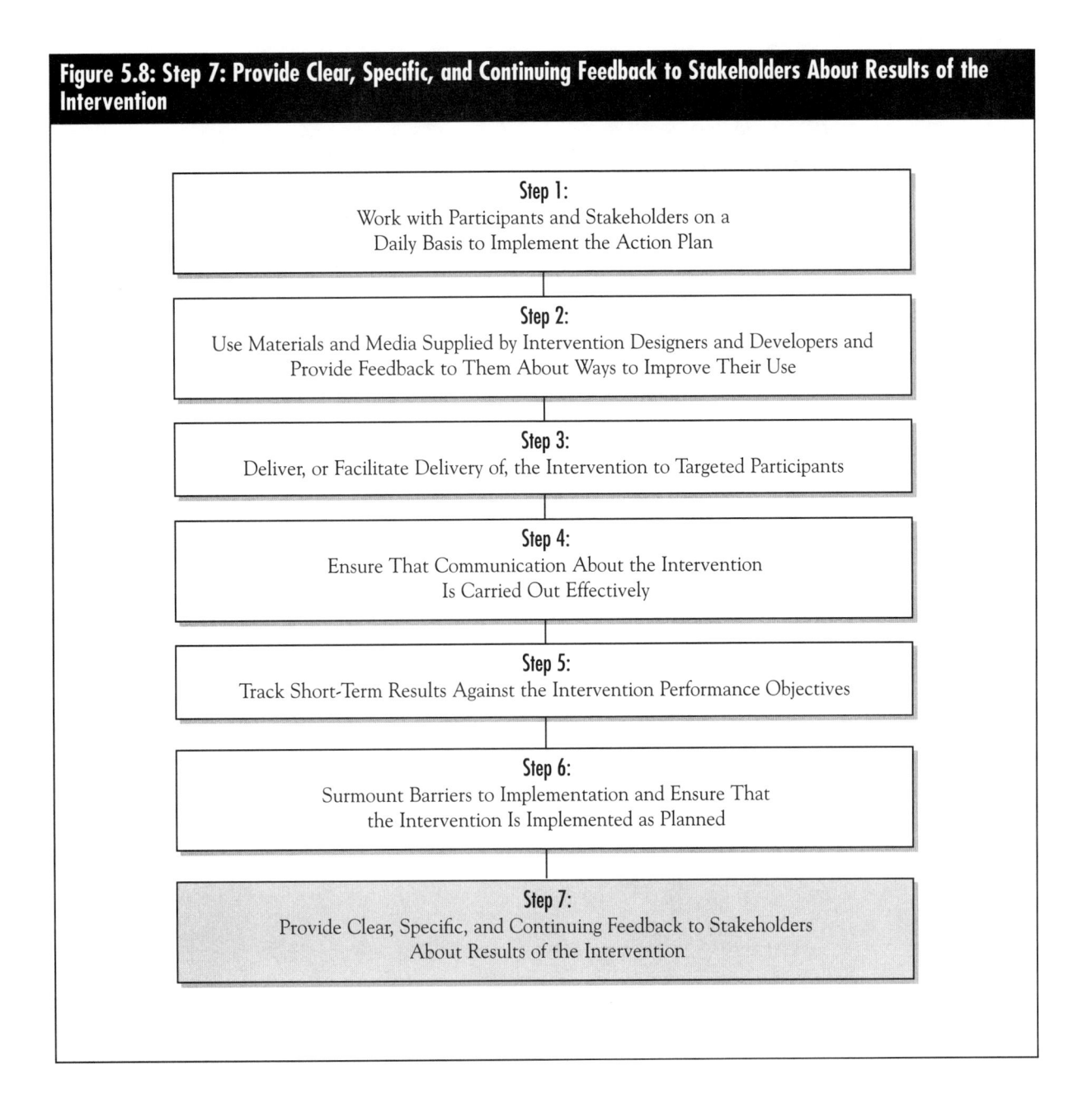

Figure 5.8: Step 7: Provide Clear, Specific, and Continuing Feedback to Stakeholders About Results of the Intervention

```
Step 1:
Work with Participants and Stakeholders on a
Daily Basis to Implement the Action Plan
            │
Step 2:
Use Materials and Media Supplied by Intervention Designers and Developers and
Provide Feedback to Them About Ways to Improve Their Use
            │
Step 3:
Deliver, or Facilitate Delivery of, the Intervention to Targeted Participants
            │
Step 4:
Ensure That Communication About the Intervention
Is Carried Out Effectively
            │
Step 5:
Track Short-Term Results Against the Intervention Performance Objectives
            │
Step 6:
Surmount Barriers to Implementation and Ensure That
the Intervention Is Implemented as Planned
            │
Step 7:
Provide Clear, Specific, and Continuing Feedback to Stakeholders
About Results of the Intervention
```

1. Work with participants and stakeholders on a daily basis to implement the action plan.
2. Use materials and media supplied by intervention designers and developers and provide feedback to them about ways to improve their use.
3. Deliver, or facilitate delivery of, the intervention to targeted participants.
4. Ensure that communication about the intervention is carried out effectively.
5. Track short-term results against the intervention performance objectives.
6. Surmount barriers to implementation and ensure that the intervention is implemented as planned.
7. Provide clear, specific, and continuing feedback to stakeholders about the results of the intervention.

SECTION 1	GETTING STARTED
SECTION 2	DEFINING THE ROLES
SECTION 3	ENACTING THE ROLE OF INTERVENTION SELECTOR
SECTION 4	ENACTING THE ROLE OF INTERVENTION DESIGNER AND DEVELOPER
SECTION 5	ENACTING THE ROLE OF INTERVENTION IMPLEMENTOR
SECTION 6	TOOLS FOR CONDUCTING INTERVENTION SELECTION, DESIGN AND DEVELOPMENT, AND IMPLEMENTATION

- Introduction to the Tools Section

SECTION 7	AFTERWORD
SECTION 8	BIBLIOGRAPHY

SECTION 6   TOOLS FOR CONDUCTING INTERVENTION SELECTION, DESIGN AND DEVELOPMENT, AND IMPLEMENTATION

Introduction to the Tools Section

This section presents five different tools:

- Figure 6.1, Worksheet to Guide Intervention Selection: Use this worksheet to guide you through the key questions to ask for effective intervention selection.
- Figure 6.2, Worksheet to Guide Intervention Design and Development: Use this worksheet to guide you through the key questions to ask for effective intervention design and development.
- Figure 6.3, Worksheet to Guide Intervention Implementation: Use this worksheet to guide you through posing the key questions necessary for effective intervention implementation.

Figure 6.1: Worksheet to Guide Intervention Selection

Directions: Use this tool to guide you from start to finish and step-by-step through intervention selection. You do not have to use every question, and you may wish to add questions when appropriate. This tool is a template to guide your questioning during the selection of performance interventions.

Step 1: Verify That the Root Causes of the Performance Problem Have Been Distinguished From the Symptoms or Consequences

1. Could the problems be caused by reasons other than those pinpointed by analysis? If so, what are those other possible causes? How much influence are they exerting on the problem?

2. Could there be more than one cause of the performance problem? If so, what are the other possible causes, and how could their influence on the performance gap be assessed?

3. If action is taken to address the identified causes, will the performance problem be solved, or will the performance gap narrow? How can we tell?

Step 2: Consider the Range of Possible Interventions to Close the Performance Gap By Addressing the Root Causes

1. Considering the root causes of the performance problem, what are the most logical solutions to that problem? Why do we think so?

2	Considering the root causes of the performance problem, how have other organizations solved the problem based on best-practice examples and benchmarking?
3	Considering the root causes of the performance problem, what does available research on the topic, if any, suggest might be the most effective approaches to solving it and the least effective?
4	What analytical, creative, or group process methods might be most helpful in identifying a range of possible interventions to solve the problem by closing the performance gap?
5	How can those methods be used?
6	Once those methods have been used, what range of possible performance interventions were identified? Was more than one necessary to address more than one root cause?
7	Are there ways that the problem can be reframed so that the range of solutions might be different or the interventions proposed might avert the problem?

Step 3: Identify Constraints or Limitations on the Choice of Interventions

1	What interventions would be most effective—that is, optimal—to close the performance gap at present?

(continued on next page)

Figure 6.1: Worksheet to Guide Intervention Selection *(continued)*

Step 3: Identify Constraints or Limitations on the Choice of Interventions *(Continued)*

2 How likely is it that the necessary resources to implement the optimal interventions can be obtained?

3 What limitations or restrictions most likely influence the choice of an intervention or interventions? (Consider limitations on time, money, people, or other necessary resources, such as tools, equipment, and incentives.)

4 What optimal interventions to solve the performance problem must be ruled out because they require resources that are not possible to secure?

5 What interventions are the best fit or nearest fit in light of the existing limitations on resources?

6 What are the trade-offs or consequences of using the best fit or nearest fit, rather than the optimal intervention? In other words, what benefits are sacrificed?

Step 4: Identify Possible Changes in the Performance Problem That May Influence the Interventions

1 What will happen if no corrective is taken to address the performance problem or to narrow or close the performance gap?

2 What changes in the future are likely to affect the organization, the industry, the performance problem, and performance interventions identified to solve the problem?

3	How will those changes influence the problem and the intervention?
4	When will the likely impact of those changes be felt?
5	Who (what groups) in the organization is most likely to be affected by these trends, and in what ways will they be affected?
6	Where in the organization will those changes have the most impact?

Step 5: Consider Possible Side Effects of Interventions if Implemented and Plan for Addressing Them

1	What will be the likely side effects of a performance intervention? What is likely to happen if the organization should implement the interventions?
2	Who (what groups) is likely to be most affected by these side effects? Why?
3	When will these side effects be felt—immediately or over the long term?
4	Where will these side effects be felt? If the organization does business internationally, what impact will the intervention have on conditions in other parts of the organization around the globe? In different cultures?

(continued on next page)

Figure 6.1: Worksheet to Guide Intervention Selection *(continued)*

Step 5: Consider Possible Side Effects of Interventions if Implemented and Plan for Addressing Them *(continued)*

5	Why are these side effects likely? What is the probability that they will happen?
6	How will these side effects influence the performance problem? How will they influence performance interventions?

Step 6: Determine Necessary Stakeholder Support, Involvement, and Ownership

1	What is the scope of the intended interventions? Will the total organization be affected, or will only part of the organization be affected? Will that scope change over time?
2	Who are the stakeholders and decision makers who stand to gain most by the interventions? Where are they located? What are their attitudes about the interventions?
3	Who (what groups) is most influenced by the interventions, and what are their attitudes about the interventions?
4	Who (what groups) can most influence the interventions, and what are their attitudes about them? (For instance, to select a performance intervention requiring a change of reward systems, it may be essential to have support from the vice president of human resources or the compensation manager.)

	Step 7: Select Appropriate Interventions to Close the Performance Gap and Thereby Address the Performance Problem
1	Who should make the decisions about the interventions?
2	What performance interventions will appropriately close performance gaps by addressing the root causes of performance problems?
3	When should the decisions about the interventions be made?
4	How should the decision be justified? On what basis will the decision be made?
5	What are the relative costs and benefits of the performance interventions, and how were they estimated?
6	How are the constraints or limitations on the interventions to be managed?
7	How will the performance interventions address possible changes in the performance problem over time?
8	How will possible side effects of the interventions be planned for, and what steps will be taken to avert side effects or minimize their detrimental effects?
9	What stakeholder and participant support, involvement, and ownership is assumed, and how will it be recognized and (when possible) rewarded?

(continued on next page)

Figure 6.1: Worksheet to Guide Intervention Selection *(continued)*

Step 7: Select Appropriate Interventions to Close the Performance Gap and Thereby Address the Performance Problem *(continued)*

10	What alternative interventions might achieve the same results at the same or lower cost?

Step 8: Clarify the Initial and Eventual Scope of the Performance Interventions

1	How will the performance interventions, once selected, be designed and developed?
2	Who (what groups) will be the focus of the performance interventions initially? Eventually?
3	What groups might improve the most in a short time if the performance interventions are focused on them?
4	Where will the performance interventions likely enjoy the most stakeholder support, involvement, and ownership?
5	How much time should be permitted for the performance interventions to be successful, and how will results be tracked and measured?

Figure 6.2: Worksheet to Guide Intervention Design and Development

Directions: Use this tool to guide you from start to finish and step-by-step through intervention design and development. You do not have to use every question, and you may wish to add questions when appropriate. This tool is a template to guide your questioning during the design and development of performance interventions.

Step 1: Examine the Characteristics of the Participants in the Intervention

1	Who (specifically) will participate?
2	To whom do the participants report?
3	What (specifically) are the participants expected to do during the intervention?
4	What do the participants think and feel about the performance problem and the intervention intended to address it? Do they believe that the problem *is* a problem? Do they support the intervention? Are they motivated to participate in it?
5	How will the participants be involved in designing and developing the intervention and in designing and developing the materials and media to implement it?
6	What disabilities, if any, might affect the intervention, and how can reasonable accommodation be made for them?
7	What physical, mental, and emotional demands will the intervention require of participants?

(continued on next page)

	Figure 6.2: Worksheet to Guide Intervention Design and Development *(continued)*
	Step 1: Examine the Characteristics of the Participants in the Intervention *(continued)*
8	How much time and effort will the intervention require, and are participants able to devote that time and effort to the intervention? Do their immediate organizational superiors support it? Do their superiors' superiors support it?
	Step 2: Examine the Competencies Necessary for Successful Achievement
1	What competencies do participants already possess that are relevant to addressing the performance problem and designing and developing the intervention?
2	What competencies do participants need that are relevant to addressing the performance problem and designing and developing the intervention?
3	How can the organization build the competencies participants require to be successful in the intervention?
4	How can the organization build the competencies required of the participants' immediate organizational superiors in the intervention?
5	What experience, if any, have the participants had with a similar intervention, and how did they feel about that experience? Was the intervention successful or unsuccessful? Why?

	Step 3: Examine the Characteristics of the Work Environment
1	What conditions in the work environment will influence the preparation and planning of the intervention? What conditions in the work environment will influence the preparation and planning of its implementation? What conditions in the work environment will influence its success in changing attitudes, behaviors, or results?
2	What conditions in the work environment are most likely to support the intervention?
3	What conditions in the work environment are most likely to pose barriers to the intervention?
4	How can the conditions supporting the intervention be intensified, and how can barriers to the intervention be surmounted?
	Step 4: Formulate Performance Objectives to Guide the Intervention
1	What specific performance problems are to be addressed by the intervention?
2	What performance gap is to be closed by the intervention?

(continued on next page)

Figure 6.2: Worksheet to Guide Intervention Design and Development (continued)

Step 4: Formulate Performance Objectives to Guide the Intervention (continued)

3 What final results or outcomes can be described that, taken together, will fully describe the final outcomes desired on completion of the intevention? (When these results are achieved, the performance gap will be closed or its effects at least minimized.)

4 What interim results or outcomes are desired at various milestones during the implementation of the intervention?

5 What results or outcomes will performers achieve on completion of the intervention?

6 What conditions or resources will be necessary for the performers if they are to demonstrate the desired results or outcomes?

7 How can the conditions or resources be measured?

Step 5: Formulate Specific Methods by Which to Measure Performance Objectives

1 What should be happening (and what should be the final measurable performance levels) upon completion of the intervention?

2 How should results be measured?

3	When should results be measured? When do the milestones occur, and what results should have been achieved by each milestone?
4	Who will conduct the measurements of the interventions?
5	Where will results be measured? Will comparison groups (such as pretest and posttest groups or experimental and control groups) be established? If so, where and how?

Step 6: Create a Detailed Project Plan

1	Who will take action during each part of the intervention?
2	What tasks should they carry out, and what measurable results are they expected to achieve?
3	What are the deadlines for achievement?

(continued on next page)

Figure 6.2: Worksheet to Guide Intervention Design and Development (continued)

Step 6: Create a Detailed Project Plan (continued)

4	What is the budget, and what other resources are available during the intervention?

Step 7: Create a Detailed Communication and Marketing Plan to Clarify What Is Happening, Has Happened, and Will Happen

1	What are the phases, steps, tasks, or events of the intervention?
2	Who has a need to know about each step?
3	What do they need to know at each step, and when do they need to know it?
4	What are the most effective ways to communicate about the intervention to participants and other stakeholders for introducing each phase, step, task, or event of the intervention?
5	How should the communication plan be prepared, approved, tested, and evaluated?

6	How many details should be provided about the interventions?
7	What should be communicated about what is happening in the intervention, what has happened (progress to date) in the intervention, and what is expected or planned to happen in the intervention?

Step 8: Make, Buy, or Buy and Modify Materials and Media to Support the Implementation of the Intervention

1	What materials are necessary for use in the intervention to help meet the performance objectives?
2	Where can the materials be obtained? Should they be made, bought, or bought and modified? If bought, from where or from whom?
3	How should the materials be most cost-effectively delivered to participants and other groups to support achievement of the performance objectives?
4	Where can media support, if required, be obtained?

Figure 6.3: Worksheet to Guide Intervention Implementation

Directions: Use this tool to guide you from start to finish and step-by-step through intervention implementation. You do not have to use every question, and you may wish to add questions when appropriate. This tool is a template to guide your questioning during the implementation of performance interventions.

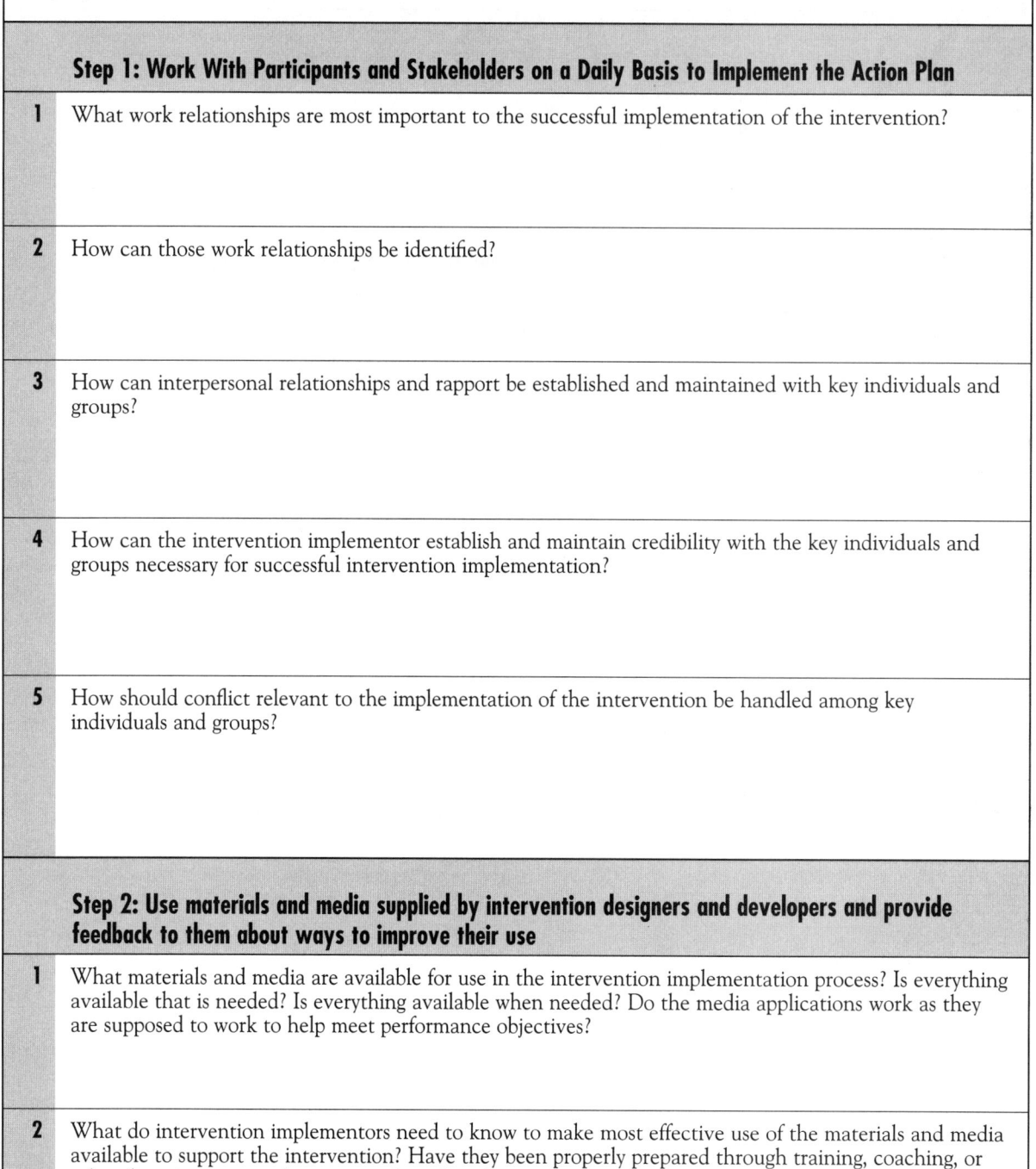

Step 1: Work With Participants and Stakeholders on a Daily Basis to Implement the Action Plan

1	What work relationships are most important to the successful implementation of the intervention?
2	How can those work relationships be identified?
3	How can interpersonal relationships and rapport be established and maintained with key individuals and groups?
4	How can the intervention implementor establish and maintain credibility with the key individuals and groups necessary for successful intervention implementation?
5	How should conflict relevant to the implementation of the intervention be handled among key individuals and groups?

Step 2: Use materials and media supplied by intervention designers and developers and provide feedback to them about ways to improve their use

#	Question
1	What materials and media are available for use in the intervention implementation process? Is everything available that is needed? Is everything available when needed? Do the media applications work as they are supposed to work to help meet performance objectives?
2	What do intervention implementors need to know to make most effective use of the materials and media available to support the intervention? Have they been properly prepared through training, coaching, or other directions to use those materials and media?

3	Who are the intervention designers and developers responsible for making modifications or revisions to materials and media devised for use in the implementation of the intervention?
4	How should intervention implementors request modifications or revisions to materials and media? How will they recognize when such changes are necessary and appropriate?
5	What processes or procedures should be established with the intervention designers and developers so that necessary modifications or revisions to materials and media can be identified and fed back, and so that corrections can be made on a timely and effective basis?
6	How can participant and stakeholder feedback about materials and media be collected by intervention implementors on a continuing basis?
7	How can the effectiveness of modifications or revisions be measured and feedback provided to intervention designers and developers?

Step 3: Deliver, or Facilitate Delivery of, the Intervention to Targeted Participants

1	What content should be delivered to participants and stakeholders during intervention implementation, and how can it be most effectively delivered?
2	How should content be delivered to participants and stakeholders during intervention implementation?
3	What methods of delivery or facilitation are appropriate for each phase of an intervention, and how can those methods be selected and used to help achieve performance objectives?

(continued on next page)

Figure 6.3: Worksheet to Guide Intervention Implementation *(continued)*

Step 3: Deliver, or Facilitate Delivery of, the Intervention to Targeted Participants *(continued)*

4	How can the effectiveness of the delivery and facilitation methods be measured and, when necessary, improved?

Step 4: Ensure That Communication about the Intervention Is Carried out Effectively

1	Who will receive communication about the intervention's implementation?
2	What kind of communication about the intervention should they receive? Is it necessary to describe activities (what is happening in the intervention) and results (what benefits were obtained)?
3	When should participants and stakeholders receive information about the intervention implementation? Should they receive reports on a continuing basis, at specific milestones, upon completion, or on some other basis?
4	How will intervention participants and stakeholders receive information? What media or methods should be used, and how should they be used?
5	How much time and money will be devoted to communicating about the intervention?
6	How might the targeted audience, level of information required, and other factors differ by stage of intervention implementation?

	Step 5: Track Short-Term Results Against the Intervention Performance Objectives
1	What are the short-term results of the intervention?
2	How often and in what ways should short-term results of the intervention be measured?
3	By whom should short-term results be measured?
4	How should short-term results be reported, and to whom should they be reported?
5	How should deviations from performance objectives be identified, and how should they be managed?
	Step 6: Surmount Barriers to Implementation and Ensure That the Intervention Is Implemented as Planned
1	What barriers to the implementation of the intervention are expected or are being encountered?
2	What are the most effective ways to surmount those barriers in the opinions of stakeholders, intervention participants, and others?

(continued on next page)

Figure 6.3: Worksheet to Guide Intervention Implementation *(continued)*

Step 6: Surmount Barriers to Implementation and Ensure That the Intervention Is Implemented as Planned

3 How can contingency plans be formulated to manage barriers as they arise?

4 How can the barriers be confronted and addressed without prompting skepticism about the intervention among participants and stakeholders?

Step 7: Provide Clear, Specific, and Continuing Feedback to Stakeholders about the Results of the Intervention

1 What feedback is necessary?

2 To whom should that feedback be reported?

3 When should that feedback be reported, and what form should the feedback take to make it most clear and specific?

4 How should the feedback be communicated?

5 What results are sought from providing the feedback? Do intervention implementors seek to increase awareness of the intervention, build continuing or additional support, demonstrate value received from the organization's investments, or achieve another end?

SECTION 1	GETTING STARTED
SECTION 2	DEFINING THE ROLES
SECTION 3	ENACTING THE ROLE OF INTERVENTION SELECTOR
SECTION 4	ENACTING THE ROLE OF INTERVENTION DESIGNER AND DEVELOPER
SECTION 5	ENACTING THE ROLE OF INTERVENTION IMPLEMENTOR
SECTION 6	TOOLS FOR CONDUCTING INTERVENTION SELECTION, DESIGN AND DEVELOPMENT, AND IMPLEMENTATION
SECTION 7	AFTERWORD

- Why Is It Important to Master These Roles and Competencies?
- How Does It Feel to Perform These Roles?
- What Should You Do Next?

| SECTION 8 | BIBLIOGRAPHY |

SECTION 7 AFTERWORD

This section addresses three key issues:

- Why is it important to master the roles of intervention selector, intervention designer and developer, and intervention implementor and the competencies associated with them?
- How does it feel to perform these roles?
- What should you do next?

Why Is It Important to Master These Roles and Competencies?

Intervention selection, intervention design and development, and intervention implementation are associated with middle steps in the HPI process model. Without these roles, WLP practitioners would not solve the root causes of performance problems, seize opportunities for improvement, or ensure effective implementation of performance interventions. Without these roles, the efforts of the analyst would be rendered pointless, and the efforts of the evaluator would not be necessary because no results would be achieved.

The key to intervention selection is to choose the right performance intervention (or combination of interventions) to address the root causes of performance problems. While there is sometimes a tendency to think that one problem deserves one solution (intervention), that is not always true. In some cases, several interventions are necessary. It may be necessary, for example, to combine off-the-job training with on-the-job changes in feedback, incentives and rewards, equipment and tools, and real-time coaching.

The key to intervention design and development is to plan one or more effective interventions.

There is sometimes a tendency to think that all that is important is the visible action the WLP practitioner takes. Planning is also essential to success. Planning must be done in a way that balances speed and results, so that decision makers and other stakeholders do not become impatient waiting for implementation. At the same time, there is value to deciding what the intervention will be, how it will be carried out, who will bear various responsibilities, and how accountabilities will be ensured for groups and individuals.

The key to intervention implementation is to ensure that the day-to-day practices of the intervention correspond to plans, address root causes of performance problems, and match up with the change objectives for the intervention, which was established during intervention design and development.

How Does It Feel to Perform These Roles?

The performance of these roles requires a bias for action, a sense of urgency, and an attention to detail, all of which are tempered with an awareness that actions have consequences. It is not enough to take action. The actions must get results, and they must get results consistent with the desired results established at the outset of the intervention. For that reason, WLP practitioners who enact these roles must focus attention on the tactical level while they remain sensitive to the big picture—that is, the strategic level. They must also remain open-minded about the criticism of the interventions they hear, because criticism often has a kernel of truth, no matter how tactlessly it may sometimes be stated by workers, managers, or others. Ultimately, WLP practitioners should not be concerned about defending or justifying what has been done, but they should focus instead on what needs to be done to get results.

What Should You Do Next?

The Intervention Selector, Designer and Developer, and Implementor is the third of several self-study job aids introduced in *ASTD Models for Workplace Learning and Performance* (1999). The other volumes focus on such other possible WLP roles as analyst, evaluator, manager, and change leader. Use all the job aids to help build your competencies.

You might find it useful as well to refer to the tools found in Section 6 of this volume to guide your daily application of the steps in demonstrating the competencies associated with these roles. Section 8 provides a comprehensive bibliography that can lead you to other helpful publications and resources on WLP roles.

SECTION 1 GETTING STARTED

SECTION 2 DEFINING THE ROLES

SECTION 3 ENACTING THE ROLE OF INTERVENTION SELECTOR

SECTION 4 ENACTING THE ROLE OF INTERVENTION DESIGNER AND DEVELOPER

SECTION 5 ENACTING THE ROLE OF INTERVENTION IMPLEMENTOR

SECTION 6 TOOLS FOR CONDUCTING INTERVENTION SELECTION, DESIGN AND DEVELOPMENT, AND IMPLEMENTATION

SECTION 7 AFTERWORD

SECTION 8 BIBLIOGRAPHY

SECTION 8 BIBLIOGRAPHY

Adams, J. (1986). *Conceptual blockbusting: A guide to better ideas* (3rd edition). Reading, MA: Addison-Wesley.

Adler, K., and Swiercz, P. (1997). "Taming the performance bell curve." *Training & Development*, 51(10), 33–38.

Alden, J. (1999). "Results-based management." In D. Langdon, K. Whiteside, and M. McKenna (Eds.), *Intervention resource guide: 50 performance improvement tools*. San Francisco: Jossey-Bass/Pfeiffer, 330–337.

Amano, T. (1999). "Performance management." In D. Langdon, K. Whiteside, and M. McKenna (Eds.), *Intervention resource guide: 50 performance improvement tools*. San Francisco: Jossey-Bass/Pfeiffer, 293–302.

Anderson, D. (1998). "Aligned values + good job fit equals optimum performance." *National Productivity Review*, 17(4), 23–30.

Atkinson, V., and Chalmers, N. (1999). "Performance consulting: Get credit from your clients." *Performance Improvement*, 38(4), 14–19.

Barbazette, J. (1999). "Employee orientation." In D. Langdon, K. Whiteside, and M. McKenna (Eds.), *Intervention resource guide: 50 performance improvement tools*. San Francisco: Jossey-Bass/Pfeiffer, 149–157.

Beeman, C. (1999). "Compensation systems." In D. Langdon, K. Whiteside, and M. McKenna (Eds.), *Intervention resource guide: 50 performance improvement tools*. San Francisco: Jossey-Bass/Pfeiffer, 98–105.

Binder, C. (1999). "Fluency development." In D. Langdon, K. Whiteside, and M. McKenna (Eds.), *Intervention resource guide: 50 performance improvement tools*. San Francisco: Jossey-Bass/Pfeiffer, 176–183.

Blair, D., and Price, D. (1998). "Persistence: A key factor in human performance at work." *Performance Improvement*, 37(1), 27–31.

BNH Expert Software. Advisor P.I., a needs assessment tool to improve performance. Demo copies available at http://www.bnhexpertsoft.com or at >www.astd.org.

Bobrow, W. (1999). "Assessment centers." In D. Langdon, K. Whiteside, and M. McKenna (Eds.), *Intervention resource guide: 50 performance improvement tools*. San Francisco: Jossey-Bass/Pfeiffer, 59–66.

Boshyk, Yuri. (Ed.). (2000). *Business driven action learning: Global best practices*. New York: St. Martin's.

Brethower, D. (1999). "Performance analysis." In D. Langdon, K. Whiteside, and M. McKenna (Eds.), *Intervention resource guide: 50 performance improvement tools*. San Francisco: Jossey-Bass/Pfeiffer, 280–286.

Bristol, S. (1999). "Human resource information systems (HRIS)." In D. Langdon, K. Whiteside, and M. McKenna (Eds.), *Intervention resource guide: 50 performance improvement tools*. San Francisco: Jossey-Bass/Pfeiffer, 184–190.

Brown, M. (1987). "Designing effective performance systems." *Performance and Instruction*, 26(3), 14–18.

Callahan, M. (1998). "The role of the performance evaluator." *Info-line*. No. 9803. Alexandria, VA: ASTD.

Callahan, M. (1997a). "The role of the performance intervention specialist." *Info-line*. No. 9714. Alexandria, VA: ASTD.

Callahan, M. (1997b). "From training to performance consulting." *Info-line*. No. 9702. Alexandria, VA: ASTD.

Carr, C. (1992). "How performance happens (and how to help it happen better)—Part 12: Ten keys to successful performance facilitation." *Performance and Instruction*, 31(1), 36–40.

Carr, C. (1990). "How performance happens (and how to help it happen better)—1: What this is—and why." *Performance and Instruction*, 29(10), 44–46.

Carter, C. (1994). "Measuring and improving the human resources function." *Employment Relations Today*, 21(1), 63–75.

Caudron, S. (1999). "Now what?" *Training & Development*, 53(9), 42–45.

Chaston, I. (1993). "Performance improvement intervention: Privatized and public sector organizations." *Leadership & Organization Development Journal, 14*(1), 4–8.

Cheney, S. (1998). "Performance consulting for better supplier management." In S. Cheney (Ed.), *Excellence in practice* (volume 2). Alexandria, VA: ASTD, 99–106.

Clark, R. (1998). "Motivating performance—Part 1: Diagnosing and solving motivation problems." *Performance Improvement, 37*(8), 39–47.

Dean, P., Dean, M., and Guman, E. (1992). "Identifying a range of performance improvement solutions through evaluation research." *Performance Improvement Quarterly, 5*(4), 16–31.

Dean, P., and Ripley, D. (1998a). *Performance improvement interventions: Culture and systems change.* Washington, DC: International Society for Performance Improvement.

Dean, P., and Ripley, D. (1998b). *Performance improvement interventions instructional design and training: Methods for organizational learning.* Washington, DC: International Society for Performance Improvement.

Dent, J., and Anderson, P. (1998). "Fundamentals of HPI." *Info-line.* No. 9811. Alexandria, VA: ASTD.

Denton, D. (1996). "Don't hire performance problems: The employment interview and the performance improvement practitioner." *Performance Improvement, 35*(9), 6–9.

Desautels, B. (1999). "Performance appraisal." In D. Langdon, K. Whiteside, and M. McKenna (Eds.), *Intervention resource guide: 50 performance improvement tools.* San Francisco: Jossey-Bass/Pfeiffer, 287–292.

Deterline, W. (1997). "The shoemaker's gap." *Performance Improvement, 36*(7), 6–8.

Dotlich, D., and Noel, J. (Eds.). (1998). *Action learning: How the world's top companies are re-creating their leaders and themselves.* San Francisco: Jossey-Bass Business and Management Series.

Dubois, D. (1999). "Competency Modeling." In D. Langdon, K. Whiteside, and M. McKenna (Eds.), *Intervention resource guide: 50 performance improvement tools.* San Francisco: Jossey-Bass/Pfeiffer, 106–111.

Dubois, D., and Rothwell, W. (2000). *The competency toolkit.* (2 vols.). Amherst, MA: Human Resource Development.

Esque, T. (1995). "Watching Tom Gilbert's feet." *Performance and Instruction, 34*(10), 16–25.

Estes, F. (1999). "Expert systems." In D. Langdon, K. Whiteside, and M. McKenna (Eds.), *Intervention resource guide: 50 performance improvement tools.* San Francisco: Jossey-Bass/Pfeiffer, 158–165.

"The few, the proud—the invisible? how to develop." (1999). *Training Directors' Forum Newsletter, 14*(8), 1–4.

Fisher, S. (1997). *The manager's pocket guide to performance management.* Amherst, MA: Human Resource Development Press.

Ford, J. (1999). "Organizational development." In D. Langdon, K. Whiteside, and M. McKenna (Eds.), *Intervention resource guide: 50 performance improvement tools.* San Francisco: Jossey-Bass/Pfeiffer, 250–258.

Galpin, T. (1994). "How to manage human performance." *Employment Relations Today, 21*(2), 207–225.

Gery, G., and Jezsik, L. (1999). "Electronic performance support system (EPSS)." In D. Langdon, K. Whiteside, and M. McKenna (Eds.), *Intervention resource guide: 50 performance improvement tools.* San Francisco: Jossey-Bass/Pfeiffer, 142–148.

Gilbert, T. (1978). *Human competence: Engineering worthy performance.* New York: McGraw-Hill.

Gilley, J., Boughton, N., and Maycunich, A. (1999). *The performance challenge: Developing management systems to make employees your organization's greatest asset.* Reading, MA: Perseus.

Green, T. (1992). *Performance and motivation strategies for today's workforce: A guide to expectancy theory applications.* Westport, CT: Quorum.

Hale, J. (1998). *The performance consultant's fieldbook.* San Francisco: Jossey-Bass/Pfeiffer.

Hallberg, C., and DeFiore, R. (1997). "Curving toward performance." *Technical & Skills Training, 8*(1), 9–11.

Harless, J. (1997). *Analyzing human performance: Tools for achieving business results.* Alexandria, VA: ASTD.

Harrington, H., and Harrington, J. (1995). *Total improvement management: The next generation in performance improvement.* New York: McGraw-Hill.

Hart, L. (1999). "Conflict management." In D. Langdon, K. Whiteside, and M. McKenna (Eds.), *Intervention resource guide: 50 performance improvement tools.* San Francisco: Jossey-Bass/Pfeiffer, 112–118.

Harvey, E. (1995). "Coaching for constant improvement." *Executive Excellence, 12*(7), 6.

Hill, J., and Brethower, D. (1997). "Ridding ourselves of "non-instruction." *Performance Improvement, 36*(8), 6–9.

Hollands, J. (1997). *Red ink behaviors: Measure the surprisingly high cost of problem behaviors in valuable employees.* New York: Blake/Madsen.

Hunter, D., Bailey, A., and Taylor, B. (1995). *The art of facilitation: How to create group synergy.* Tucson, AZ: Fisher Books.

Hutchison, C., and Stein, F. (1997). "A whole new world of interventions: The performance technologist as integrating generalist." *Performance Improvement, 36*(10), 28–35.

Jackson, S., and Tosti, D. (1999). "Organizational scan." In D. Langdon, K. Whiteside, and M. McKenna (Eds.), *Intervention resource guide: 50 performance improvement tools.* San Francisco: Jossey-Bass/Pfeiffer, 259–265.

Jorgensen, M. (1999). "Why go to a trainer for non-training solutions?: Eight reasons why trainers make good performance technologists." *Performance Improvement, 38*(1), 20–24.

Kaminski, E. (1999). "Automated resume tracking system." In D. Langdon, K. Whiteside, and M. McKenna (Eds.), *Intervention resource guide: 50 performance improvement tools.* San Francisco: Jossey-Bass/Pfeiffer, 67–71.

Kaufman, R., and Watkins, R. (1999a). "Needs assessment." In D. Langdon, K. Whiteside, and M. McKenna (Eds.), *Intervention resource guide: 50 performance improvement tools.* San Francisco: Jossey-Bass/Pfeiffer, 237–242.

Kaufman, R., and Watkins, R. (1999b). "Strategic planning and visioning." In D. Langdon, K. Whiteside, and M. McKenna (Eds.), *Intervention resource guide: 50 performance improvement tools.* San Francisco: Jossey-Bass/Pfeiffer, 348–356.

Kearny, L., and Smith, P. (1999). "Cognitive ergonomics." In D. Langdon, K. Whiteside, and M. McKenna (Eds.), *Intervention resource guide: 50 performance improvement tools.* San Francisco: Jossey-Bass/Pfeiffer, 82–90.

King, S., King, M., and Rothwell, W. (2000). *The complete guide to training delivery: A competency-based approach.* New York: AMACOM.

Kirrane, D. (1997). "The role of the performance needs analyst." *Info-line.* No. 9713. Alexandria, VA: ASTD.

Koehle, D. (1999). "The role of the performance change manager." *Info-line.* No. 9715. Alexandria, VA: ASTD.

Kravetz, D. (1989). *The directory for performance improvement.* Rolling Meadows, IL: Dennis J. Kravitz and Associates.

LaBonte, T., and Robinson, J. (1999). "Performance consulting: One organization, one process." *Training & Development, 52*(8), 32–37.

Langdon, D. (1997). "Selecting interventions." *Performance Improvement, 36*(10), 11–15.

Langdon, D. (1999a). "Job aids." In D. Langdon, K. Whiteside, and M. McKenna (Eds.), *Intervention resource guide: 50 performance improvement tools.* San Francisco: Jossey-Bass/Pfeiffer, 191–196.

Langdon, D. (1999b). "Process mapping." In D. Langdon, K. Whiteside, and M. McKenna (Eds.), *Intervention resource guide: 50 performance improvement tools.* San Francisco: Jossey-Bass/Pfeiffer, 311–317.

Langdon, D. (1999c). "Selecting interventions." In D. Langdon, K. Whiteside, and M. McKenna (Eds.), *Intervention resource guide: 50 performance improvement tools*. San Francisco: Jossey-Bass/Pfeiffer, 15–25.

Langdon, D., Whiteside, K., and McKenna, M. (Eds.). (1999). *Intervention resource guide: 50 performance improvement tools*. San Francisco: Jossey-Bass/Pfeiffer.

Mackin, D. (1999). "Teaming." In D. Langdon, K. Whiteside, and M. McKenna (Eds.), *Intervention resource guide: 50 performance improvement tools*. San Francisco: Jossey-Bass/Pfeiffer, 372–380.

Mager, R. (1997a). *Measuring instructional results or got a match?* (3rd edition). Atlanta: The Center for Effective Performance.

Mager, R. (1997b). *Preparing instructional objectives: A critical tool in the development of effective instruction* (3rd edition). Atlanta: The Center for Effective Performance.

Mager, R., and Pipe, P. (1997). *Analyzing performance problems or you really oughta wanna* (3rd edition). Atlanta: The Center for Effective Performance.

Manzoni, J., and Barsoux, J. (1998). "The set-up-to-fail syndrome." *Harvard Business Review*, 76(2), 101–113.

Marquardt, M. (1999). "Action learning." In D. Langdon, K. Whiteside, and M. McKenna (Eds.), *Intervention resource guide: 50 performance improvement tools*. San Francisco: Jossey-Bass/Pfeiffer, 52–58.

Marquardt, M., and Revans, R. (1999). *Action learning in action : Transforming problems and people for world-class organizational learning*. Palo Alto, CA: Davies-Black.

Marsh, L. (1992). "Good manager: Good coach? what is needed for effective coaching?" *Industrial & Commercial Training*, 24(9), 3–8.

Marx, R. (1999). *The ASTD media selection tool for workplace learning*. Alexandria, VA: ASTD.

"Matrix of interventions." (1999). In D. Langdon, K. Whiteside, and M. McKenna (Eds.), *Intervention resource guide: 50 performance improvement tools*. San Francisco: Jossey-Bass/Pfeiffer, 36–38.

McCauley, C. (1999). "Leadership development programs." In D. Langdon, K. Whiteside, and McKenna, M. (Eds.), *Intervention resource guide: 50 performance improvement tools*. San Francisco: Jossey-Bass/Pfeiffer, 197–203.

Meier, D. (1999). "Accelerated learning." In D. Langdon, K. Whiteside, and M. McKenna (Eds.), *Intervention resource guide: 50 performance improvement tools*. San Francisco: Jossey-Bass/Pfeiffer, 47–51.

Microsoft. Microsoft Project 2000, for project management. Demo copies available at http://agent.microsoft.com/office/project/trial.htm.

Murray, M. (1999). "Mentoring/coaching." In D. Langdon, K. Whiteside, and M. McKenna (Eds.), *Intervention resource guide: 50 performance improvement tools*. San Francisco: Jossey-Bass/Pfeiffer, 220–226.

Musselwhite, W., and Ingram, R. (1999). "Change style preference models." In D. Langdon, K. Whiteside, and M. McKenna (Eds.), *Intervention resource guide: 50 performance improvement tools*. San Francisco: Jossey-Bass/Pfeiffer, 77–81.

Nelson, B. (1999). "Recognition programs." In D. Langdon, K. Whiteside, and M. McKenna (Eds.), *Intervention resource guide: 50 performance improvement tools*. San Francisco: Jossey-Bass/Pfeiffer, 318–323.

Nowack, K. (1999). "360-degree feedback." In D. Langdon, K. Whiteside, and M. McKenna (Eds.), *Intervention resource guide: 50 performance improvement tools*. San Francisco: Jossey-Bass/Pfeiffer, 39–46.

O'Mara, J. (1999). "Leveraging diversity." In D. Langdon, K. Whiteside, and M. McKenna (Eds.), *Intervention resource guide: 50 performance improvement tools*. San Francisco: Jossey-Bass/Pfeiffer, 211–219.

Robinson, R. (1999). "Outplacement." In D. Langdon, K. Whiteside, and M. McKenna (Eds.), *Intervention resource guide: 50 performance improvement tools*. San Francisco: Jossey-Bass/Pfeiffer, 266–272.

Robinson, D., and Robinson, J. (1995). *Performance consulting: Moving beyond training*. San Francisco: Berrett-Koehler.

Rosenheck, M. (1997, May-June). "Closing the gap between training and performance." *CBT Solutions*, 50–53.

Rossett, A., and Tobias, C. (1999). "A study of the journey from training to performance." *Performance Improvement Quarterly, 12*(3), 31–43.

Rothwell, W. (1996a). *ASTD models for human performance improvement: Roles, competencies, and outputs.* Alexandria, VA: ASTD.

Rothwell, W. (1996b). *Beyond training and development: State-of-the-art strategies for enhancing human performance.* New York: AMACOM.

Rothwell, W. (1999a). *The action learning guidebook: A real-time strategy for problem solving, training design, and employee development.* San Francisco: Jossey-Bass/Pfeiffer.

Rothwell, W. (1999b). "On-the-job training." In D. Langdon, K. Whiteside, and M. McKenna (Eds.), *Intervention resource guide: 50 performance improvement tools.* San Francisco: Jossey-Bass/Pfeiffer, 243–250.

Rothwell, W., and Dubois, D. (Eds.). (1998). *In action: Improving human performance.* Alexandria, VA: ASTD.

Rothwell, W., Hohne, C., and King, S. (2000). *Human performance improvement: Building practitioner competence.* Houston: Gulf.

Rothwell, W., and Kazanas, H. (1998). *Mastering the instructional design process: A systematic approach* (2nd edition). San Francisco: Jossey-Bass.

Rothwell, W., and Lindholm, J. (1999). "Competency identification, modelling and assessment in the USA." *International Journal of Training and Development, 3*(2), 90–105.

Rothwell, W., Sanders, E., and Soper, J. (1999). *ASTD models for workplace learning and performance: Roles, competencies, and outputs.* Alexandria, VA: ASTD.

Rothwell, W., Sullivan, R., and McLean, G. (Eds.). (1995). *Practicing organization development: A guide for consultants.* San Francisco: Jossey-Bass/Pfeiffer.

Rummler, G. (1996). "In search of the holy performance grail." *Training & Development, 50*(4), 26–32.

Ruona, W., and Lyford-Nojima, E. (1997). "Performance diagnosis matrix: A discussion of performance improvement scholarship." *Performance Improvement Quarterly, 10*(4), 87–118.

Saunier, A., and Mavis, M. (1998). "Fixing a broken system." *HR Focus, 75*(3), 1, 3–4.

Schein, E. (1999). "Cultural change." In D. Langdon, K. Whiteside, and M. McKenna (Eds.), *Intervention resource guide: 50 performance improvement tools.* San Francisco: Jossey-Bass/Pfeiffer, 125–130.

Schermerhorn, J., Jr., Gardner, W., and Martin, T. (1990). "Management dialogues: Turning on the marginal performer." *Organizational Dynamics, 18*(4), 47–59.

Schwartz, R. (1994). *The skilled facilitator: Practical wisdom for developing effective groups.* San Francisco: Jossey-Bass.

Sharpe, C. (1998). *The Info-Line Guide to Performance Improvement.* Alexandria, VA: ASTD.

Sink, D., Scott; T., Suttle, T. (1990). "The performance management question in the organization of the future." *Industrial Management, 32*(1), 4–12.

Sloat, K. (1999). "Safety management." In D. Langdon, K. Whiteside, and M. McKenna (Eds.), *Intervention resource guide: 50 performance improvement tools.* San Francisco: Jossey-Bass/Pfeiffer, 338–341.

Sorohan, E. (1996). "The performance consultant at work." *Training & Development, 50*(3), 34–38.

Spitzer, D. (1996). "Ensuring successful performance improvement interventions." *Performance Improvement, 35*(9), 26–27.

Stalik, S. (1999). "Reengineering." In D. Langdon, K. Whiteside, and M. McKenna (Eds.), *Intervention resource guide: 50 performance improvement tools.* San Francisco: Jossey-Bass/Pfeiffer, 324–329.

Sugrue, B., and Fuller, J. (Eds.). (1999). *Performance interventions—selecting, implementing, and evaluating the results.* Alexandria, VA: ASTD.

Sujansky, J. (1999). "Partnering agreements." In D. Langdon, K. Whiteside, and M. McKenna (Eds.), *Intervention resource guide: 50 performance improvement tools.* San Francisco: Jossey-Bass/Pfeiffer, 273–279.

Swenson, J. (1999). "Communication." In D. Langdon, K. Whiteside, and M. McKenna (Eds.), *Intervention resource guide: 50 performance improvement tools.* San Francisco: Jossey-Bass/Pfeiffer, 91–97.

"Tactics to try, land mines to leap when moving training to 'performance' focus." (1996). *Training Directors' Forum Newsletter, 12*(7), 5.

TeamWave Software Ltd. TeamWave Workplace, groupware for online interactive decision making. Demo copies available at http://teamwave.com.

Thiagarajan, S. (1999a). "Challenge Education." In D. Langdon, K. Whiteside, and M. McKenna (Eds.), *Intervention resource guide: 50 performance improvement tools.* San Francisco: Jossey-Bass/Pfeiffer, 72–76.

Thiagarajan, S. (1999b). "Simulation." In D. Langdon, K. Whiteside, and M. McKenna (Eds.), *Intervention resource guide: 50 performance improvement tools.* San Francisco: Jossey-Bass/Pfeiffer, 342–347.

Thorlakson, A. (1997). "Performance improvement counselling." *Canadian Manager, 22*(4), 16, 26.

"3-step model for offering performance consulting services in your company." *Training Directors' Forum Newsletter, 11*(12), 4.

Warrick, D. (1995). "Action planning." In W. Rothwell, R. Sullivan, and G. McLean (Eds.), *Practicing organization development: A guide for consultants.* San Francisco: Jossey-Bass/Pfeiffer, 171–202.

Weinstein, K. (1998). *Action learning: A practical guide for managers* (2nd edition). Hampshire, England: Gower.

Weiss, E. (1999). "Usability assessments." In D. Langdon, K. Whiteside, and M. McKenna (Eds.), *Intervention resource guide: 50 performance improvement tools.* San Francisco: Jossey-Bass/Pfeiffer, 387–394.

Wells, R. (1999). "Critical thinking systems." In D. Langdon, K. Whiteside, and M. McKenna (Eds.), *Intervention resource guide: 50 performance improvement tools.* San Francisco: Jossey-Bass/Pfeiffer, 119–124.

"What to avoid when shifting from training to performance consulting." (1996). *Training Directors' Forum Newsletter, 12*(3), 1–2.

"What you can learn from IBM's transformed education model." (1996). *Training Directors' Forum Newsletter, 12*(6), 1–2.

Whiteside, K. (1997). "Implementing performance interventions." *Performance Improvement, 36*(10), 6–10.

Whiteside, K. (1999a). "Implementing interventions." In D. Langdon, K. Whiteside, and M. McKenna (Eds.), *Intervention resource guide: 50 performance improvement tools.* San Francisco: Jossey-Bass/Pfeiffer, 26–34.

Whiteside, K. (1999b). "Work group alignment." In D. Langdon, K. Whiteside, and M. McKenna (Eds.), *Intervention resource guide: 50 performance improvement tools.* San Francisco: Jossey-Bass/Pfeiffer, 395–400.

Wilburn, K., and Wilburn, R. (1998). "Eleven techniques to jump-start performance dialogue." *Performance Improvement, 37*(1), 24–26.

Wood, J. (1999). "Team performance." In D. Langdon, K. Whiteside, and M. McKenna (Eds.), *Intervention resource guide: 50 performance improvement tools.* San Francisco: Jossey-Bass/Pfeiffer, 365–371.

Wydra, F., and McKenna, M. (1999). "Learner-controlled instruction." In D. Langdon, K. Whiteside, and M. McKenna (Eds.), *Intervention resource guide: 50 performance improvement tools.* San Francisco: Jossey-Bass/Pfeiffer, 204–210.

Zemke, R. (1999). "Customer feedback." In D. Langdon, K. Whiteside, and M. McKenna (Eds.), *Intervention resource guide: 50 performance improvement tools.* San Francisco: Jossey-Bass/Pfeiffer, 131–141.

Zenger, J. (1997). "The invisible wall." *Training & Development, 51*(10), 24–27.

ABOUT THE AUTHOR

William J. Rothwell is professor of human resource development in the Department of Adult Education, Instructional Systems, and Workforce Education and Development in the College of Education on the University Park Campus of the Pennsylvania State University and director of Penn State's Institute for Research in Training and Development. He also is president of Rothwell and Associates, a private consulting firm with more than 30 multinational corporations on its client list.

Previously, Rothwell was assistant vice president and director of management development for the Franklin Life Insurance Company, Springfield, Illinois, and training director for the Illinois Office of Auditor General. He holds a Ph.D. from the University of Illinois at Urbana-Champaign and has worked full-time in human resource management and employee training and development since 1979, combining real-world experience with academic and consulting experience.

Rothwell's latest publications include *The ASTD Reference Guide to Workplace Learning and Performance* (with Henry J. Sredl, 2000); *The Analyst* (2000); *The Evaluator* (2000); *The Complete Guide to Training Delivery: A Competency-Based Approach* (with S. King, M. King, 2000); *Human Performance Improvement:Building Practitioner Competence* (with Carolyn K. Hohne, and Stephen B. King, 2000); *Building In-house Leadership and Management Development Programs* (with H. Kazanas, 2000); *The Competency Toolkit* (with D. Dubois, 2000); *ASTD Models for Workplace Learning and Performance* (with E. Sanders and J. Soper, 1999); *The Action Learning Guidebook* (with K. Sensenig, as editors, 1999); *Sourcebook for Self-Directed Learning* (as editor, 1999); *Creating, Measuring and Documenting Service Impact: A Capacity Building Resource: Rationales, Models, Activities, Methods, Techniques, Instruments* (1998); *In Action: Improving Human Performance* (with D. Dubois, as editors, 1998); *Strategic Human Resource Leader: How to Help Your Organization Manage the Six Trends Affecting the Workforce* (with Prescott and Taylor, as editors, 1998); *In Action: Linking HRD and Organizational Strategy* (as editor, 1998); and *Mastering the Instructional Design Process: A Systematic Approach* (with H. Kazanas, 2nd edition, 1998).

Letters can be addressed to the author at 305C Keller Building, University Park, PA 16803. He can be reached via email at wjr9@psu.edu.

NOTES

NOTES

NOTES

NOTES

NOTES

NOTES